CW00566850

THE BATTLE

OF THE

SOMME: A

LAYMAN'S

GUIDE

SCOTT ADDINGTON

OTHER BOOKS BY SCOTT ADDINGTON:

WW1: A Layman's Guide
WW2: A Layman's Guide
D-Day: A Layman's Guide
The Third Reich: A Layman's Guide
Waterloo: A Layman's Guide
The Great War 100
Heroes of World War One
Five Minute Histories: First World War Battles
Five Minute Histories: First World War Weapons
Heroes of The Line
1001 Fantastic First World War Facts
1001 Sensational Second World War Facts
Reaching For the Sky. The RAF in 100 Moments
Invasion! D-Day in 100 Moments

Visit www.wordsofwarfare.com for more details and the opportunity
to get a free First World War Factbook.

EPILOGUE: THIS WAS WAR

The Somme area was a God-forsaken battleground created by earnest staff officers now slightly hysterical about their still incomplete labours. An atmosphere of over-elaborated brusque inefficiency pervaded the hinterland of slaughter. Too many men, too many officers, far too many generals, and a thousand times too many jacks-in-office, railway transport officers, town majors, assistant provost marshals, traffic control officers, laundry officers, liaison officers, railway experts, and endless seas of mud. And no more estaminets.

This was war.

Captain Douglas Jerrold, Hawke Battalion, 189th Brigade, 63rd (Royal Naval) Division.

CONTENTS

Introduction

I currently own forty-five books that are dedicated to the Battle of the Somme. These include massive one-volume tomes, panoramic then/now photographs of the battlefield, eye-witness accounts, battlefield tour guides, war diaries, old narratives, modern takes, and books that look at the battle exclusively from the German, French or British point of view.

I have just typed in 'The Battle of the Somme' into the book section of Amazon UK and there are 999 results. It would seem that I have still quite a bit of reading to do, and it kind of begs the question, 'why write another book on the Battle of the Somme?'

I blame two people - Mr. Peter Barton and Mr. Jeremy Banning. Two of the finest military historians on the planet as well as being two of the most genuine and nicest human beings you are ever likely to meet. A number of years ago I had the privilege of joining them at La Boisselle as they investigated some of the tunnels dug underneath the old *No Man's Land* in an untouched crater field in an area known as The Glory Hole.

The tour of the tunnels was fascinating, as was the walking tour of the battlefield they took me on. It got me hooked on the battle and the battlefields of the Somme. I go back every year with my son to walk the fields and visit the graves and memorials of three family members that fell during the fighting. It is my favourite four days of the entire year.

I also collect the medals and militaria related to the men who fought in the battle. I even have an image from the movie ' The Battle of the Somme' tattooed on my arm. (Yes, really). Did I mention the books? There are forty-five of them, if you recall. Although I think I am going to buy some more later.

I guess writing this book was inevitable.

Following in the style of other *Layman's Guides,* this book a straightforward history of one of the most destructive battles in history that is more akin to a chat over a cup of tea than a heavy historical text. That being said, I have worked hard to make this book stand out on its own merit, and is, I think, different to many of the books already published on the subject:

- I have included views from both sides of the wire! This is not a description of the battle from just the side of the Allies. This book also looks at things from the German point of view too. After all, it takes two (or more) to make a fight!

- I have included a number of mini-biographies of some of the remarkable characters that took part in the battle and were rewarded for their bravery.

- The book covers the run up to the battle and covers in detail the dreadful events of the infamous first day of battle. However, we don't stop there. We go on to cover every major move and shake, right up to mid-November.

- Maps – there are many maps in this volume, so you have an idea of where all the place names are located and their relevance to the battle.

Ultimately, this *Layman's Guide* is my attempt at telling the story of one of the greatest battle of all battles in an engaging and entertaining way that will appeal to both new readers and seasoned campaigners alike.

I hope I have done the memory of The Somme justice.

SMA 2023.

1

NIEDERWERFUNGSTRATEGIES AND SCHWERPUNKTS: IMPERIAL GERMAN STRATEGY

To understand the German methodology of battle during the first eighteen months of the First World War, we need to travel back in time and catch up with a chap called Carl Philipp Gottfried von Clausewitz – a Prussian General who cultivated a reputation as one of the greatest military thinkers of his time.

Born in 1780, Clausewitz joined the Prussian army at the age of twelve and saw plenty of action in the Rhine Campaigns and Napoleonic Wars. However, he is mostly known for his military theories, and his unfinished three-volume *Magnus Opus - Vom Krieg* (On War) - was influential amongst German military planners right through to the nineteenth and twentieth centuries.

Within *Vom Krieg*, Clausewitz discussed and dissected many military ideas and theories, but one critical idea which resonated loud and clear with subsequent Prussian and German military leaders had to do with the concept of the *centra gravitatis* (centre of gravity) of any military opposition. The idea of a *centra gravitatis* was relatively simple: find out the one thing – whether it be a fortress, a city, a military leader, or some other token of nationality – that lies at the very centre of an enemy's being and focus everything you have on destroying it.

By doing this, the enemy in question will quickly crumble, turn in on itself, and collapse.

Clausewitz was not just advocating simple victory here. No sir, he was banging the drum for complete and utter annihilation of the enemy using devastating speed and overwhelming destructive force.

> *The best strategy is always to be very strong, first generally, then at the decisive point. Therefore, apart from the energy which creates the army, a work which is not always done by the general, there is no more imperative and simpler law for strategy than to keep the forces concentrated. No portion is to be separated from the main body unless called away by some urgent necessity.*[1]

Thirty-eight years after *Vom Krieg* was posthumously published by Clausewitz's wife, this was exactly the process followed by Helmuth von Moltke (Moltke the elder) when he utilised simple mathematics to smash the French armies at Sedan on 1-2 September 1870. The maths principle employed being the one that said that 500,000 German soldiers is more than 300,000 French soldiers. Moltke summarised his mathematic genius thus:

> *The concentration of all our forces in the Pfalz protected both the lower as well as the upper Rhine and allowed an offensive into enemy territory which, timed carefully, meant that it forestalled any attempt by the French to set foot on German territory.*[2]

Who said maths isn't fun?

By winning so emphatically, Moltke proved that Clausewitz's concept was more than just theory. Using focussed brutality, he was able to successfully execute his *Niederwerfungstrategie* (strategy of annihilation) and laid a blueprint for victory that was lauded for the next seventy years. Given Germany's location in the middle of the European landmass, a long-drawn-out war of attrition was not something she fancied. If ever the temperature in Europe approached boiling point again, Germany would need to act fast and punch hard if she wanted to repeat the glory of 1870.

Enter Alfred Graf von Schlieffen, who served as Chief of the Imperial General Staff between 1891 – 1906. Schlieffen was the latest in a long line of Clausewitz fanboys and after Germany's failure to renew the 'Reassurance Treaty' with Russia in 1890, dedicated a lot of time to solving a German nightmare scenario – a war fought simultaneously on two fronts. Specifically, France in the west and Russia in the east.

Not surprisingly, his ideas and preparations were centred around his own *Niederwerfungstrategie* which saw France dealt with in swift fashion during the first phase of battle, before transferring attention east to deal with Russia. A key part of his plan, and one which became somewhat diluted over time, was Schlieffen's insistence of a concentration of total force against the *centra gravitatis* of France. When the time came for the German army to act against France in the summer of 1914, the current Chief of Staff Field Marshall Helmuth von Moltke reduced the size of the northern wing of the advance to protect against potential French retaliation on the border. This caused the advance to lose momentum near the Marne river. The *Niederwerfungstrategie* had failed.

The big question now was how would an army that had grown up on the concept of large-scale, decisive manoeuvres adjust and cope with the new reality of static trench warfare? The answer was once again found deep within the writings of our old friend, Clausewitz.

While the concept of *centra gravitatis* was used to pinpoint a priority target at a very high strategic level, the German translation (*Schwerpunkt* – translated as point of main effort or focal point) was used within the army to help pinpoint priority targets at a more tactical or local level. Every level of command, from the highest staff offices right down to individual infantry companies or artillery batteries could identify their own *Schwerpunkt* and they would get the support of any service or logistical organisation that was helping them (such as ammunition columns, engineers, labour groups etc.) Everyone knew what their focus point was, and this helped all decision makers use their resources in the right way to benefit their own personal *Schwerpunkt*.

In 1916, the *Schwerpunkt* of the German High Command was Verdun and to keep this particular *Schwerpunkt* alive, it forced the rest of the Western Front to survive on the bare minimum of resources. Not surprisingly, this had repercussions up and down the line, not least for the German Second Army, commanded by *General der Infanterie* Fritz von Below, which was bracing itself for a major Allied attack on either side of the Somme river.

2

---•---

SIT REP: THE WESTERN FRONT, 1916

A s the first anaemic tentacles of dawn danced across *No Man's Land* on 1st January 1916, things were not looking all that rosy for the Allies. The war had been raging for the best part of sixteen months, and despite tremendous efforts and massive loss of life, the German army had not budged. Vast swathes of French and Belgian territory remained in German hands and there were no signs of them packing their bags and heading back to the Fatherland.

The Western Front, 1916

This situation was not lost on the top brass of the Allies. French Commander-in-Chief General Joffre had been pushing for more co-ordination in Allied attacks since the first Inter-Allied Military Conference at Chantilly on 7th July 1915. Later that year, Joffre issued a memo called *The Plan of Action Proposed by France to the Coalition* in which he proposed simultaneous large-scale attacks by French, British, Italian, and Russian troops as soon as conditions were favourable in 1916.

From a British point of view, a couple of decisions made in 1915 had reduced any offensive options in 1916 to a short list of one. After agreeing to evacuate Gallipoli and ruling out increasing activity in Salonika, this left France or Belgium on the Western Front as the only alternatives.

Throughout 1915, both Britain and France had tried valiantly to break through the German defensive lines on the Western Front. The vision of the Allies was a glorious one: Orchestrate a decisive breakthrough of the German defences, liberate Lille and other important French cities, free up French industry, kick the Germans out of Brussels, re-instate the Belgian King and push the dastardly Hun all the way back to Berlin. It all sounded so easy, but none of it happened. They didn't even get close.

The only thing the main Allied offensives of 1915 – in Artois, the Champagne region, Neuve-Chappelle and at Loos – succeeded in doing was to add thousands upon thousands of names to the already swollen casualty lists. Mix into the pot some choice German attacks such as those at Hill 60 and the Second Battle of Ypres and we can quickly see what a miserable place the Western Front was for the Allies in 1915.

Despite the effort and sacrifice of the men in the trenches, by the time the military leaders were tucking in to more vol-au-vents at Chantilly for the second Inter-Allied Military Conference in December, the positions of trenches along the Western Front were practically the same as at the start of the year – only the barbed wire entanglements were thicker, the machine-gun posts more numerous, the dug-outs were deeper and the mud thicker.

3

GRASPING THE NETTLE: BATTLE PLANNING

The failure to smash the Germans at Loos was embarrassing for both British military leaders and the politicians of the War Committee. They immediately started looking for a suitable scapegoat and, after much hand wringing and moustache smoothing, decided that it had taken too long to get the reserves up to the front line to take advantage of initial successes. As a result, Field Marshall Sir John French was cancelled on 19th December 1915 and asked to clear his desk. His replacement was General Sir Douglas Haig.

Haig took over the British Expeditionary Force (BEF) when it was just beginning to flex its muscles on the Western Front. People all over the country had heard the rally cries for men to enlist, and by January 1916 the army had deployed thirty-eight infantry divisions in France and Flanders – amounting to almost a million men. If that wasn't enough, Britain's manufacturing industry had finally got into a rhythm and was now supplying a decent number of guns, ammunitions and supplies to keep these new soldiers in the show. It had taken almost two years, but Britain had finally found her fighting boots.

From a French point of view, all of this had taken Britain two years too long and still paled into insignificance when compared to the French deployment of ninety-five Divisions. Whatever noises came out of London, the French were still the masters of the Allied disposition on the Western Front – a situation that General Joffre was never shy of mentioning. Indeed, it was Joffre who insisted that the British should take more of a front-line position during 1916 and by the time Haig had settled into his new office Joffre had already decided that the main Allied attack of the summer would take place down by the River Somme with the French and British armies linking arms and giving the Germans a jolly good Anglo-French beating.

It was an ambitious plan. The proposed attack would take place across a 60-mile front along a stretch of the Western Front which had not seen a great deal of action so far - giving the Germans plenty of opportunity to perfect their positions and construct formidable defences. Despite that, Joffre was convinced that if the British and French pooled their resources, they would smash the Germans to pieces on the Somme, use up all their reserves and achieve a stunning breakthrough. The battle on the Somme would never be a subtle, tactical affair. No, this would be a lesson in brute strength and power winning the day.

From a British point of view, there was little direct strategic reward for mounting such an assault on the Somme. Haig preferred to have a go in Flanders, where he at least had a chance of liberating the Belgian coast. However, being the new boy at the top table meant he had little choice but to take one for the team for the sake of the Allied alliance.

There were lots of details to iron out, and one such detail that caused significant back and forth between Haig and Joffre was the subject of preliminary operations to be carried out before the main event. Joffre was adamant that the British would put together at least two spring attacks to soften up the Germans before the big show on the Somme, whereas Haig was only willing to commit to one. Tensions rose within the Allied corridors of power; however, it all became a touch irrelevant on 21st February when Falkenhayn launched a surprise assault on the French fortress city of Verdun.

Whilst Joffre concerned himself with making sure his French army could cling on to Verdun, Haig got busy with his plans for the *Big Push* in the summer. On 24th March, he put together detailed training instructions for his cavalry divisions - he wanted them ready to take advantage of any gap that appeared in the enemy's defences. A week later, a brand-new casualty clearing station was erected in the village of Heilly, just eight miles from La Boiselle. Within eight weeks, ten more stations were up and running.

The sheer scale of the scheduled offensive was enough to give the planning team severe migraines. Somehow facilities needed to be found that could put a roof over the heads of 400,000 men and 100,000 horses. Roads had to be reinforced with chalk so they could handle the huge numbers of boots, hooves and wheels that would traverse them. An entire water system needed to be designed and built to deliver water as near to the front as possible, filling up massive water tanks of 2,000 gallons each at pre-designated watering holes.

To supplement the road network, work began on a new standard-gauge railway line to enable fifteen trains a day to deliver supplies to the front and evacuate the wounded. In addition, the existing rail network behind the lines was extensively improved and extended. All in all, seventeen rail-heads were constructed, and fifty-five miles of new track laid down.

As the preparations continued, so did the fighting at Verdun. By the beginning of May, the situation in the fortress city was causing serious alarm. The French were suggesting casualties were already close to 115,000, but there were many senior Allied staff officers convinced they were sandbagging and that the real number was significantly higher. There was a real and present danger that the Germans were on the cusp of breaking through.

France needed Britain to launch their offensive to divert German focus away from Verdun, and they needed it now. And while they were at it, those forty French divisions that Haig was counting on would have to be reduced to twenty-five and even then, there was no guarantee that the French could muster that number of men. It was situation critical, and Joffre was getting very excited, demanding that Haig launch his attack in July at the very latest. In response, Haig re-iterated his support to help bail out the French, but, having kept a close eye on the training of his men, he was not convinced they would be ready for a July show.

Ultimately, Joffre overruled Haig, famously shouting that "the French Army would cease to exist if we did nothing until then!" Haig had no choice but to defer to French demands. Haig's *Big Push* was pencilled in for 29th June.

4

ALMOST AGREEING: DEFINING SCOPE AND OBJECTIVES OF THE BATTLE

O nce it became obvious that this would be largely a British-led show, Haig got busy with the preparations. The Somme frontline he had earmarked for the British ran from Gommecourt in the north to Maricourt in the south, with the French straddling the River Somme from Maricourt down to Foucaucourt. General Sir Henry Rawlinson was put in charge of sorting it all out.

Rawlinson moved into his new HQ at Querroeu on 25th February and immediately got to work, undertaking some reconnaissance of the battlefield to see for himself the German defences. He was initially quite upbeat about the whole show, but his corps commanders didn't share his optimism and went out of their way to impress on their commander their preference for a smaller scale attack with limited objectives. They had even taken it upon themselves to draft up a full plan for such an offensive.

Their plan outlined a two-step *bite and hold* operation, which had the express aim of killing as many German soldiers as possible. It would take place on a front of 20,000 yards and would follow a lengthy preliminary bombardment of around sixty hours to cut the enemy wire. This was not about huge thrusting advances and penetrating deep inside enemy territory, this was about wearing down the enemy while enduring as little loss as possible.

Rawlinson agreed to put the plan forward to Haig, and did so on 4th April, although he knew the Commander-in-Chief would not like it.

He was right. Haig hated it. Ten days later, Haig wrote a formal reply disagreeing with the long bombardment and suggesting a more aggressive plan to capture the German second line all at once. Haig believed the artillery support would be enough to protect the advancing men, despite the long distances involved.

Rawlinson wrote back on 19th April. He agreed that extending the line north and south, as per Haig's initial requests, would be sensible in an ideal world, but he did not have the manpower or artillery resources to support such notions. He also kicked back on Haig's insistence on extending the scope of the objectives, re-iterating his nervousness surrounding effective artillery support to such distant activities. Although he conceded that in these matters, he would carry out Haig's instructions if he were insistent.

Regarding other matters, Rawlinson was more stubborn. He was not about to back down regarding a lengthy bombardment, repeating his conviction that they needed fifty to sixty hours of shelling to cut enemy wire sufficiently. There was also a misunderstanding regarding the use of cavalry – Rawlinson proposed to use the cavalry *en masse* south of Grandcourt to help protect the northern flank of the attack, while Haig wanted them spread across the front, ready to exploit any gaps in the line.

Over the coming weeks, the commanders agreed on compromises - Haig's plan to attack at Gommecourt in the north was reduced to a diversionary tactic and handed over to the Third Army. Haig also agreed to release five additional siege artillery batteries to help with the extension of the southern flank down to Montauban, and he agreed that the length of the preliminary bombardment should be extended. Rawlinson got his five-day smash-up.

By early May, the British aspect of the attack was clearly defined; Eleven divisions would attack along a front of 24,000 yards that stretched from Serre in the north to Montauban in the South (where they would link arms with the northern element of the French attack).

North of the Pozieres-Albert road, the primary objective would be the German second line – somewhere between 3,000-4,000 yards from the jumping-off points.

South of the road, the objectives were slightly shorter, varying between 2,000 and 3,000 yards distant. The infantry assault would be aided where possible by smoke screens and would be preceded by a five-day artillery bombardment which would clear wire and destroy enemy strong points. Gas would be used to clear villages.

Battle objectives north of the Somme River. 1st July 1916.

Cavalry would be used to protect the northern and southern flanks of the attack and also to assist the infantry where needed. When all of this had been accomplished, the focus would move south to help bolster the French.

It all sounded very simple on paper, but no sooner had Haig and Rawlinson shook hands on the detail the situation at Verdun meant that the French contingent of 39 Divisions would now only be 30. By the end of the month, that number had reduced to 20 and by the beginning of June, the French contingent was down to just 12

Divisions. It was very late in the day, but Rawlinson was forced to re-evaluate his plans for the attack.

On 14th June, Rawlinson issued his new set of battle objectives. The first objectives remained unchanged although the second line was modified, and a third set of objectives were added – namely the capture of the prominent ridge from Martinpuich to Ginchy, via High Wood. The overall aim of the offensive was changed too – it was no longer to assist the French, it was now to breach the enemy's defences and carry out a full-on breakthrough, using cavalry to rout the beleaguered enemy and chase them all the way back to Bapaume. Some fifteen kilometres (nine and a bit miles) distant.

So much for Rawlinson's cautious *bite and hold* strategy of April.

In a war where most large advances were being measured in yards, an objective of almost ten miles seems somewhat optimistic. Europe hadn't seen that kind of advance since Napoleon, and when the Emperor was busy giving most of Europe a very French kicking, trivial things such as machine-guns, heavy artillery, trench mortars, barbed wire, underground mines and deep fortifications had yet to be invented or perfected.

5

FRESH MEAT: KITCHENER'S NEW ARMY

On 5th August 1914, Field Marshall Earl Kitchener of Khartoum assumed the position of Minster of War and promptly implemented strategies to substantially grow the British Army. Unlike most people of the time, he did not think that the war would be over by Christmas, instead he foresaw a long, drawn-out conflict that would require a lot more men than the BEF currently had.

He didn't fancy using the Territorial Army as a basis to increase British military strength, as members of the Territorials could opt to avoid overseas service. In Kitchener's opinion, Britain didn't need a big home service army, she needed men on the Western Front, giving Fritz what for. He therefore decided to expand the regular army by raising a new version of wartime volunteers aged between 19 and 30 who would sign up for the duration of the war and, more importantly, would agree to be sent anywhere the army needed them.

On 6th August, parliament agreed to an increase of 500,000 men of all ranks.

The call went out to the men of Great Britain: *Your King and Country needs you!* General Sir Henry Rawlinson wondered if men would be more inclined to enlist in the Army if they knew they would serve alongside their mates. To test his theory, he appealed to London stockbrokers to raise a battalion of men from workers in the City of

London. A week later, 1,600 men had enlisted in the 10th (Service) Battalion, Royal Fusiliers, the so-called "Stockbrokers' Battalion".

A few days later, Edward Stanley, the 17th Earl of Derby, followed this example and organised the formation of a battalion of men from Liverpool. Within two days, 1,500 Scousers had joined the new battalion. Speaking to these men, Lord Derby said: "This should be a battalion of pals, a battalion in which friends from the same office will fight shoulder to shoulder for the honour of Britain and the credit of Liverpool." Three more battalions were raised in Liverpool within the next few days.

The country had listened and acted. Two weeks after Kitchener's Call to Arms, the first 100,000 men had signed up. Kitchener had his first Army (named 'K1') made up of six Divisions. On 28th August, Kitchener asked for another 100,000 men. To help the recruitment effort, the idea of the Pals Battalion was heavily hyped up and down the country; also, the age limits were lowered to thirty-five for men with no experience, forty-five for ex-soldiers and fifty for old Non-Commissioned Officers (NCO's).

By the end of September 1914, over fifty towns had formed one or more Pals Battalions and there were enough men for another army ('K2'). The War Office sanctioned three more Armies by October. Altogether, thirty new Divisions (in 1915 a single Division included about 19,500 men) were in the process of being built. It was, quite simply, an incredible achievement.

In March 1915, an order was issued to create a sixth Army. By the end of December 1915, many original regular battalions had a large contingent of volunteers who had replaced the losses of the previous eighteen months of fighting.

The men were now in place, but what about the weapons, uniforms, medical centres, accommodation, vehicles, animals, ammunition, guns, training centres, experienced officers and commanders needed to transform these men into a professional and effective fighting unit?

In reality, no regiment had the required amount of equipment for the new intake. Many men trained in their own clothes and some regiments dug out old uniforms dating from earlier wars for recruits (or at least NCO's) to wear. Regarding guns, there weren't many of those around either. All available artillery was already at the front, and many regiments had to make do with wooden replica rifles for training purposes.

By spring 1915, many of these issues had been overcome and Kitchener's Armies trained hard. Training this lot was tough. Few of the volunteers had any soldiering experience, and the majority had never held a rifle, let alone fired an artillery piece or a machine gun. The progress was slow, and British Commanders were not convinced that these new recruits would perform very well on the Western Front.

Only time would tell if Kitchener's idea would prove successful. The first *Pals'* battalions would see fighting on the Western Front around the town of Loos in just a few months' time. The rest would have to wait until 1916 and the *Big Push* on the Somme to get a piece of the action.

6

ALMOST DISASTROUS: FALKENHAYN'S FOOLISHNESS

For Falkenhayn and the rest of the chaps at *OHL* (*Oberste Heeresleitung* – The German High Command) the strategic *Schwerpunkt* for 1916 was obviously Verdun. German deployments elsewhere significantly felt the impact of this decision as the High Command systematically diverted guns, men, and resources from the rest of the Western Front to strengthen the Verdun offensive. Consequently, German positions elsewhere were spread dangerously thin - none more so than those holding the line in the Somme region.

It was the German Second Army, under the watchful gaze of *General der Infanterie* Fritz von Below, who held residency on the Somme. At the beginning of 1916 it was a relatively quiet part of the line, but no sooner had the Germans fired their opening salvos at Verdun, Second Army reconnaissance aircraft were reporting a significant increase in enemy activity just north of the Somme river that indicated the British were planning something heavy.

These kinds of reports caused Below to get understandably twitchy. Although his men had held this section of the line for over a year and had developed a network of powerful defensive positions, he could only muster eleven divisions. If the British did kick off on his doorstep, he wasn't in great shape to do anything about it.

Below believed it would be in his interest to take the fight to the British sooner rather than later – before they were ready. On 2nd March Below sent a request to *OHL* asking permission to launch a pre-emptive attack that would catch the enemy off guard and help straighten out a kink in his line – making it easier to defend. To make this attack work, he asked for reinforcements of twelve infantry divisions and 130 heavy artillery batteries.

Falkenhayn's response was brief and to the point. *Nein!* He would allow nothing to dilute the Verdun *Schwerpunkt.*

As spring turned into summer, the activity behind the British lines was being ramped up to eleven and it was proving almost impossible to hide from German observers. Below's advisors were now suggesting that the British could have as much as a 3-1 superiority in infantry. On 26th May Below submitted a fully worked out attack plan for his Somme sector, which called for an advance on a twenty-five-kilometre front designed to capture as much land and cause as much disruption to Allied preparations as possible. Knowing that resources would be tight, Below proposed a phased approach, attacking in the north first before redeploying his forces to the south for round two.

The response from *OHL* was deafening in its silence.

Getting desperate, Below sent another option to *OHL* suggesting he could still disrupt Allied attack plans by launching a minor attack just a few kilometres wide from St. Pierre Divion to Ovillers. This plan would need only one additional infantry division, thirty heavy howitzers and a handful of other artillery batteries. This time he did hear back from OHL. The answer was no. Again.

There was no doubt that the fancy brass at *OHL* knew Below was about to be attacked in a rather large way, but blinded by the Verdun *Schwerpunkt,* they refused to help him. Then, on 4th June, the Russians launched their own attack in the east - now there was no hope for Below to get any reinforcements for his Second Army on the Somme.

It was now clear that Below had to deal with whatever the Allies were going to throw at him without help from the *OHL*. He now needed to make a very important decision; where was his *Schwerpunkt* going to be?

He plumped for the north side of the Somme, specifically the high ground running from Ovillers, across the Thiepval and Hawthorn Ridges and along to Serre. There were a couple of reasons for this decision; first, this high ground had long been identified as having real strategic significance in the area and since October 1914, the German regiments holding that sector had worked tirelessly to make it as impregnable as possible. Second, Below presumed the French would struggle to launch anything major to the south of the Somme, mainly because of the demands of the Verdun battle on their men and resources, but also because he knew that if they advanced too far, they would march straight into huge swampy marshlands which would prove almost impossible to cross under-fire.

With the decision on the whereabouts of his *Schwerpunkt* made, Below set about doing everything he could to protect it, and this meant moving significant resources north, leaving the southern sector dangerously thin on the ground. However, he did have one little trick up his sleeve, which meant the situation wasn't quite as hopeless as it seemed on paper.

One of the many peculiarities of the German Army was the way it was organised. Although it tried very hard to behave as a single 'Imperial' entity, the reality was somewhat different. Prussia was the obvious dominating force within the Army, but there were several other army contingents that originated from other kingdoms across the country, such as Bavaria, Saxony, and Württemberg. These different groups enjoyed a certain degree of independence from Mother Prussia and as a result, Below and his Staff could circumnavigate some of the Prussian hierarchy and take the matter of reinforcements up with directly with the Württemberg command structure.

By the end of May, a request for reinforcements was approved, the Reserve Field Artillery Regiment 27 was formed and started marching straight for the Somme. Happy days!

In the same way, two new Field Artillery Regiments, a new Reserve Field Artillery Regiment and several infantry battalions were formed via the Grand Duchy of Baden to help reinforce the 28th Reserve Division, which held the line between La Boisselle and Mametz. Within a matter of weeks, Below had a raft of new guns and fresh men in position and ready to go.

Yet, despite all of this, thanks to the continual refusal of Falkenhayn and his *OHL* cronies to strengthen the region, the German positions to the north and south of the Somme were hopelessly outnumbered. Below and his men had no choice but to strengthen their defences where possible and wait anxiously for the inevitable Allied assault.

7

BIG GUNS: ARTILLERY

Whatever way you looked at it, the Battle of the Somme was always going to be a battle of the big guns. As soon as the fighting on the Western Front had settled down in early 1915 to a static trench-based affair, the army big-wigs on both sides of the wire quickly figured out that it was the artillery gun that held the key to success – although neither side had quite figured out how to pick the lock just yet.

As part of their plan, both Haig and Rawlinson had put a lot of emphasis on the role of the artillery. Their approach was simple: gather up more guns than had ever been gathered up before and use them to fire more shells than had ever been fired before in a five-day preliminary bombardment that would quite literally smash the enemy to pieces. The guns would cut the enemy's barbed wire, smash German defensive positions and strong-points and neutralise any return artillery threat. When the infantry attack began, the men would simply saunter across *No Man's Land* behind a protective curtain of shells and occupy the shattered German front line.

It would be a beautiful, albeit brutal, sight to behold.

Yet as the Somme planners went through the gears, back in London, the War Committee was nervous. The scandal of the 1915 artillery shell shortage for the spring battles was still a painful memory, and all eyes were on the Minister of Munitions, David Lloyd George, to see if he could conjure up the required number of guns and shells needed for such an epic shoot-out. On 2nd June, all British munitions workers were given the glorious news that their traditional Whitsun holiday of 11th June was to be postponed until later in the year. Every munitions factory in the land was working round the clock to meet War Office demand. But would it be enough?

The proposed start date for the *Big Push* was a matter of weeks away. Preparations had reached a crescendo; thousands of men were being trained to attack dummy trenches in France, artillery teams were being put through their paces and millions of tonnes of supplies were being hauled up to the front to feed the fighting machine. Yet the War Office had not actually given the attack their seal of approval. That all depended on a rather important meeting with Mr Lloyd George on 21st June. They needed to be convinced that he was going to deliver the hardware necessary for the preliminary bombardment.

They need not have worried. An upbeat Lloyd George produced some great numbers that proved that Britain had finally tied up the laces on her gun-making shoes. 140-150 heavy guns a month were leaving British factories bound for the France – compare that to the paltry 20-30 heavy guns coming out of France each month and you could understand Lloyd George's optimism. And as for shells, Lloyd George told the War Committee that Haig could order enough shells for his guns to lob over 300,000 shells onto the German lines each week. The War Committee was suitably impressed and signed the entire show off there and then.

In those final weeks running up to the whistle, some of the busiest soldiers on the Western Front were the artillerymen who were preparing for a massive five-day long bombardment designed to soften up the enemy defences before the infantry did their thing.

Lloyd George had famously promised the infantry that they would be backed up by guns standing 'wheel to wheel' along the entire front line. A bold claim, but when the bombardment began, there was an artillery gun, howitzer, or mortar for every seventeen yards of the enemy front line to be attacked. Compared with Loos, there were almost three times as many guns and six times the number of shells. In the eyes of many, Lloyd George had delivered.

But had he? Really?

Yes, he had assembled over three times as many guns compared to the Loos caper, but the Somme battle front was more than twice that as Loos, as such the men doing the fighting on the Somme would be only slightly better off than their counterparts from 1915. Another thing to consider is the German defences on the Somme were often three lines deep compared to a much flatter disposition at Loos – this meant that the Somme guns had up to six times the number of enemy positions to knock out when compared to Loos.

Six times the number of targets with only three times the number of guns. Looking at it like this, Lloyd George wasn't perhaps as successful as he would have us think.

That said, the number of guns being brought up to the line during early June was a formidable sight. Each gun was manhandled into position during the night to avoid enemy eyes. After they had settled in, each gun would fire a few shots to register targets and give the crew some practice, aided by forward observation officers positioned out in the front line or by observers from the Royal Flying Corps in either planes or balloons. Once this had been completed, they had nothing more to do other than wait.

By the time the first rounds of the great bombardment hurtled through the air towards the German lines on 24th June, there were an impressive (on paper at least) 1,437 guns ready and primed to give the enemy what-for. Over the next five days, the guns were scheduled to lob over 150,000 shells into enemy positions. Each day.

They would fire more shells in this single bombardment than had been fired in the first year of the war.

8

— • —

THE GREAT BOMBARDMENT

T he preliminary bombardment for the *Big Push* began on 24th June across the entire battle front. At this time the plan was still to have a five-day bombardment, with the infantry going over the top on 29th June.

Over the coming week, British artillery was to fire an eye-watering 1.7 million shells onto enemy positions. It was going to be a gargantuan effort, but would it be enough? Rawlinson had issued his gunners with three primary objectives: cut the wire laid in front of the German positions, smash those aforementioned German positions to pieces, and destroy as many enemy artillery positions as possible. He was confident his boys could do it and the men at the guns were determined not to let him down.

They quickly settled into a routine that comprised a morning blitz of eighty minutes where every available gun barked at the enemy lines, and a steady, continuous barrage fired throughout the rest of the day. At night, half of the guns were rested, in their place heavy machine-guns put down harassing fire behind the enemy's front line to disrupt the delivery of rations, supplies and reinforcements.

The gunners worked their guns until they either ran out of ammunition or the gun gave up the ghost. They fired to order, religiously following the barrage tables issued to each battery. The shelling was relentless and repentless. They fired until the gun breeches were so hot they had to be prised apart with an axe. They fired until the recoil buffers on some guns simply snapped under the strain. Surely nothing could survive such a pounding?

Unfortunately, plenty could and did survive. Despite the impressive show and the hard work and gusto of the gunners, the bombardment wasn't quite having the desired effect.

Of Rawlinson's three primary objectives, the cutting of the wire was perhaps the most achievable. It was also the task that had the most resources thrown at it, with almost two-thirds of the available guns dedicated to wire cutting. It was also the easiest of the three tasks to monitor progress using both Forward Observation Officers and the odd cheeky raid into *No Man's Land* to get a close-up view of the state of the enemy's wire defences.

That being said, cutting the wire wasn't without its difficulties. The undulating nature of the ground meant that direct observation was not always possible, poor light and weather also affected the ability to report back accurately on the state of the enemy wire. Then there were the big elephants in the room. The shells themselves.

Most of the shells that were put aside for wire-cutting work were 18-pound shrapnel or high explosive shells. When the shrapnel shell exploded, they scattered hundreds of lead balls forwards and downwards, so for these to work, they needed to be fired with great accuracy, so they detonated in just the correct spot for maximum impact. Not a straightforward thing to do and only a fraction of the gun teams had the pre-requisite experience and knowledge to lay down such accurate fire shell after shell. The high explosive shells did not demand shrapnel-levels of accuracy, but as they were designed to explode on impact with the ground, they tended to just throw great clumps of wire up in the air without cutting any of it.

Cutting the wire that lay between the German first and second lines was even more difficult, as the gunners had to rely on photographs from airplane spotters to help them understand if they were being successful. Most gunners agreed it was just down to luck if they cut any wire beyond a 5,000 yard range.

The only sure-fire way of checking the actual state of the enemy wire was to send men out into *No Man's Land* and get up close and personal with the wire itself.

Each patrol could only realistically be out in *No Man's Land* for a short period of time given the immense danger of such excursions, therefore only short lengths of the wire could be inspected at any given time – on a good night a patrol might have been able to check on 100 yards of wire. In the army records that covered the time period of the *Great Bombardment*, there were 50 such raids recorded. Optimistically, the maximum amount of wire that could have been checked would have been around 5,000 yards out of the 24,000 yards of front – a smidge over 20% of the total frontage. Hardly what you would call a thorough examination, but even so, half of those raids reported that the enemy wire seemed undamaged.

It would seem that the bombardment was not having the desired effect upon the enemy wire.

OK, so maybe the enemy wire would not be as cut-up as first expected, but even so, surely enemy front-line trench systems and dugouts would be obliterated? This was the artillery's second aim, but again, it was quite difficult to ascertain its effectiveness.

One option was to get the chaps from the Royal Flying Corps to take photos of the enemy front line and examine the images for damage. Thousands of photos were taken, but they were not detailed enough and were often difficult to interpret. Yet again it was down to infantry raiding parties to see at first-hand what was going on in the enemy's trenches.

In the south, the information coming from such raids was encouraging, with reports suggesting much damage being done to enemy front-line positions, including the destruction of many deep dugouts.

In the north, however, the situation was slightly different. Much of the wire was not cut, so raiding parties had trouble even getting to the enemy lines, and even when they managed to get through, they often faced strong enemy retaliation - especially from machine-guns - which made it impossible to check the conditions of enemy positions.

Third on the artillery's 'to-do' list was counter-battery work, (i.e., destroy Germany artillery so they couldn't fire on the advancing Allied infantry during the attack). This was another tough gig for the gunners, as the accuracy required to destroy relatively small targets over such long distances was difficult to achieve. That being said, the biggest issue facing the gunners here was simply a lack of hardware with which to carry out this work.

Rawlinson had allocated just 180 guns for counter-battery duty and many of these were old and worn-out pieces. On top of that, the demands from HQ to smash not only enemy front-line positions but also their second and even third lines of defences meant that many artillery commanders were forced to divert guns that should have been concentrating on counter-battery fire to distant wire cutting and trench bombardment.

Those that carried out counter-battery operations were further hampered by the weather, especially during the early days of the bombardment. Because of the distances involved, successful counter-batter fire depended on the RFC to be the eyes of the gunners and to report back on the accuracy of their fire and the positions of the enemy guns. When the weather turned on 26th June, low cloud and rain forced the RFC to ground their planes, forcing the gunners to use old map references to hit their targets.

All of this added up to a lacklustre counter-battery operation that ultimately failed to deliver results. When the whistles blew early in the morning on 1st July, the Germans had 850 guns of varying size and shape all aimed squarely on the advancing Allied infantry.

9

— ∙ —

WAR SPORT: TRENCH RAIDING

D uring brief lulls in the Allied drumfire, small raids were carried
out on enemy positions up and down the line. These had
two primary functions; to figure out how the enemy's front line was
coping with the bombardment and to grab a few prisoners for some
gentle interrogation.

A British intelligence report for 25th - 26th June noted ominously
that many of the raids carried out that night were unsuccessful because
of intense enemy machine-gun and rifle fire. One patrol of the Royal
Dublin Fusiliers navigated their way through the German wire and
got close enough to see that the German front-line positions were
totally smashed up, but they couldn't get much closer because of
sweeping machine-gun fire from positions behind the front-line. This
was not news to inspire confidence. If the Germans were moving their
machine-gunners to positions behind their front line, but they still
enjoyed a clear field of fire into *No Man's Land*, the assaulting troops
were going to be in all sorts of trouble come Zero hour.

On 26th June, heavy rain dampened the mood throughout the
British front line, but the weather didn't stop the raiding. That
night, fifty-seven men of the Newfoundland Regiment crossed *No
Man's Land* with the express aim of bringing back German prisoners
for a grilling. They were armed with Bangalore torpedoes - twen-

ty-foot-long steel tubes stuffed full of explosives – designed specifically to blow holes in enemy wire. As they approached the German wire, the first torpedo worked swimmingly, blowing a big enough gap in the wire to get everyone through safely, but once through the wire, they were faced with... yet more wire.

A second thick belt of wire had been placed right behind the first tranche. The second Bangalore torpedo was used but failed, leaving the group trapped in between two thick lines of wire. To make matters worse, their activities had alerted the Germans, who immediately sprayed the area with machine-gun bullets. The Newfoundlanders had no choice but to retreat to their own lines empty handed.

The next night, a second Newfoundland raiding party skirted out into No Man's Land to bring back prisoners. Despite torrential rain, they got through the German wire and into their front-line positions, but they were quickly spotted. Once more, they took zero prisoners, and this time lost six men in hand-to-hand fighting.

More raids took place during the night of 29th / 30th but with mixed fortunes. The Newfoundlanders went over once more, but this time ran into German trenches that were choc-full of enemy soldiers, forcing them once more to beat a hasty retreat empty-handed. Forty-two men of the 18th West Yorkshire Regiment volunteered to take part in a raid on the same night, but despite the artillery barrage, the enemy were in place and on full alert. Thirteen of the Yorkshires were killed, twelve were wounded and one was taken prisoner. Towards the southern limits of the front, there was, however, cause for some optimism. Raid reports in this area seemed to suggest that it was easier to get into enemy positions and that they were badly damaged, with many dug-outs being destroyed.

Getting prisoners was proving to be a very tough ask. Just twelve Germans were captured and interrogated in the week before the assault, and their feedback was less than conclusive. Some said that the German dug-outs were being destroyed left, right and centre. Others reported the dug-outs to be in good condition and providing adequate shelter for the men. One prisoner even mentioned new dugouts being constructed in the support lines.

If the results of the raids and the information gleaned from the tiny group of prisoners were telling Haig and his cronies one thing, it was that despite all the artillery action, in many parts of the line the Germans were far from being smashed up, especially in the north.

This was not the conclusion reached by the chaps at Fourth Army Intelligence, however. In their daily intelligence report for 30th June, they optimistically stated that "From the examination of prisoners, it is apparent that our artillery fire has been most effective. Most of the dug-outs in the (enemy) front line have been blown in or blocked up."

Quite how they gleaned this conclusion from the evidence of just twelve prisoners is anyone's guess.

10

— • —

JUST LET THEM COME! THE GERMAN FRONT
LINE – JUNE 1916

A t the beginning of June, the Germans manning their front-line
positions throughout the Somme sector were in a relatively
positive frame of mind. Yes, it seemed inevitable that the British were
going to launch some kind of summer attack in the area, but over the
last eighteen months they had built themselves some very nice, sturdy
defensive fortifications across the sector.

Deep solid trenches zig-zagged across the front line, some up to
twelve feet deep, with strong wicker and wooden revetments to help
them absorb shock waves and stop them collapsing under pressure
from shellfire. Fortified strong-points were dotted along the front
line, cleverly concealed and blended into the fire-trenches so they
became practically invisible to any attacking force until it was too late.
Machine-gun positions were chosen specifically to give the gunners
excellent fields of fire across all approaches. Twenty feet underground
there was a veritable warren of inter-connected wood panelled living
quarters, and medical bunkers.

The Germans had long since had an inkling that the Somme would
see some kind of Allied action, and nothing had been left to chance.
Not only did the German know every inch of the ground, they controlled the high ground. Extra trenches had been built across the ridges

that dominated any likely Allied approach, and all villages in the area had been fortified.

These dominating positions meant they could see well into the rear of the British lines, and the specific design of the defences meant that the second and third lines could fire over the heads of those in the front line into any on-rushing attack. All of this added up to a serene confidence that they could beat down any Allied attack that came their way. And anyway, at least they had not been sent to the killing grounds of Verdun.

Their attitude to their surroundings would have changed significantly at the commencement of the Great Bombardment, for it would be the start of a living nightmare that would continue unabated for a full week and push the men's nerve, spirit, and determination to survive to the very limit and beyond.

It wasn't just the sheer number of shells that fell on their positions that was shattering their sanity – it was the certainty - and yet at the same time, uncertainty - of the impending attack that was equally nerve-shredding. They knew it was all going to kick off at some point, but when? No one could say for sure.

The constant shelling was also causing utter chaos behind the lines. Food rations, equipment and reinforcements struggled to get anywhere near the men in the trenches as German infrastructure was systematically smashed to pieces. After a couple of days of constant bombardment, the overall situation on the German side of the wire was approaching crisis levels, yet they found a way.

While the front lines soldiers were forced to break into their emergency iron rations just to survive, towards the rear everyone was frantically figuring out how to feed them. Roads were rebuilt and food rations were brought up as far as possible by columns of motor transport that were forced to take significant detours to avoid the shelling. Once unloaded, the rations were brought up to the front by hand. It was slow, arduous, and dangerous, but by day three of the bombardment, warm food rations were once again reaching the front line.

The conditions being endured by the Germans were excruciating, but most of the men were not directly exposed to the shellfire in the open trenches. Most were tucked up deep underground in huge, reinforced bunkers and dugouts. Conditions down there were not going to worry the Ritz, but it was much safer than being out in the open. They were physically and mentally exhausted, but those men lucky enough to see out the bombardment in these dugouts remained relatively unscathed and were primed to be deployed in a matter of minutes into whatever remained of their trench system above ground.

Corporal Friedrich Hinkel, 7th Company, 99th Reserve Infantry Regiment summed up the general mood in these cramped German dug-outs when he recalled:

> ... on the 27th and the 28th there were gas attacks on our trenches. The torture and the fatigue, not to mention the strain on the nerves was indescribable! There was just one single heart-felt prayer on our lips: "Oh, God, free us from this ordeal; give us release through battle, grant us victory; Lord God! Just let them come!" And this determination increased with the fall of each shell. You made a good job of it, you British! Seven days and nights you rapped and hammered on our door! Now your reception was going to match your turbulent longing to enter![1]

11

RECONNAISSANCE AND DOMINANCE: THE ROLE OF THE ROYAL FLYING CORPS

An often-overlooked aspect of the Battle of the Somme is that of the air battle. Both sides were building out their respective air forces as quickly as possible. Tactics were evolving and many senior military planners on either side of the wire were realising the advantages of fully integrating their respective air corps into their land-based battle plans.

As the Battle of the Somme was a British-led attack, the onus was on Sir Hugh Trenchard's administration to squeeze as much out of their flying machines as they possibly could and work 'wing to muzzle' with the army chaps to take the fight to the Germans in all areas.

The biggest challenge facing the Royal Flying Corps (RFC) was that the scrap on the Somme would be on a much grander scale than anything that it had been part of before. As preparations for battle ramped up in late 1915, the rate of expansion in the RFC was so great that many of the new squadrons that were popping up in France all over the place were dominated by pilots and observers who had received precious little formal training and whose combat experience was practically zero.

Regardless of experience, the Royal Flying Corps was an integral part of battle planning and was given four principal objectives: first, they were tasked with winning and maintaining air superiority over the battlefield; second, they were to carry out detailed reconnaissance over enemy territory, searching out and reporting on enemy strong points, fortifications and artillery positions; third, they were to help British artillery find and range specific targets and finally they were given the not insignificant task of photographing the entire enemy front from above so the army intelligence group could do their thing.

As leader of the Royal Flying Corps, Trenchard was keen for his men to dominate the skies and be proactive in taking the fight to the enemy by any means possible. No opportunity to take down an enemy machine should be passed by but it wasn't until the introduction of three new planes in early 1916 – the de Haviland 2 (DH2), the FE2 B and the Sopwith 1 ½ Strutter (the first British aircraft to boast a synchronised Vickers machine gun that could fire through the propeller) – that the pendulum of aerial superiority swung over to the British. Finally, the brave pilots had possession of a new generation of aircraft that could compete on equal terms with the German Fokker machines.

In May and June, the pace of aerial combat grew ever more frenetic as both sides became increasingly desperate to take control of the air. To maximise damage and destruction, all RFC pilots were ordered to carry two 20lb bombs and drop them on any enemy position they thought was worthwhile. As well as causing maximum violence, this order also ensured all pilots actually made it across to the enemy lines, as some were reluctant to do so.

This combative direction continued throughout the entire battle. By November 1916, the RFC had dropped over 17,600 bombs onto enemy territory (that's almost 300 tonnes of explosives) and had accounted for 370 enemy aircraft.

As well as trying to smash the German air force to bits, the Flying Corps boys were also asked to help the artillery seek potential targets and assist with aiming and ranging the big guns. Pilots were asked to fly deep into enemy territory to spot artillery placements – although they were often well camouflaged, their location were sometimes given away by muzzle flashes or smoke. Once discovered, the pilot would then mark the position on a large-scale map he carried with him in the cockpit.

During a typical reconnaissance mission like this, a pilot might locate two or three gun batteries. Once back on the ground the information was either telephoned through to the artillery batteries concerned, or the pilot may see the battery commanders in person to take them through what he had discovered from the air. By early 1916, this method of aerial observation was well established and very successful.

Another way the Royal Flying Corps helped the gunners on the ground was with ranging their guns. When firing on targets that were out of sight, it was obviously difficult to know if you had scored a hit or not, but with a spotter in the air reporting back on how far away from the target you shot was, and in which direction, the gunners could home in on targets with decent accuracy.

To help orchestrate the whole programme of ranging guns, a 'clock code' had been developed back in 1915, which allowed the pilot and gunner to use the same frame of reference when talking about a specific target. Rather than me try to describe it, why don't we hear from someone who was directly involved – Captain Archibald James, 2 Squadron, Royal Flying Corps:

> *"The system of correcting faults (in the firing) was this. You had imaginary circles drawn around the target, 25 yards, 50 yards, 150, 200, 250, 300, 250, 400 – and you had a simple letter and figure code to indicate two things: the clock-face point at which the shells were falling, in other words whether they were falling at one o'clock or three o'clock from the target; and the distance expressed in the imaginary circles which you visualised*

without much difficulty. With a good battery – batteries varied enormously – you should get them right on target at about the third salvo.[1]

Captain James makes it sound easy, but to be a good aerial spotter took a lot of practice, and some ranging projects were easier than others. For example, ranging on to a large enemy gun battery would be slightly easier that trying to get shrapnel shells to burst in just the right place to cut through enemy wire belts.

There was then the small matter of egos. Many artillery officers hated they fact that they were being advised and told what to do by non-artillery personnel and often ignored or sabotaged the information being given from the air.

The final piece of the British air-war jigsaw was photographic reconnaissance. Such intelligence gathering from the air began the minute the British took over the Somme front in July 1915, but only really got serious in March 1916. From this date, the Royal Flying Corps set about photographing the whole of the German front to a depth of around 1,000 yards every month to keep track of any new structures or defensive posts. The RFC used box cameras with an infinity lens which were attached to the outside of the plane and operated by the pilot.

The cameras were not the handheld 'point and click' pieces of technology we are used to today. Oh no, these were slightly more cumbersome and complicated than that. They were big and bulky wooden box cameras with a leather concertina pull out lens which were strapped to the outside of the plane pointing down towards earth.

There was a small handle that needed to be pushed and pulled to change the glass plates and to take an actual photo the pilot (yes, the pilot!) needed to lean over the side of the cockpit, look down through the camera sight, push and pull the lever to get the plates into position with his right hand while steering the plane with his left. To complete the shot, he had to pull a small piece of string that was flapping about in the wind – preferably while avoiding being shot at. Once one photo had been taken, the handle was pushed and pulled again. The pilot then carried on flying for a bit, judged the overlap and did it all again.

It was far from simple work, and the pilots were forced to spend two or three hours over enemy lines for each reconnaissance mission, but the results were hugely important.

With good, clear photos taken from a reasonable height of between 6,000 and 8,000 feet, the detail was quite something to the trained eye. The location of the German defences could be pinpointed, including machine-gun posts, dug-outs, strongpoints, and supply dumps. Although photographic interpretation was far from being an exact science in 1916, the information brought back by the pilots of the Royal Flying Corps was incredibly valuable.

Although the alignment and the co-operation between land and air forces were far from perfect in 1916, the Battle of the Somme was the first large-scale attack in which Britain consciously tried to integrate her airborne capabilities directly with the ground battle. Lessons learned on this battlefield would ultimately prove invaluable in the design and deployment of the full air/land co-operation that would be so effective in 1918.

12

RED TABS AND LONG DAYS: THE VIEW FROM HQ

British GHQ (General headquarters) was transferred from Saint-Omer to Montreuil-sur-Mer in March 1916. The tranquil surroundings of this place were set back towards the French coast – over one hundred kilometres from the filth and tension of the front line trenches.

Not that life in the Staff was without stress. The logistic and administrative burdens heaped upon the staff officers charged with getting everything ready for the *Big Push* were enormous. Many such men worked fourteen hours a day, every day, in the run up to the offensive and dozens of regimental men drafted in to give a hand struggled to cope with the relentless pressure of the job. With just forty-eight hours to go before the whistles blew, the combined force of the officers and men of the British Staff had literally moved mountains to ensure that the largest British fighting force ever assembled had enough weapons, ammunition, food, water, animal fodder and fuel to ensure victory.

Wells had been dug to ensure a reliable source of vital water, new roads and rail links had been constructed to enable supplies to be brought up to as close to the front line as possible, dozens of extra medical facilities had been built, as had numerous prisoner of war stations to hold captured enemy troops.

It was an unprecedented organisational effort and had been carried out with remarkable competency.

Sir Douglas Haig summed it up nicely when he wrote to his wife from his forward HQ at the Château Val Vion at Beauquesne (twelve miles behind the lines) on the eve of battle.

> *The attack is to go in tomorrow at 7.30am... I feel that everything possible for us to do to achieve success has been done.*[1]

Despite the stress and workload, life at GHQ wasn't a bad gig. Most HQ's based themselves within large stately homes or château's which were well out of range of the enemy big guns. The houses were palatial for good reason – such bases required living quarters, working space and copious amounts of stabling for horses. The men were worked hard but were also well looked after – the wine cellars of HQ's were never empty.

There were eighteen British Divisions in the front line poised and primed for the attack. Divisional HQ's were dotted along the battle front, mostly situated close behind the artillery gun line. Corps Commanders were situated about eight miles back and General Rawlinson, head of the Fourth Army, had positioned his HQ around twelve miles behind the front line.

Haig could sometimes be accused of issuing orders that lacked clarity and definition. He was not the best speaker in the world and quite often his subordinates, including Rawlinson, mis-interpreted his instructions. For the Battle of the Somme, Haig and Rawlinson needed five separate meetings to agree and define the battle objectives for the Fourth Army. These orders were cascaded down to the five Corps commanders of the Fourth Army, few of whom had the experience or guts to question the plans even if they had their own reservations.

Even If they had pushed back a little, Rawlinson made it apparent right from the start that any criticism of orders would not be tolerated – they had no choice but to just suck it up and get on with it.

Communication lines between the various headquarters were sorely inadequate – it was often easier and quicker for Haig to send and receive messages to and from London than it was for him to get information on what was happening at the front line. Telephone links running in and out of Montreuil were intermittent at best but provided somewhat acceptable connections up to Divisional HQ level, but collaboration with Battalion HQ's and any other command posts nearer the line had to rely on despatch riders, runners, and good ole pigeons.

The relationship between Corps and Division could often become strained. Divisional and Brigade HQ's represented the transition between General Staff aspirations and the reality of the front line – there was precious little human interaction between any group, it was just an endless stream of orders and instruction. Rawlinson's HQ sent 10,000 telegrams, 20,000 phone calls and 5,000 messages to Corps and Divisional headquarters a day. The Divisional Staffers had a hard time responding to the top's communication, let alone devise their own plans.

On the other side of the wire, the German command set-up was in decent shape. They had had a lot of time to choose the perfect positions for the various HQ locations. Battalion HQ's were all located in the second and third lines of the German trench system. Regimental HQ's were also well forward, often within the third line of defences, with Brigade HQ close by.

Telephone lines were buried deep underground, out of the way of even the heaviest of British shells, and linked all HQs with each other, including von Soden's own HQ at Château de Biefvillers just outside of Bapaume, some ten miles behind the line. This telephone system was also backed up with a system of both light and siren signals in case wires were cut.

Apart from a more robust inter-HQ communications system, there were two other key differences between the German and British General Staff. A British staff officer in the front line trenches was a very scarce bird indeed, whereas their German counter-parts were encouraged to visit the front line on a weekly basis – they were very much the eyes and ears of their Commanding Officer and were specifically asked to report back on such matters as soldier morale, the state of the trenches, supplies reaching the men, etc.

The second difference was a matter of prescription. British GHQ controlled every element of the attack plan through the minutiae of orders and they expected their orders to be carried out to the letter. The Germans were a bit more relaxed with the option of letting local leaders in the front line make on-the-spot decisions during the heat of battle as they saw fit.

13

CLAY KICKERS AND CANARIES: THE UNDERGROUND WAR

We know a great deal about the battle fought on the surface, with its massive trench systems, massive guns and even more massive infantry assaults. However, there was another war taking place simultaneously that is less well known; a brutal war of nerve and patience, carried out in total silence in cramped, claustrophobic conditions with precious little light and even less good air to breathe.

This was the underground war. A fascinating and fearful war where highly skilled tunnellers worked tirelessly to detonate huge explosive mines under enemy positions to blow them quite literally off the face of the earth.

By the end of 1914, activity on the Western Front had settled down somewhat and both sides set about building highly fortified and static positions right opposite each other, separated by a sliver of *No Man's Land*. It was the perfect environment for an underground war and for a specialist team of underground miners and tunnellers to show the world what they could do.

At about the same time, a very different group of men were hard at work beneath Manchester, England. They were known as Clay Kickers and they were working on a project to extend the sewerage system of the city under the watchful eye of wealthy engineer, businessman and MP; Major John Norton-Griffiths, who affectionately called these men his 'moles'.

Norton-Griffiths was an interesting character. He formed the 2nd King Edward's Horse cavalry regiment at the beginning of the war, but later he realised the military potential of his 'moles' and offered their services to the War Office for digging tunnels under enemy positions. His offer was politely turned down by however the Wart Office quickly changed its attitude when the Germans successfully mined a Indian-held position during the Battle of Givenchy in December 1914, with ten minor charges totalling just over 1,000lbs of explosives. The Givenchy mines were tiny compared to future explosions, but still killed many of the Sirhind Brigade who were holding the trench. Even though the Germans ultimately failed to make a decisive breakthrough at Givenchy, the whole show had a substantial impact on British morale.

More German mines followed in short order and by January 1915 panic was spreading among both front-line soldiers and the sharp suits of the War Office who were quickly back on the phone to Norton-Griffiths to enquire if his offer regarding his 'moles' was still on the table. It was, and a relived Lord Kitchener immediately put in a request for 10,000 clay kickers to be dispatched to France at the earliest opportunity.

He was to be disappointed – there just wasn't that amount of clay kickers in existence, but on 18th February 1915, the first group of twenty kickers were lifted out of the Manchester sewers and transported to the London office of Norton Griffiths. Here they were signed up and given a military medical - eighteen out of the twenty passed the tests – and those eighteen were immediately packed off to Victoria Station and then on to Brompton Barracks, the home of the Royal Engineers.

Within 24 hours these men had been catapulted from the sewers of Manchester to one of the most illustrious corps of the British Army

– they didn't know how to salute, parade or present arms, and they were more likely to address an officer with 'hey, mate' rather than 'sir', but all of that was of little consequence. That same evening, they were on the way to France, where they had one task and one task only – to dig. Within 36 hours, they were beneath the Western Front, kicking themselves towards the enemy.

It wasn't quite the 10,000 that Kitchener wanted, but it was a start.

As part of the deal to get the clay kickers in the Army's service, Norton-Griffiths was appointed liaison officer between the newly formed tunnelling companies and the Engineer-in-Chief's office and could often be seen touring the British reserve lines across France in his old Rolls Royce loaded with crates of fine wine which he used to persuade Commanding Officers to release men who Norton-Griffiths believed to be well suited to mining – such as former coal miners or engineers.

It was an unorthodox recruitment strategy, but it worked. By March 1915, five tunnelling companies had been formed and more were on their way.

A clay kicking team comprised three men and would work in either 6- or 12-hour rotating shifts. A 'kicker' would loosen earth and clay from the tunnel face using a kicking iron; then a 'bagger' would take the lump of clay that has been loosened, prise it away from the tunnel face and place it into a sandbag before passing the full sandbags to a 'trammer' whose job it was to get rid of the sandbags, often using a small rubber-wheeled trolley.

The team would work in utter silence until they had taken 9 inches (22.5cm) of mud and clay out of the tunnel, they would then insert a wooden brace to support the walls before going again for another nine inches.

In essence, they were moving towards the enemy 9 inches at a time.

Tunnellers worked in cold, dark, cramped galleries that were often flooded with water and trench foot and other similar ailments were rife. The air in the tunnels was also often terrible. At first, a candle was used to see if there was enough air to work, then coal miners started using 'miners' friends' like mice and canaries. These small animals were highly susceptible to gas and if they fell unconscious, it would give the miners an early warning to evacuate.

Despite the destructive power of mines, the primary job of the tunnellers was a defensive one. It was to protect their own infantry from being under-mined by the enemy and blown to bits. To do so, British miners had to intercept the German tunnels and blow them up underground – and vice versa. The key here was to pinpoint enemy activity. At the beginning of the war, the British used a civilian listening rod, originally designed for finding water, as well as biscuit tins filled with water, which were placed around the tunnels. Any vibrations made by enemy activity would cause ripples in the water and alert the miners.

In November 1915, Norton-Griffiths delivered the miners an early Christmas present in the shape of the Geophone. It looked like an over-sized doctor's stethoscope but could pick up enemy activity up to 100 feet away, allowing the miners to plot and track the progress of enemy mining activity and help plan their own counter-mining operation. It revolutionised the detection of enemy mines overnight.

Once the decision to blow a mine had been taken, an underground chamber was cut out of the clay or chalk into which explosives were packed in. Once the chamber was filled with the pre-requisite number of explosives, the gallery or tunnel behind the chamber was packed tightly with chalk filled sandbags to deflect the force of the blast upwards and outwards, towards the enemy.

The trick was to wait until there was the maximum amount of enemy personnel in the target chamber before the plunger was pushed to spark the charge – to cause the largest amount of damage possible. Yet the job wasn't necessarily done after the first explosion. No, sir. If you were feeling particularly feisty, you would get some more explosives ready in anticipation for the rescue party that would inevitably clamber down to the blown-in chamber to rescue their comrades. Once this rescue party was busy digging out their mates, you set off explosive number two and blow the rescue party to pieces, too.

The war below ground was as barbaric as it was claustrophobic.

After the very first shafts were sunk in late 1914, both sides set about constructing a complex underground network of tunnels and galleries.

Each major combatant approached the business of tunnelling in slightly different ways. The British tended to dig long defensive tunnels that ran parallel to their front-line trenches. From this main tunnel, they would then drive fighting tunnels deep into No Man's Land.

The French were often a bit more direct and dug smaller, shallow tunnels to minimise their underground footprint. As was to be expected, the Germans went bigger and deeper than anyone else and lined their tunnels with timber for extra stability. If we were to use an automotive analogy for a minute here, the German tunnels would be like a big spacious Audi Q7, the British tunnels would be akin to a long and slender Jaguar XJ and the French tunnels would be like a narrow little Citroen 2CV.

You may never look at an Audi Q7 in the same way again...

Underground activity on both sides of the wire peaked in 1916 – during this time, it is estimated that around 120,000 men were involved in this sub-terranean war. In 1916 alone, it is estimated that around 1,500 mines were detonated with the express intention of blowing enemy front-line positions to bits, plus many more thousands of smaller charges, designed to blow up enemy tunnels.

Three of the largest of those mines were ready and primed to explode in the early hours of 1st July 1916. One was located under the Hawthorn Redoubt and two were placed either side of the village of La Boisselle – smack in the middle of the Somme battlefront.

When the plungers were pushed, it would be those three mines that would signal the beginning of the Battle of the Somme.

14

BOOM! HAWTHORN RIDGE, LOCHNAGAR, Y-SAP AND ASSORTED MINES

There were nineteen mines of varying sizes blown on the first day of the Battle of the Somme. When the collective plungers were pushed, the joint explosion of these mines produced the loudest man-made sound in history. Reports suggest the boom was heard way back in London.

Most of the nineteen mines were relatively minor affairs, dug in shallow tunnels designed to remove local German strong-points and machine-gun nests. The three mines clustered around Fricourt and Mametz - Trambour, Bulgar Point and Hidden Wood mines – were slightly bigger, with a combined potency of almost 22,000kg (49,000Ib) of explosives. There was another decent sized mine detonated just north of Carnoy, containing 2,300kg (5,000Ib) of explosives.

Then there were the three real biggies: the mine under the Hawthorn Ridge, near Beaumont Hamel and the two mines that straddled the village of La Boisselle - Lochnagar and Y-Sap. Between them, these three mines would use an eye-watering 63,400kg (140,600Ib) of explosives to blow the enemy to kingdom come.

The Hawthorn Redoubt, situated on a substantial ridge in front of Beaumont Hamel, was deemed such a strong fortification that it was decided it would be easier to blow it up from underneath rather than try a full-frontal assault with infantry.

It would be the pleasure of 252nd Tunnelling Company to carry out the excavation for H3 (the official name for the Hawthorn Ridge Mine) under the watchful gaze of Captain Rex Trower. Digging commenced in the spring of 1916.

The geology in the tunnels some 57 feet (17 metres) under the Hawthorn Ridge was so tough the tunellers were forced to soak the flinty chalk with water to soften it up enough to allow them to silently pick out small chunks with their bayonet. Their efforts paid off, however, and by the end of May, the main tunnel of about 1,000 yards (910m) was finished. By the end of June, the 900ft long (270 metres) mine gallery was also complete and chock full of thousands of ammonal-filled petrol tins, adding up to a whopping 40,600lb (18,400kg) of prime explosives – all ready to blow the Hawthorn Redoubt to smithereens.

Back at HQ, there was much discussion over the best way to utilise H3 in the coming attack. Most of the other mines that were being readied for the attack were going to be detonated just moments – a matter of two or three minutes – before the infantry went over the top, however, VIII Corps Commander Hunter-Weston thought that blowing the mine a wee bit earlier would give his men a bit of extra time to occupy the crater.

He originally wanted to push the plunger at 3.30am, some four hours before H-Hour, and although some staff officers baulked at such a plan, many members of the underground fraternity actually lent this idea their support, suggesting that if the crater could be occupied and consolidated, it might lull the Germans into thinking it was an isolated incident and not part of a wider, co-ordinated assault.

After much back-and-forth, Fourth Army HQ waded into the argument and decreed that all mines planned for the 1st July were to be detonated no earlier than eight minutes before zero. Hunter-Weston challenged this and eventually a compromise was reached where H3 would be blown ten minutes before the assault. As it turned out, this was quite possibly the worst timing choice that could have been made.

Such a blast – the explosion flung an immense column of mud and earth into the air hundreds of metres high – was hard to hide, even with the roar of the artillery guns. It was a solid sign to the Germans that something heavy was about to go down and, not surprisingly, alarm bells were rung, and whistles were blown up and down the German lines. The men were herded out of their dugouts and cellars and ordered to man their battle-stations to prepare for the inevitable.

The explosion of H3 produced a crater some 140m long, 90m wide and 25m deep, and as soon as the dust had settled, the race to control the crater began. The 2nd Btn. Royal Fusiliers captured one side of the crater, but the Germans secured the opposite side and set up machine-guns to defend against any attack.

In the end, as impressive as H3 looked when it was blown, it achieved precious little in the grand scheme of things. Even prisoner reports suggested that the casualties from the initial blast were very light and nothing like pre-battle hopes.

Approximately 9km (5.5 miles) to the south, two other massive mines were all set to go off on either side of the small village of La Boisselle.

The village of La Boisselle was no stranger to mining activity. Here, the two opposing front lines came dangerously close to one another - at one point, *No Man's Land* was just 50 yards (46 metres) wide. Such a situation was perfect mining territory and in the first eighteen months of the war, the French and German forces were locked in a constant battle of mining and countermining to get the upper hand.

When the British took over this part of the line from the French, they found the Germans had out-tunnelled the French, constructing a network that was significantly deeper and more extensive. To reset the subterranean equilibrium, two specialist tunnelling companies –

the 179th and, later, the 185th - were drafted into the sector and immediately set about making plans to dig deep underneath the enemy front-line positions.

Similar to the Hawthorn Ridge position, the village of La Boisselle was a prime target for the Somme offensive, but was too heavily fortified for a straightforward infantry attack. Once again, it would be down to the specialist miners to give the infantry a bit of a helping hand. At La Boisselle, that helping hand came in the shape of two gigantic mines on either side of the village that would blow the German defences to bits and give the advancing infantry a couple of very wide doors to advance through.

The tunnellers immediately got busy and opened up a brand-new tunnel on 11th November 1915, way back behind the British front line at a communication trench called Lochnagar Street. The ultimate target of this tunnel was a German strongpoint called the *Schwabenhöhe* which was positioned to the south of the village and to get there, the main tunnel would need to be the thick end of 1000 feet long.

It was slow progress, with the miners advancing around 17 feet per day, but even at that pace, the men struggled to remove all the spoil. For every foot dug, there were about forty-eight sandbags of spoil and by early December, a trolly system was built and in place to help with the removal of the chalk. The British struggled to conceal the resulting mountain of chalk spoil, which was frequently shelled by German spotter planes.

Lochnagar wasn't the only mining operation the 179th was busying itself with at La Boisselle. On the other side of the village, a second major mine gallery had been started under the British front line near where it crossed the Albert to Bapaume road. Its main purpose was to eliminate several pesky machine-gun posts that were situated to the north of the village, in an area the British called Y-Sap.

By early summer excellent progress was being made, but the tunnellers of both mines were now getting perilously close to the Germans' own network of tunnels and were in earshot of enemy listening posts. It suddenly all got very tense underground as the danger of detection was getting very real indeed. New instructions were given to the miners to ensure absolute silence.

Their trusty pick was replaced by the bayonet which was used to ease out lumps of chalk which was then handed over to a carrier who would move the chalk up and out of the tunnels manually. Spoil trucks were simply too noisy to use, so everything was carried out by hand. Work was halted often for everyone to listen out for sounds of enemy activity. Not surprisingly, the rate of progress slowed dramatically – the average daily advance fell to less than twelve inches a day.

Air quality in both tunnel networks was becoming an issue, too. To ventilate such long tunnels properly was incredibly difficult – large blacksmith bellows were connected to a hose which ran up to the working face, but the air quality was still dangerously poor. The final stretches of tunnel were reduced in size to four and a half feet high by two and a half feet wide to speed things up, but that made things even more uncomfortable.

Despite these challenges, the miners kept inching forwards. Once the Lochnagar mine tunnel had progressed to within 135 feet (41 metres) of the target, the tunnel was split into two separate branches, the ends of which were to be enlarged to form chambers ready to house the explosives. The initial intention was to have these two chambers about 250 feet apart, but as the miners started excavating the forks, they heard the enemy overhead, digging down from their own front line. As a result, they were forced to stop digging about 100 yards short of their target position.

To compensate for this, the decision was taken to 'overcharge' the mine with more explosives than originally planned to create the same desired effect. A massive thirty tonnes of high explosives were squeezed into the twin chambers underneath the *Schwabenhöhe* strongpoint with another twenty tonnes stuffed beneath Y-Sap.

The original plan was to blow the Y-Sap mine a couple of days early to destroy the German machine gun placements. The idea being to give the infantry an advanced jumping off point for the main attack and reduce the distance to the German front line by some 150 metres. Unfortunately, Corps commanders ultimately said no to the idea, citing that the early detonation would give too much warning of the impending attack.

As the countdown to Zero Hour – now locked in for 7.30am on 1st July - drew ever closer, the British did everything they could to keep the exact time and date of the *Big Push* a secret. But in the end the attack was compromised, and it happened deep under La Boisselle.

15

'GOOD LUCK FOR TOMORROW.' PLANS REVEALED.

Anyone with a German pulse knew that the British attack was imminent. The 'old sweats' among the German ranks also knew that once the whistles had been blown, speed would be of the essence – especially in those areas where *No Man's Land* was narrow. Every second would count, and all men were on high alert, waiting for the attack.

What the British were not aware of was that the Germans had their own listening process set up deep under La Boisselle. It was called the Moritz System, and it was specially designed to pick up electrical impulses that passed through the earth. Impulses such as telephone messages.

On the night of 30th June, an unscrambled message was sent from a chamber under La Boisselle to one of the local Brigade headquarters. The message signed off with a well-meaning but unnecessary piece of motivation wishing all ranks the best of luck for the morning, re-it-erating the importance of holding on to every square inch of ground gained and reminding them of the massed artillery that was backing them up in the attack.

Not surprisingly, the interception caused a considerable amount of excitement among German ranks and the transcript was quickly and widely distributed all along the German front line before morning. After being on the receiving end of an eight-day artillery beat-down, the Germans knew that a large attack was pending. They just didn't know exactly when it was all going to kick off.

The British had just told them.

16

— • —

LORD, I SHALL BE VERY BUSY THIS DAY: MOVING ON UP

D uring the evening of 30th June, over 100,000 British soldiers emerged from their village billets scattered around the Somme countryside and began the slow trudge up to the front line. The rain that had delayed the original assault date had subsided, and the wind had dropped, making life much more tolerable for everyone. As the men marched through gently undulating farmland, across small woodland streams and along quiet country lanes, they sang vociferously:

> *We beat them on the Marne,*
> *We beat them on the Aisne,*
> *We gave them hell at Neuve Chappelle,*
> *And here we are again!*

Towards the north of the British line, in a small courtyard surrounded by the noise and activity of men getting ready to move out, a group of officers from 12th Btn. London Regiment shook hands.

One of those officers was Lieutenant Edward Liveing. As he paused to let a group of London Scottish soldiers move past, he wondered if he was witnessing his last ever sunset. As he sat there, he was reminded of the seventeenth century Cavalier prayer by Sir Jacob Astley, which his father had enclosed on a card in his last letter:

> *Lord, I shall be very busy this day.*
> *I may forget Thee, but do not Thou forget me.*[1]

The men making their way to the front line were loaded up to the max with all kinds of ammunition and supplies.

An infantryman's battle kit weighed in at 40lbs without their packs. Rifle, bayonet and 200 rounds of ammunition added another 25lb of weight. But that was just the start of it. Almost every man carried 'extras' – whether it was coils of signal wire, extra entrenching tools, or huge field telephones. By the time they got to the front line they were already exhausted from lugging all that equipment for miles and miles.

The men finally approached the network of communication trenches during the early hours of the morning. If the march-out from the villages wasn't tiring enough for the 158 battalions moving to the front, trying to navigate the maze of cramped, crowded trenches would be even worse. Getting into their jumping-off positions was often more effort than the fight itself.

Even in the pitch dark, the men knew they were approaching the trenches because of the terrible smell. It was a noxious blend of latrine buckets, putrid mud, chloride of lime, rotting sandbags, cordite from the guns and hundreds of bodies that were gently decomposing all around. Immediately inside the trench system, all men were given the order to 'load' - to insert nine bullets into their rifle, with one primed in the chamber, and put the safety catch on. This way they were just a second away from being able to fire, without having to load their rifle first. Once all the men were loaded, they were picked up by guides to help them navigate the warren of communication trenches.

They trudged in single file through the trenches, struggling under the weight and bulk of their personal load and seeing nothing but the pack of the man in front. Very quickly the trench system narrowed and soon became jammed packed with men stumbling and slipping on the mud or tripping over wires as they desperately tried to get to their allocated positions.

Upon arrival at their ultimate positions, the men tried to snatch some rest, but the cold of the night and the soreness from carrying such heavy loads for hours meant that, for many, sleep was impossible. Some men chain-smoked to while away the time, some oiled their rifles again and again. Many simply stood still, contemplating what was to come, lost in their own thoughts, gazing intently at nothing in particular.

There was nothing to do but wait for dawn.

17

– : –

COUNTDOWN TO ZERO

4 a.m. As the first streaks of watery light appeared in the east above the German lines, the British soldiers crammed into their trenches got their first glimpse of the ground they would attack over later that morning. It was only now that they were told the precise time of the assault. Company commanders did the rounds, sharing news that only intensified the tension in the trenches. Zero Hour would be 7.30am - they would be conducting a full-frontal assault on the German lines in broad daylight.

The arrival of a warm breakfast did much to reinvigorate the men. But even more welcome than the food was the sudden appearance of petrol tins full of hot coffee laced with rum. For the men standing in water-logged trenches feeling cold and apprehensive, this was a great pick-me-up and morale improved significantly, which was just as well – because the German artillery had just woken up.

Enemy shelling had been a factor all night, but at around 5.30 a.m. they started to really turn up the gas and poured an intense barrage onto the British trenches, supply routes and gun batteries. The sudden enemy activity shocked many on the British side of the wire as they were convinced the Germany artillery guns had been all but destroyed over the last week. Many of the men took this as a sign that the Germans knew they were coming. In those parts of the line that were directly under fire, morale once more ebbed away.

At 6.25 a.m. it was the turn of the British artillery to return the compliment. For many of the British infantry, it was the first time they had witnessed a British bombardment – and they were mightily impressed. Some men sat on top of their parapet and cheered as the shells whizzed overhead and crashed into the German positions a few hundred yards away. Any doubts they had about German resistance suddenly vanished – surely nothing could withstand such a pounding?

As the minutes ticked down to Zero, it was last thirty-or-so minutes when the tension in the trenches started to move off the scale. Officers and NCO's did their best to calm and encourage the men, but many were too pre-occupied with their own thoughts to take notice. Some prayed, some filled in Section 13 of their paybook (a page for setting out an informal will), others looked through cherished family photographs.

For some, the strain of the moment became too much – there were quiet tears, there was uncontrollable sobbing or shaking, and there were men that went completely crazy – shouting and screaming as finally their nerves couldn't take it any longer.

By 7.20 a.m. the British barrage was approaching a stupefying crescendo as the gunners, ably joined by scores of trench mortar batteries, went eyeballs-out to fill the German positions with as much high explosive as humanly possible. Once more it had a rousing effect on the morale of the infantry – there were just a few minutes left to wait now.

Up and down the attacking lines there were flurries of activity as some unit commanders opened up the entrances to Russian Saps (shallow tunnels that stretched out into *No Man's Land* to allow the assaulting troops to begin their trip slightly closer to the enemy line). If they had no such tunnels, they let their leading waves climb up the trench ladders over the parapet and file through their own wire before lying down in *No Man's Land*.

The continued artillery bombardment meant that most units who made these moves did so in relative safety, but in some areas, the Germans were already in position. An officer of the 4th Middlesex Regiment estimated his men were targeted by at least six separate machine-gun posts while they took up their starting position. It was an ominous observation, but it was too late to do anything about it now.

18

PRIVATE WILLIAM FREDERICK
MCFADZEAN VC, ROYAL IRISH RIFLES

William "Billy" Frederick McFadzean was born at Lurgan, County Armagh, Ireland on 9th October 1895. His father, William Senior, was a linen salesman who married Annie Pedlow in 1895. The family also lived in Ormeau, County Down, and later moved to Belfast.

The young Billy attended Mountpottinger Boy's School from 1904 to 1908 before moving to the Trade Preparatory School in Belfast. After his education, he was offered an apprenticeship with Spence, Bryson & Co. a major manufacturer of cotton and linen handkerchiefs. Billy was tall and well-built and enjoyed playing junior rugby for the Collegians Rugby Football Club. He was part of the Ulster Volunteer Force, his regiment being known as the "Chocolate Soldiers" because of their commercial and well-off family backgrounds.

He enlisted on 22nd September 1914, joining 'C' Company, 14th Battalion, Royal Irish Rifles. After being put through his paces at various training camps, McFadzean and the rest of the 14th Royal Irish Rifles finished their training in England before finally moving out to France on 5th October 1915.

Billy's adventure in France would lead him to Thiepval Wood during the summer of 1916, where he and his mates were knee deep in preparations for the *Big Push*. Given his height and stature (6ft tall and weighing around 13 Stone / 83kg) he was ideally suited to the role of bomber. Part of the role of a bomber was to look after boxes of bombs and ensure they were all primed, prepped and distributed to the men before the assault.

The night of 30th June 1916 found Billy and his battalion in their assembly trenches at Elgin Avenue in Thiepval Wood. It was 6.45am and Billy was busy with the distribution of bombs to the men.

He picked up a box of grenades and cut the surrounding cord. Somehow, he lost grip and the box suddenly overturned, spilling its contents of bombs onto the trench floor, with two of them losing their safety pins. In just four seconds, those two bombs would explode and cause utter carnage. Without a moment's thought, Billy immediately threw his body over the bombs and a second later they exploded, with Billy taking the full force of the impact. He died instantly, but in giving up his own life, he saved the lives of dozens of his friends – only two other people were injured in the incident.

Some accounts suggest that when his remains were later carried away on a stretcher, the men removed their helmets in respect – many openly wept.

McFadzean's heroic actions were recognised by a posthumous award of the Victoria Cross (VC). His was the first VC of the Battle of the Somme and the first to be awarded to a member of the Ulster Division.

William McFadzean's Victoria Cross was gazetted on 9th September 1916:

> *For most conspicuous bravery. While in a concentration trench and opening a box of bombs for distribution prior to an attack, the box slipped down into the trench, which was crowded with men, and two of the safety pins fell out. Private McFadzean, instantly realising the*

danger to his comrades, with heroic courage threw himself on the top of the bombs. The bombs exploded blowing him to pieces, but only one other man was injured. He well knew his danger, being himself a bomber, but without a moment's hesitation he gave his life for his comrades.

A week later, his commanding officer, Lieutenant Colonel F C Bowen, wrote to William Senior:

Dear Mr McFadzean, It is with feelings of great pride that I read the announcement of the granting of the VC to your gallant son and my only regret is that he was not spared to us to wear his well-earned decoration. It was one of the finest deeds of a war that is so full of big things, and I can assure you that the whole battalion rejoiced when they heard it. Your gallant boy, though gone from us, his deeds will forever live in our memories and the record will go down for all time in the regimental history which he has added fresh and great lustre to.

The family also received a letter from Buckingham Palace on 18th December 1916.

It is a matter of sincere regret to me that the death of Private McFadzean deprived me of the pride of personally conferring upon him the Victoria Cross, the greatest of all rewards for valour and devotion to duty. (Signed George R I)

As he never married, the VC was presented to his father by King George V at Buckingham Palace on 28th February 1917. When handing over the VC, the King said, "Nothing finer has been done in this war for which I have given a Victoria Cross than the act committed by your son to save many lives in giving his own so heroically."

In addition to his VC, he was awarded the 1914-15 Star, British War Medal and Victory Medal. His VC was donated by the McFadzean family to the Royal Ulster Rifles Regimental Museum in March 1980, where it is still on display in Belfast.

Pte. McFadzean is commemorated on the Thiepval Memorial.

19

— • —

OVER THE TOP

Those final ten minutes of concentrated mortar fire made even the hardiest of British soldiers wince on behalf of their German counterparts. But there was little to time to dwell on any thoughts of compassion as the men took up their positions for the attack.

Across the twenty-two miles of trenches that provided the theatre for the coming battle, fourteen of those miles were under British command, with the remaining eight miles falling under the auspices of the French.

The British had two full armies ready for action: General Rawlinson's Fourth Army and General Gough's Reserve Army, with a total of thirteen divisions in the front line. From a French perspective their hand on the Somme had been much reduced due to the shenanigans of Verdun – they had eight divisions from the French Sixth Army positioned south of the River Somme ready to go.

On the other side of the wire stood the German Second Army under the command of General Otto von Below. Man for man we are looking at 200,000 British and French troops facing off against 150,000 Germans – although the Germans could draft in another 200,000 – 300,000 men from the Eastern Front and Verdun if they needed. Something which both France and Britain hoped they would do – it was, after all, the main purpose of this entire show.

At exactly 7.30a.m. the British artillery bombardment stopped so the gunners could readjust their gun sights for their next planned targets. The German counter barrage had also stopped, resulting in an eerie silence descending on the battlefield just moments before all hell was let loose.

The calm was short-lived. After a few seconds, the British guns barked into life once more. This time, the maelstrom was accompanied by the shrill of whistles and the barking of orders for the men to begin the advance. The first men to get going were those already positioned out in *No Man's Land*. Long lines of men rose, adjusted their equipment, and set off at a steady, well-rehearsed pace towards the enemy. There was no rush, there was no commotion and no fuss – they just got on with it.

In the trenches, the Platoon Commanders were already up the ladders and on top of the parapets, encouraging their men to follow them and offering their hand to those who were struggling under the burden of their kit to clamber over the sand-bags.

Before these men could get on with the business of advancing on the enemy, they had to negotiate their own belts of defensive wire. Some units placed duckboards on top of the wire to make temporary foot bridges, but most had to make do with passing through narrow corridors that had been pre-cut into the wire belts. Once through this first obstacle, they re-grouped, lined up in formation, and strode across *No Man's Land*.

> *At zero hour, everybody climbed out of the trenches. Two platoons formed the first wave. Every man climbed out of the trench at the officers' whistles, and not a man hesitated. I was lucky; I was at a part of the trench where the parapet had been battered down, and when I ran out of the trench, I was under the hail of bullets that were whizzing over my head. Most of our fellows were*

killed, kneeling on the parapet.[1]

Pte. Arthur Pearson, 15th Battalion, West Yorkshire Regiment.

The Battle of the Somme had begun.

20

THE BRITISH BURDEN OF BATTLE

As the men clambered over the top on 1st July, the average British Tommy was hauling sixty-six pounds (almost 30KG) of equipment over with him. Basic assault gear included (but was not limited to) the following:

- Fully functioning Lee Enfield SMLE rifle with fixed bayonet

- Ammunition for the aforementioned rifle – anywhere between 170 and 220 rounds

- Two No.5 Mills bombs (grenades)

- A waterproof cape

- Two sandbags

- Steel helmet

- Two gas masks in a satchel

- A pair of goggles in case of tear gas

- First aid field dressings and iodine

- Rolled waterproof groundsheet

- Water bottle (filled)

- A haversack with mess-tin, shaving kit, extra socks, and rations

For the show on the Somme, almost half the men would carry shovels or picks which were strapped to their backs. If that lot wasn't enough, each battalion issued some more supplies throughout its 1,000 men:

- 1,600 flares for communicating with Royal Flying Corps observers

- 512 haversacks containing extra ammunition for Lewis guns

- 64 bundles of 5ft wooden pickets to act as trench supports

- 10 trench bridges – each 10ft long and to be carried by two men

- 16 sledgehammers

- 1 tin of grey paint to paint the unit's identification on any German artillery guns that were captured

As a result of these extra delights, some men carried up to seventy-six pounds (34.4kg) of kit into battle. Such a burden meant many men struggled to get out of their own trench at Zero Hour. Once out into *No Man's Land* the weight of their packs meant it was impossible to stumble along any quicker than a steady walk – they would prove easy targets for German machine-gunners.

I went carrying a full kit, blanket in the pack, a rifle, helmet, a full-size navvy's pick across my shoulders, the pack on my back, two hundred rounds of ammunition and twenty Mills bombs. I could have been a mule, you know, not a human being! We had to jump out of the trenches with that, and not only did I carry my own twenty bombs, but I collected two bags of twenty each from one fellow that was wounded, and another that come down with shell shock. So, I went in with sixty bombs. I was a moving arsenal! A bit of shrapnel would have shot me into the clouds![1]

Pte. Herbert Hall, 12th Battalion, York and Lancaster Regiment.

In contrast to the ordinary rank and file, officers led their men carrying only gas masks, ammunition pouches and their trusty Webley pistol. They wore the same uniform as the men in an effort to appear inconspicuous, but as they were invariably at the head of their unit, urging their men on, they were easily singled out for special attention from the German machine-gun teams.

21

THE FILM MEN: DOCUMENTING THE BATTLE

A t the beginning of the war, the British Army's top brass were dead against any front-line film making and were quick to issue a blanket ban on any kind of filming or photography during live operations. This meant that news reel companies who were trying to document the early stages of the war had to make do with either training footage, film shot far behind the lines, or resort to staging mock fight scenes after the event. It was not an ideal situation.

Back home in Britain, the chaps at the War Office slowly realised they might be missing a trick by not responding to the growing public demand to see actual war footage. A well-produced film could do wonders for home front morale and give a much-needed boost to conscription numbers. There was also a growing international perception that Germany was winning the propaganda war – and that would just not do.

Negotiations between the War Office and the newsreel industry took place during 1915 and it was eventually agreed that just two *kinematographers* (as video cameramen were called at the time) would be allowed to film in the front lines of the British Army. On 2nd November of that year, two cameramen - Geoffrey Malins and Edward Tong - set off for France. Both carried the rank of Lieutenant.

It wasn't the first time Malins had been on the Western Front. Working as a freelance film cameraman, he saw the war as an opportunity to make a name for himself and quickly secured himself film projects such as filming the Belgian Army near the coast at Nieuwpoort and recording a French attack in the forests of the Vosges.

Tong was invalided home after just a month or so, but Malins continued to travel around the front, filming the British soldiers in the Ypres Salient, at Neuve Chapelle and in Arras throughout late 1915 and the first half of 1916. In June 1916, Malins was positioned at the Somme sector of the front to film the forthcoming *Big Push*. As the British Army organised itself for the attack, Malins got busy filming as much of the preparation as he could, including the movement of men and guns up to the front before John McDowell, a cameraman with the British & Colonial Film Company, joined him in the sector on 23rd June 1916.

Malins was attached to the 29th Division near Beaumont Hamel, while McDowell worked with the 7th Division near Mametz. Over the next two weeks, they would go on to film some of the most iconic and remarkable footage in British military history.

Fortunately for us, Malins documented his adventure in a detailed journal. He was fanatical in his pursuit of the perfect image and, despite having to carry his heavy and unwieldy film equipment, was often seen setting up his camera in some of the liveliest positions on the front line. With hours to go before the attack on the Somme, Malins was invited to film a group of Lancashire Fusiliers who had sneaked out into *No Man's Land* un-detected and were huddled together in a sunken road...

> *"Keep low as you run across the road, sir. The Bosche*
> *can see right along it; make straight for the other side."*
> *With that he ran across, and I followed. Then I set my*
> *camera up and filmed the scene. I had to take every*

precaution in getting my machine in position, keeping
it close to the bank, as a false step would have exposed
the position to the Bosche, who would have immediately
turned on H.E. shrapnel, and might have enfiladed
the whole road from either flank. I filmed the waiting
Fusiliers. Some of them looked happy and gay, others sat
with stern, set faces, realising the great task in front of th
em.[1]

Within a few brief hours, most of the men he filmed in that sunken
road would be dead or wounded.

At 6.30am – just one hour before the whistles were due to be blown
– Malins packed up his kit and was quickly on the move again. He
wanted to capture some scenes of the men in the trenches taking up
their final positions before he got to his grandstand position opposite
the Hawthorn Redoubt. He travelled back through the front-line
trenches where he managed to film men fixing their bayonets ready for
the attack. After wishing the men good luck he headed off towards a
position he had earlier earmarked for recording the mine explosion –
called Jacob's Ladder due to the many steps cut into the white chalk.
He got there with just twenty minutes to spare, but when an enemy
shell struck the parapet nearby, he had to quickly scramble to find
another position.

He quickly fixed his camera on the side of a small bank, pointing
towards the Hawthorn Redoubt, where, unbeknown to the many
German soldiers stationed there, would soon be the scene of an unprecedented explosion that would signal the beginning of the offensive.

Time: 7.19 a.m. My hand grasped the handle of the
camera. I set my teeth. My whole mind was concen-

trated upon my work. Another thirty seconds passed. I started turning the handle, two revolutions per second, no more, no less. I noticed how regular I was turning. (My object in exposing half a minute beforehand was to get the mine from the moment it broke ground.) I fixed my eyes on the Redoubt. Any second now. Surely it was time. It seemed to me as if I had been turning for hours. Great heavens! Surely it had not misfired.

Why doesn't it go up?

I looked at my exposure dial. I had used over a thousand feet. The horrible thought flashed through my mind, that my film might run out before the mine blew. Would it go up before I had time to reload? The thought brought beads of perspiration to my forehead. The agony was awful; indescribable. My hand began to shake. Another 250 feet exposed. I had to keep on.

Then it happened.

The ground where I stood gave a mighty convulsion. It rocked and swayed. I gripped hold of my tripod to steady myself. Then, for all the world like a gigantic sponge, the earth rose in the air to the height of hundreds of feet. Higher and higher it rose, and with a horrible, grinding roar the earth fell back upon itself, leaving in its place a mountain of smoke. From the moment the mine went up my feelings changed. The crisis was over, and from that second I was cold, cool, and calculating. I looked upon all that followed from the purely pictorial point of view, and even felt annoyed if a shell burst outside the range of my camera. Why couldn't Bosche put that shell a little nearer? It would make a better picture. And so my thoughts ran on.

The earth was down. I swung my camera round on to our own parapets. The engineers were swarming over the top and streaming along the sky-line. Our guns redoubled their fire. The Germans then started H.E. Shrapnel (which) began falling in the midst of our advancing men. I continued to turn the handle of my camera, viewing the whole attack through my view-finder, first swinging one way and then the other.

Then another signal rang out, and from the trenches immediately in front of me, our wonderful troops went over the top. What a picture it was! They went over as one man. I could see while I was exposing, that numbers were shot down before they reached the top of the parapet; others just the other side. They went across the ground in swarms, and marvel upon marvels, still smoking cigarettes. One man actually stopped in the middle of "No Man's Land" to light up again.[2]

Both Malins and McDowell continued to film for the rest of the day. The filming of battle scenes was often highly dangerous and for much of the footage they had to rise above the trench parapet and remove sandbags to place the camera into a position where it could record the action. Both cameramen experienced near missed throughout the day, with Malins' tripod damaged by shrapnel.

McDowell followed the successful advance of the 7th Division and was able to take actual footage of captured German trenches near Fricourt and Mametz. The following day, Malins captured the action around La Boisselle before returning to London on 9th July. He was back in France capturing more footage between 12th - 19th July and it was during this period where he filmed some of the controversial staged close-up footage of soldiers disembarking from their trenches and clambering over wire before being shot and fading out of the picture.

Editing started immediately and a rough cut of the film was shown at British General Headquarters and at Fourth Army Headquarters where commander Henry Rawlinson commented it was good but didn't show enough of the horror of the war.

On 2nd August, the film was shown to the Secretary of State for War, David Lloyd George, as well as to the Royal Family via a private screening at Windsor Castle.

On 10th August, at the Scala Theatre in London, the film received its first public screening for a select audience of journalists and officials. Before the film started, a letter from Lloyd George was read out to the audience, compelling them all to "see that this picture, which is in itself an epic of self-sacrifice and gallantry, reaches everyone. Herald the deeds of our brave men to the ends of the earth. This is your duty."

By 21st August, it was being shown in theatres across London and a week later was being shown practically nationwide. It is estimated that in the first six weeks of its release, some twenty million people went to see it. Eventually, the film was shown internationally and became a huge commercial success, even if the images of injury and death shocked many. To this day, it remains as one of the most important documentaries ever filmed. In 2005, it appeared on the UNESCO Memory of the World Register, the first British document to be included.

Buoyed by this success, Malins went out to France again to film the autumn stage of the battle. The result was *The Battle of the Ancre and the Advance of the Tanks*, and although it didn't achieve the phenomenal success of his first film, it still attracted large cinema audiences when it was released in 1917. Containing disturbing scenes of trench warfare, the poor conditions of the front line and giving the public their first view of the new super weapon – the Tank – in action, many critics consider it to be technically a much better film than The Battle of the Somme.

In June 1918, Malins was awarded an OBE for his troubles. The citation commended his work as official photographer "in circumstances of great difficulty and danger."

22

---·---

1ST JULY: GOMMECOURT - AN EXPENSIVE DIVERSION

The main thrust of the British attack on 1st July was to be car-ried out by eleven infantry divisions from General Rawlinson's Fourth Army. However, two miles to the north, a couple of territorial divisions from General Edmund Allenby's Third Army (VII Corps) were all set to launch their 'diversionary' attack on the village of Gom-mecourt, designed to attract as much German artillery and infantry attention as possible away from the northern flank of the Fourth Army assault around Serre.

The attack on Gommecourt would follow a classic 'pincer' move-ment with the 46th (North Midland) Division attacking from the north and the 56th (1st London) Division coming up from the south. All being well, they would both make progress through the second and third lines of German defences, meet up on the east side of the village and force the German garrison to surrender.

It was a hugely ambitious plan. Facing Allenby's men were the German 2nd Guard Reserve Division, made up of pre-war conscripts of various Guards Divisions. These men were proper soldiers, and they just happened to be looking after some of the most robust defensive fortifications the Germans had put together along the whole of the Somme front.

Gommecourt. 1st July 1916

A major fortification, the *Kernwerk* (known as *The Maze* to the British), was built towards the east of Gommecourt village and heavily equipped for all-round defence. The men in the front line enjoyed deep dugouts, many with electric lighting and kitchens. These dugouts were also inter-connected so that men and equipment could be moved around in relative safety, despite the best efforts of the Royal Artillery to smash them all to bits.

Whilst the German defenders were relatively safe from the dangers of enemy artillery, the same could not be said for the British infantry. A woeful allocation of just 20 shells per artillery gun for counter-battery fire and just one aircraft available for aerial observation in this sector meant that German artillery in the Gommecourt area was still in fine fettle, and was about to steal the show.

The attack of the North Midland's Division started off terribly and then got substantially worse as the morning drew on. Everything that could go wrong for the North Midlanders did so. They were manning trenches that had seen the worst of the recent bad weather, and many had spent the previous night up to their knees in mud and water. The enemy artillery was also active all night – as this attack was merely a diversion, the powers that be had purposely decided not to hide the build-up of men and equipment in this sector – they wanted the Germans to think something was cooking – however, that lack of counter-battery artillery work was about to come back and haunt them.

At 7:20am, ten minutes before Zero-Hour, white smoke was poured onto the battlefield across the front of both divisions to act as a safety screen for the infantry as they crossed *No Man's Land*. On paper this was a smart thing to do, and in some parts of the line it helped, but for the 46th Division the smoke became so dense the men became disorientated and could not get to their jumping-off points. If that wasn't bad enough, the wisps of smoke rolling over *No Man's Land* had alerted the Germans and they immediately started lobbing over dozens of heavy shrapnel shells which caused nothing but havoc and mayhem to the men trying desperately to launch their advance.

The attack had faltered before it had even started.

The delay and confusion in setting off, combined with the muddy conditions of *No Man's Land* meant that progress towards the German lines was painfully slow. When the smoke suddenly started to clear after just thirty minutes, the first waves of the attack were only halfway across *No Man's Land* and presented the German defenders with perfect targets. They could hardly miss.

Despite the carnage, pockets of men managed to get to the German wire, but most found the wire uncut or repaired - a situation very much contrary to leadership predictions. Three groups of Sherwood Foresters did manage to dodge the machine-guns, get through the wire and break into a German front-line trench, with a handful of them even sneaking into the enemy's second line. Unfortunately, subsequent waves failed to get across *No Man's Land* in the face of renewed German machine-gun vigour, leaving the Sherwood's isolated and cut off.

By 9am it was obvious that the attack by the 46th Division had failed. A fresh attack under cover of another barrage was ordered for 12.15pm to allow time for the reorganisation of the men and procurement of smoke bombs. The attack was postponed several times due to a lack of smoke bombs until it finally went ahead at 3.20pm. The smoke screen was woefully inadequate and eighteen out of the first twenty men who went over the parapet were cut down by machine-gun fire. Shortly afterwards, the attack was thankfully called off.

Meanwhile, to the south, the 56th (1st London) Division launched their attack along a 900-yard front with the aim of getting to the third line of German defences before swinging round behind Gommecourt (taking out some pretty impressive strongpoints on the way) and linking up with the 46th Division. Easy.

Their attack plan mirrored that of the 46th Division. At 07.20am smoke was discharged and within five minutes was laying heavy across the entire 900-yard front. Also mirroring what was happening to the north, as soon as the Germans saw the smoke, they let rip their artillery guns onto the British first and second-line trenches. Ignoring the artillery fire, the first and second attacking waves clambered out of their trenches to take up their assault positions in *No Man's Land*, still under cover from the smoke.

At 07.30am they rose together and began their advance – the smoke hiding them from enemy view much more effectively than it did for their comrades from the 46th Division. They progressed much quicker across *No Man's Land* and also found that, although much of the initial wire cutting had been repaired over night by the Germans, there were enough gaps to get through relatively quickly.

Consequently, the Londoners were jumping down unopposed into the enemy's front-line trench system in relatively short order. Across their front, the first two German lines were secured quickly, but the enemy had retreated to their third defence line and were packed onto their fire-step, armed to the teeth with rifles, bombs and ma-chine-guns. This line was going to be trickier to get hold of and only fell after an intense and prolonged fire fight.

By 9am, practically all aspects of the three German forward defence lines were in possession of the London Division. It was all going swimmingly until the Germans unleashed the full might of their ar-tillery onto their lost front line trenches and *No Man's Land*.

The first casualties of this intense barrage were, ironically, captured German prisoners who were being herded back across *No Man's Land* towards the British lines for processing, but the artillery fire also meant British reinforcements struggled to get forward to help bolster the attack.

At around 9am, a small band of men, along with a machine-gun crew, managed to get across to lend a hand, but these were the last successful group to make the journey unscathed. Despite many valiant attempts to reinforce the assault, they all failed. *No Man's Land* was now full of the dead and wounded.

The failure of the 46th Division to make any headway on their front had disastrous consequences for the 56th, who were now desper-ately hanging on to their hard-fought gains despite energetic enemy counter-attacks coming in from all sides. Gradually, they were forced to succumb to the pressure and had to give up their hold on the third line.

From about 1pm, although they were still holding the German first and second lines, groups of wounded men started to crawl across *No Man's Land* back towards the British lines. It was about now that they really needed their mates from the 46th Division to help out and push on – but they couldn't. The situation was becoming hopeless for the men still holding out behind enemy lines.

By 4pm the Germans had re-taken their second line positions and had already got a toe-hold in their first line – by nightfall, the British foothold within the German lines comprised a single position held by five officers and seventy men. They had no choice but to beat an organised retreat with their single Lewis Gun providing cover. The last men from the party clambered back into the British trenches around 9.30pm. The attack was over.

In total, the two Divisions suffered 6,769 casualties (killed, missing, wounded, or taken prisoner) and ended the day in exactly the same position as they had started.

Whichever way you look at it, the attack on Gommecourt was a very expensive diversion.

23

— · —

LT. DOWNMAN'S DAMNING DECREE ON THE DISASTER OF GOMMECOURT

Lieutenant Theodore Frank Cyril Downman took part in the attack on Gommecourt with 1/5th Sherwood Foresters and was one of the few men from the 46th Division that got across *No Man's Land* safely and occupied German front-line positions. During the attack, he sustained a gunshot wound to his arm and was taken prisoner.

In a series of notes made in June 1918 and attached to the Regimental War Diary of the period, Lieutenant Downman eloquently summed up his thoughts on the reasons for failure at Gommecourt thus:

The attack failed through various causes of which the following are the chief:

The absurdly inadequate strength of some of the attacking units; my own battalion went over between 500 and 600 strong. My own platoon consisted of 15.

Lack of knowledge on the part of the higher commands of the conditions prevailing in the trenches and of what was likely to take place in an attack on trenches from trenches.

The absurd distribution of equipment; those in 1st waves who got into German lines having to wait for 4th waves who never got there.

Overloading of all attackers, especially 'carriers'.

Very bad management regarding cutting of German barbed wire; this was absolutely uncut on a 2-battalion front, letting down our right flank and the 56th Division's left flank. The wire on my own front was sufficiently cut owing to the energies of Lt. Lilley who had taken patrols out to do this work, the artillery not being sufficiently competent to do it properly.

Half-heartedness in regard to the attack by Divisional General (46th Division). Only 4 battalions went into attack at 7.30am. They were not supported, and no reinforcements were sent. I understood that subsequent attacks by the rest of the division took place during the day, none of which reached the German lines. If these troops had all attacked between 7.30 and 8am we should have gained our objectives and held them, presuming that the wire was cut.[1]

It is difficult to argue against any of his points.

24

—·—

1ST JULY: PREMATURE DETONATION AT SERRE AND BEAUMONT HAMEL

S tand on the top of the Hawthorn Ridge today and you can see for miles. Its tactical value during the First World War is still obvious – the German defenders positioned within the Redoubt (strong point) perched on top of the ridge would have had an uninhibited view across *No Man's Land* and down to the British positions dug into the valley. It was machine-gunning heaven, and this danger was not lost on the top man of the British VIII Corps, Lieutenant-General Sir Aylmer Hunter-Weston and his staff, which is why his men went to so much trouble to dig under Hawthorn Ridge, pack it full of high explosives and blast the position out of existence.

The importance of the ridge was also front-and-centre in the thoughts of the German defenders. Not only would they lose a delightful view if they got kicked off the ridge, it would also expose their forward artillery lines and render their grip on the nearby villages of Beaumont-Hamel, Beaucourt, Thiepval, Grandcourt and Miraumont sketchy to say the least. Not surprisingly then, the German commander in the region, *Generalleutnant* Franz Freiherr von Soden, spared no effort in beefing up the defences of his lines.

Once the Hawthorn Redoubt had ceased to exist, Hunter-Weston's plan was to breach the German lines with a full-frontal infantry attack using three full divisions which were to push on through the enemy defences to a depth of around 3,000 yards before all linking arms on their final objective: the Serre-Grandcourt Spur.

Serre and Beaumont Hamel battlefield. 1st July 1916

The most northerly division in the attack was to be the 31st Division – made up largely of Pals Battalions from the north of England - who would capture Serre before moving on to the high ground beyond. Immediately to their south, the 4th Division would attack up the Redan Ridge, smashing up the Redan Redoubt, the Heidenkopf Redoubt, and the Soden Redoubt before linking up with their chums

from 31st Division. Finally, the 29th Division was to capture Beaumont-Hamel, Y-Ravine, Grallsburg, Beaucourt Redoubt and Beaucourt village before arriving at the southern edge of the Serre-Grandcourt Spur.

The infantry would be backed up by the chaps of VIII Corp Artillery who had three primary tasks. In no particular order, these were
to smash the German defensive line to bits, including machine-gun
posts, trenches, and barbed wire entanglements; account for as many
infantry casualties as possible and neutralise enemy artillery batteries.

A lot of this work was carried out during the *Great Bombardment*
– VIII Corps artillery lobbed almost 363,000 shells onto German
positions between 24th - 30th June. On 1st July they fired another
61,500. These were impressive numbers – impressive enough to convince Hunter-Weston that his men simply had to just 'walk into Serre'.

Regardless of the mighty artillery support, this was an ambitious
plan. Some would call it highly optimistic; others might call it highly
stupid. But the plan was approved by Brigadier-General John Char-
teris (General Sir Douglas Haig's Chief of Intelligence) on 28th June.
As far as Hunter-Weston was concerned, it was all systems go.

The task handed out to 4th and 29th Divisions was especially daunting. They were being asked to carry the advance straight into a natural amphitheatre towards Beaumont Hamel and then climb up onto
the Beaucourt Spur towards the enemy's second line of defence. The
key to success here was the 40,000Ibs of explosives sitting under the
Hawthorn Redoubt, just in front of Beaumont Hamel on the 29th
Divisional front. But the discussion regarding the best time to blow
the mine had been going on for weeks and was contentious to say the
least.

After much back and forth, a compromise was arrived at where the
mine was to be blown at 7.20am - ten minutes before the main attack
at. It was a time that very few of Hunter-Weston's staff agreed with

and senior artillery leaders tried in vain to get him to change his mind, but the General was unmoved.

To add insult to injury, Hunter-Weston also fiddled with the artillery timetable to accommodate the mine blast. He wanted to ensure the men racing to the Hawthorn crater were not smashed up by their own artillery – this, everyone must agree, was frightfully sensible, however instead of just ordering the artillery in the Hawthorn Ridge sector to lift at 7.20am and target the German rear lines, he ordered all his heavy artillery across his entire front to lift. As it turned out, this decision wasn't quite as sensible.

Even before the dust had settled on the massive mine-crater now in place of the Hawthorn Redoubt, German forces in rear positions rushed forwards to occupy the lip of the crater nearest to them, just as two companies of Royal Fusiliers were crossing *No Man's Land* to occupy the other side of the crater lip. Unfortunately for the British, the Germans got there first and directed withering machine-gun fire onto the advancing men, making it very difficult, if not impossible, for the British men to capture the entire crater as planned.

As the British artillery switched their attack to the German rear lines as per their direction, the leading waves of Pals from the 31st Division moved up to as close to the German wire as they dared, here they lay down ready to rush the enemy lines as soon as the whistles blew. It was at about this time that the men in these lead battalions realised that their artillery cover had all but disappeared – one soldier from the Durham Pals stole a quick peek out towards the enemy positions:

> Out on the top (of the trench) came scrambling a German machine-gun team. They fixed their gun in front of their parapet and opened out a slow and deadly fire on our front.[1]

Within minutes, heavy machine-gun fire was ripping through the men lying out in *No Man's Land*. It was not even Zero Hour, and the first waves of the attack were already getting cut to pieces. One battalion had no functioning officers by 7.28am., two minutes *before* the official start of the attack.

When the whistles did finally blow at 7.30am, those men who had not yet been hit stood up and moved off towards the German lines, only to find their path obstructed by enemy wire which had not, despite all the promises, been cut. *Musketier* Karl Blenk watched the attack unfold from his defensive position and later recollected:

> *When the English started advancing, we were very worried; they looked as if they must overrun our trenches. We were very surprised to see them walking, we had never seen that before... When we started firing, we just had to load and reload. They went down in their hundreds. You didn't have to aim, we just fired into them. If only they had run, they would have overwhelmed us.*[2]

The men making up the second and third waves of the attack fared little better. As well as murderous machine gun fire, the Germans were also dropping a fantastic artillery barrage onto the British front line and assembly areas to the rear.

The result was carnage, with many units simply wiped out before they had even reached their own front line. Those that got over the parapet had a very similar experience to the men of the 12th York & Lancasters (Sheffield Pals) who found that:

> *They had to pass through a terrible curtain of shell fire, and German machine guns were rattling death from two sides. But the lines growing ever thinner, went on*

unwavering. Here and there a shell would burst right among the attackers... Whole sections were destroyed; one section of 14 platoon was killed by concussion, all the men falling to the ground without a murmur. The left half of 'C' Company was wiped out before getting near the German wire...

The third and fourth wave suffered so heavily that by the time they reached No Man's Land they had lost at least half their strength... The few survivors took shelter in shell-holes in front of the German line and remained there until they could get back under cover of darkness.[3]

Despite the odds, pockets of men did manage to get through the German wire and into the enemy front-line trenches and even on towards Serre itself, however the Germans quickly closed in on these isolated groups, cutting off all escape routes and quickly snuffing out any danger. By noon, VIII Corps leaders had issued an order to cease any further attempts at attack and put all energies into consolidating the current front line in case of German counter-attack.

The fate of the 31st Division is one of the most tragic stories from a day full of tragedy. The ifs, buts and maybes of Hunter-Weston's decisions regarding the timing of the mine and the lifting of the barrage will rage on in perpetuity.

What is undeniable is that, through no fault of their own, the men of the 31st Division suffered over 3,500 casualties and gained zero objectives.

25

— · —

1ST JULY: 'FOR GOODNESS' SAKE, SEND REINFORCEMENTS!' ATTACKING THE QUADRILATERAL.

I mmediately to the south of 31st Division, Hunter-Weston's 4th Division attacked the gap that lay between the villages of Serre and Beaumont Hamel. Even though the 4th Division was a proud and noble regular division that had been on the Western Front since 1914, this was a tough gig.

The divisional front was 1,500 yards wide and ran astride the Redan Ridge, a piece of high ground that, like the neighbouring Hawthorn Ridge, offered a splendid panoramic view of the area on all sides and as such had been fiercely protected by the Germans since they first occupied the position back in October 1914.

As well as enjoying a naturally higher position to aid their defensive cause, the Germans had also been busy fortifying their positions. The *Heidenkopf* (known to the British as the Quadrilateral) was a powerful redoubt that jutted out into *No Man's Land* on the left flank of this sector and a few hundred yards to the south-east was another similarly designed strong point - the Redan Ridge Redoubt. Both positions were put together specifically to allow *enfilade fire* across *No Man's Land* (i.e. allowing the ability for machine-gunners to fire across the longest axis of the attacking formations – in this instance, from the sides or flanks).

The British plan of attack was simple enough – the first wave would be carried out by the 11th Brigade – with three primary attacking battalions and three further battalions in support. They were to capture the first and second objectives, after which the 10th and 12th Brigades were to pass through and carry on to the third line of objectives.

The enemy wire situation across the Division front of 1500 yards was better than most. It had been cut up enough to not hinder advancement. The German front-line positions had also taken a decent pounding, with most trenches being badly battered.

However, they weren't battered enough. Even during the final crescendo of British artillery, German machine-guns had fired intermittently, but as the heavy artillery lifted and the British first wave formed up in *No Man's Land*, deadly enfilade fire poured down from the Redan Ridge Redoubt, targeting not only the front-line attackers but also the reserve trenches where thousands of men were getting ready to support the assault.

Helping out the 11th Brigade were two Territorial Battalions borrowed from the 48th Division, namely the 1/6th and 1/8th Royal Warwickshire Regiment – both of whom would have the dubious honour of leading the attack on the Quadrilateral. To aid the men, several Russian Saps had been dug out into *No Man's Land,* which drastically cut the distance to the enemy's front line. This meant that 1/8th Warwicks, advancing with minimal equipment, could approach quickly. Within minutes they were occupying German positions and after just forty minutes they had reached their objectives and immediately started to consolidate their position.

The 1/8th Warwicks were the lucky ones. Subsequent attempts to support and reinforce their positions broke down disastrously as the German machine-gunners made hay in the early morning sunshine.

The 1st Hampshire's suffered 500 casualties trying to get across *No Man's Land*. The 2nd Royal Dublin Fusiliers were decimated as they tried to leave their assembly positions and move up to their jumping-off points. When ordered at noon to attack enemy positions, they could muster just 60 men from an original roster of 503. They had been practically wiped out before reaching their own front-line position.

Back inside the Quadrilateral, a mixed group of Warwicks and Seaforth Highlanders were involved in a bitter fight to hang on to their hard-fought gains. A senior officer of the Seaforth Highlanders was trying to organise the defence of the redoubt. The Germans in a nearby trench were firing directly onto their positions and it was becoming obvious to everyone around that they needed to be quietened in whatever way was practicable.

The order was put out that on the whistle, each man would let go five rounds rapid fire and charge the enemy position. But before the whistle was blown, a Seaforth corporal took matters into his own hands. He collected up an armful of bombs and walked steadily towards the enemy position, shouting and swearing in his broad Scottish accent while throwing his grenades. He caused confusion amongst the enemy ranks, but as he approached their position, he fell dead, collected by numerous rifle bullets.

Inspired by this action, the rest of the British line rose and charged the enemy as one, clearing the trench with bullet and bayonet until the redoubt was secure once more.

It is unknown if this soldier received a posthumous gallantry award or recommendation. He surely deserved one. But despite isolated heroics such as this, the sit-rep at 9am for the 4th Division was grim: apart from capturing small areas of the Quadrilateral and a few, isolated breakthroughs which saw some parties fight their way through to the German second line, the German defences were generally winning the day:

We started out as arranged, and things seemed (to be) going quite well till we, or rather our first wave, reached the German front line, they slowed, and we bunched rather and the most fearsome hail of rifle and machine-gun fire with continuous shelling opening on us. Most of us seemed to be knocked out.[1]

Unfortunately, communications were such that Divisional HQ had a very different view of proceedings. By 7.42am they were under the impression that the entire German front line in their sector had been captured. At 10.07am the leading brigade was thought to have been well on its way to capturing its ultimate objective – Munich Trench – some 4,000 yards behind the German front.

By noon it was understood that deployments of men from 2nd Battalion, Essex Regiment were in Munich Trench and engaging with the enemy. It was only after 1.14pm that the true situation became clear. It was at this moment a further message was received from the men from Essex. They were not in Munich Trench, but were fighting with the Warwicks to hang on to part of the Quadrilateral strong point. The message was short and to the point, it read *'for goodness' sake send reinforcements!'*

Half an hour later, two battalions reported into HQ to say they had been forced to retreat to their original jumping-off positions. By 2.15pm it was becoming obvious that hardly any of the German front line had been taken and indeed it was only at the Quadrilateral where there had been even a glimmer of a breakthrough.

With communications so up in the air, it was impossible for anyone in HQ to have an accurate and clear view of what was going on in the thick of battle. Their attempts to reinforce what they thought were successful breakthroughs only added to the body count and any attempt to redirect artillery support onto areas where they thought it might be needed (i.e. Munich Trench) was actually counter-productive. By the time the true situation had come to light, it was simply too late.

A few brave souls from the 10th Brigade had indeed made it through to Munich Trench, but any success achieved was short-lived because of the failures of the neighbouring Divisions – the 31st Division to the north and the 29th Division to the south – to make any inroads on their sectors.

The men of the 4th Division were isolated and alone and despite desperate attempts to send up reinforcements, numerous aggressive German counter-attacks eventually forced them back until all they could do was cling on to the Quadrilateral. Despite being practically surrounded by swarms of angry Germans, they held out until the early hours of 2nd July, after which they reluctantly abandoned their hard-fought positions and returned to their original lines.

Before reaching their billets at Mailly-Maillet, both Warwick battalions had a roll call in a quiet leafy lane. The 1/8th could only muster 47 men out of the 600 that went into the attack. Of the 830 men of the 1/6th who went over the top, just 95 men answered to their names. Only 25 of them were not wounded.

The Commanding Officer of 11th Infantry Brigade was Brigadier-General Prowse. He was mortally wounded as he crossed *No Man's Land* with his men. As he lay dying, he gave his opinion on the part-time soldiers from Birmingham: *"I did not think much of Territorials before, but, by God, they can fight!"*

Overall, the 4th Division suffered 5,752 casualties.

26

DRUMMER WALTER POTTER RITCHIE VC, SEAFORTH HIGHLANDERS

Walter Potter Ritchie was born at 81 Hopefield Road, Glasgow on 27th March 1892. He was the fifth child out of six for ironworker dad Walter senior and mum Helen, who worked in the warehouse of a local muslin manufacturer.

After completing his schooling at Normal School (later Dundas Vale) in the Cowcaddens district of Glasgow, he followed in his father's footsteps and gained a blacksmith apprenticeship as a young teen, but by the summer of 1908 his thoughts were turning towards a military career – despite him being just 16.

By that time, he had already joined up with the part-time territorials of the 8th Scottish Rifles as a boy drummer, but in August 1908 he joined the colours for real, forgetting his age in the process and joining the rank and file of the 8th Cameronians before being transferred to the Seaforth Highlanders. His parents were less than impressed and tried to force him to return home, but young Walter was having none of it. He wanted to be a soldier – and that (as they say) was that.

His first few years with the 2nd Battalion, The Seaforth Highlanders saw young Ritchie sent off to such glamourous places as Shorncliffe in Kent, and Fort George near Inverness, but at the outbreak of war in 1914 he soon found himself on his way to France, disembarking onto the Continent as part of the original British Expeditionary Force (BEF) on 23rd August, 1914, seeing action in some of the Western Front's earliest skirmishes – including the Battles of the Marne, Aisne, Messines and Armentieres where he sustained a nasty head wound which saw him evacuated back to Blighty during October.

He recovered sufficiently to return to his unit before the end of the year though and even witnessed first-hand the famous Christmas 1914 truce, before being shipped off to Belgium to endure the Second Battle of Ypres during the spring of 1915.

The Seaforth Highlanders were later moved down to the Somme sector of the front, being stationed near Mailly-Maillet.

During the early hours of 1st July 1916, Walter Junior and the rest of the Seaforths lined up in their front-line trenches ready to launch the greatest British infantry assault in the history of British infantry assaults. As part of the 4th Division, they were tasked with capturing enemy positions towards the north of Beaumont-Hamel, including the formidable German strongpoint nicknamed the Quadrilateral.

After the fearsome artillery barrage finally ceased, the infantry of the 4th Division clambered over their parapets and advanced on the enemy. Ritchie's battalion was part of the second wave and went over the top at approximately 9.30am.

By late morning, pockets of the 2nd Seaforths had made a bit of progress, small parties of men had penetrated the German defences and were flirting with the third line of enemy trenches, but by this time the Battalion had taken such a beating that the huge loss of men (especially from within the officer class) meant the attack was faltering. The few soldiers who had got to the German lines in one piece were pinned down and rapidly running out of ammunition.

Some men started to retreat and head back to their own lines. Drummer Ritchie, however, wasn't about to retreat anywhere and, despite a nasty wound to his knee, rushed forward from his position through a hailstorm of enemy machine-gun and grenade fire, jumped onto the parapet of a German trench and, in full view of defenders and attackers alike, took out the captured German bugle he was not meant to have and repeatedly sounded 'The Charge'.

The effect was startling. The bugle call rallied all British soldiers within earshot, nipping any ideas of withdrawal in the bud. A potentially precarious situation had been avoided.

It was an extraordinary act of bravery that showed utter disregard for his own safety and, not surprisingly, he was recommended for the Victoria Cross. The Official Citation appeared in the London Gazette on 9th September 1916 and read:

> *For most conspicuous bravery and resource, when on his own initiative he stood on the parapet of an enemy trench, and, under heavy machine gun fire and bomb attacks, repeatedly sounded the "Charge," thereby rallying many men of various units who, having lost their leaders, were wavering and beginning to retire. This action showed the highest type of courage and personal initiative. Throughout the day Drummer Ritchie carried messages over fire-swept ground, showing the greatest devotion to duty.*

Yet, despite his heroics, a lack of men and ammunition meant the forward position was extremely hazardous, with the enemy closing in on three sides. By about 5pm the attackers withdrew to the original German front line position and fifteen minutes later, the order was given to return to the British lines as quickly as possible. By this time there were about forty men of the Battalion left.

The King presented Drummer Ritchie the Victoria Cross personally at Buckingham Palace on 25th November 1916. After receiving his

VC, Ritchie returned to Scotland for a period of leave but declined all offers to reminisce about his past heroics – instead he could often be heard to say: "I like to forget about these things this side of the Channel."

In December 1916 Ritchie also received the French *Croix de Guerre*, which was presented to him by Lieutenant General Sir Aylmer Hunter-Weston, but it wasn't long before Ritchie returned to front-line duty with the Seaforth Highlanders where he was involved in many more signification battles including those at Arras and Passchendaele in 1917 and the fight for the Hindenburg Line in the final year of the war. By the end of it all, he had been wounded no less than five times and gassed twice – but he had survived.

Ritchie stayed in the army after the war, transferring to the 1st Battalion, Seaforth Highlanders. He was promoted to Sergeant and took up the position as the Battalion's Drum-Major. He was also part of the VC guard of honour for the internment of the Unknown Soldier in Westminster Abbey on 11th November 1920.

Drum-Major Ritchie retired from the army in 1929 but kept close ties with the military by working as a recruitment officer in Glasgow. When the Second World War came knocking, Ritchie re-joined the colours and served as a Staff Sergeant in the Royal Army Ordnance Corps in Scotland until he was discharged in 1941 on health grounds.

Walter Ritchie VC died on 17th March 1965, ten days short of his 74th birthday.

Although his medals are in the hands of private collectors after being sold at auction several times over the years, the bugle with which he rallied the men during the Battle of the Somme is held at the Queen's Own Highlanders Museum in Inverness, Scotland.

On 1st July 2016, a hundred years to the day of Ritchie's VC action, a centenary paving stone outside the People's Palace in Glasgow was unveiled in his memory. Fifty members of his family were present at the ceremony.

27

1ST JULY: BEAUMONT HAMEL

M ajor-General Sir Henry de Beauvoir de Lisle's 29th Division had made a name for themselves in Gallipoli, winning six VC's before breakfast at Helles on 25th April 1915. Fast forward fifteen months, and they were being thrown into the fire of battle once more – this time on the Somme – with some of the toughest objectives of the entire British attack, namely, to capture the fortified village of Beaumont Hamel, as well as Hawthorn Ridge and surrounding positions.

The village of Beaumont Hamel was between the German front-line positions and their second line of defences (known to the British as Munich Trench). The village comprised just 162 houses, but below ground were a labyrinth of caves, underground shelters, and storage areas, ideal for ammunition, kitchens, and general supplies. Every slope, ridge and gradient had been carefully utilised by the German defenders for maximum defensive protection – and don't forget the *Bergwerk* redoubt towards the north of the village, the Hawthorn redoubt perched on top of the Hawthorn ridge to the west and Y-Ravine to the south which had naturally steep sides and was rammed with dugouts.

Hawthorn redoubt had been earmarked for some special attention prior to the infantry advance. The small matter of 40,000Ib of ammonal had been lovingly placed, primed and charged deep within the ridge by the men of 252 Tunnelling Company, Royal Engineers and it would be blown at 7:20am– ten minutes before the whistles would blow to signal the general infantry attack.

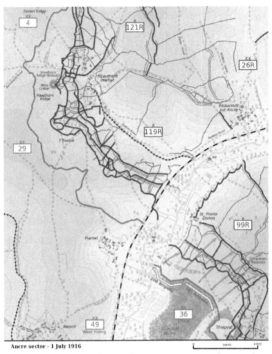

29th Division in front of Beaumont Hamel. 1st July 1916

On paper, such timing would still allow for the main crater to be occupied before the main assault got going, but concessions needed to be made regarding artillery support to make sure those men rushing for the bomb crater were not flattened by friendly fire.

In the end, those concessions would leave the entire attacking force woefully bereft of artillery support and give the enemy ample opportunity to man their defences.

The attack towards Beaumont Hamel would be fronted by three brigades – but it would be the 86th Brigade (comprising the 1st Lancashire Fusiliers, 16th Middlesex, 2nd Royal Fusiliers and 1st Royal Dublin Fusiliers) that would have the pleasure of carrying a direct assault on the centre of the village.

To help matters, Russian Saps similar to those dug at Serre were excavated beneath *No Man's Land* to within thirty yards of the German front-line trench to be used as temporary Stokes Mortar positions. The idea being that as soon as the Hawthorn Ridge mine was blown and the heavy artillery moved towards the second line of Germany defences, the Trench Mortar boys would get busy with a furious bombardment of their own to keep the German front-line defenders on their toes. The Stokes Mortar teams were in position and ready by 2:00am. There was nothing left to do but wait.

Meanwhile, on the other side of the wire, the German defenders were also patiently waiting.

> *Our regimental positions were ready to be stormed, but everyone was in cheerful spirits even if the preliminary bombardment, which had lasted 7 days, had left its mark on the nerves of the men. Many weeks of hard labour strengthening and reinforcing our positions had paid off. 7 days of constant shelling had cost the regiment only 20 dead and 83 wounded. A couple of days' earlier 10th company had taken a prisoner who had told us about an impending attack that was going to start on the 1st of July.[1]*

The men of the 119th RIR were ready and waiting. They had their weapons to hand, extra ammunition available, and were ready to spring from their dugouts at a moment's notice. And at 7.20am on 1st July, that notice was duly served, courtesy of an almighty explosion deep within the Hawthorn Ridge.

As well as the huge mine explosion, four other things happened simultaneously at 7:20 that morning: two platoons from 'D' Company, 2nd Royal Fusiliers rushed forward to occupy the huge mine crater on top of the Hawthorn Ridge; British heavy guns lifted from their German front line targets to move towards new targets in the rear; Every available Stokes Mortar in the area lit up and poured fire onto the German front-line positions as a replacement for the heavy guns; and finally, every single German soldier within earshot of the Hawthorn explosion instinctively sprang into action and readied themselves for the coming attack.

The resulting mine crater was some 130 feet across and 40 to 50 feet deep. The redoubt that was once there was completely destroyed, along with three sections of the accompanying German garrison. Before the rubble had returned to earth from the explosion, 'D' Company of the 2nd Royal Fusiliers were on their toes, rushing towards the crater armed with machine-guns and mortars. The Germans were no slouches either and as they had less ground to cover, could get set up on their side of the crater and pour machine-gun fire into the on-rushing Fusiliers. Amazingly, about 120 men avoided the German bullets and reached the British side of the crater safely – they occupied and consolidated a smashed up German position and stumbled upon a partially buried dugout where the German defenders were desperately trying to dig themselves out. *Vizefeldwebel* Davidsohn recalled the incident:

> *The English had managed to break into our trench.*
> *We had only just opened the exit of the dugout when*

they were upon us. A bayonet thrust killed the man who
was holding the shovel, his body fell down the stairs of
the dugout... I had no rifle with me but managed to
fire a signal flare into the face of one of the attackers.
The English answered by throwing some hand grenades
which forced us to withdraw.[2]

The British attackers optimistically called for the German defenders to surrender, but enemy reinforcements were quick to appear, and the Royal Fusiliers were forced to retreat to another part of the crater lip. Meanwhile, the rest of the 2nd Royal Fusiliers were advancing directly upon Beaumont Hamel. The attack was a fiasco as the men tried to pass through withering machine-gun fire. They didn't stand a chance and only a handful of men got as far as the enemy wire – which was completely uncut.

The 16th Middlesex Regiment should have followed the Royal Fusiliers into the fight for Beaumont-Hamel but could not get to their jumping-off positions at the front line in time due to heavily congested communication trenches full of dead and dying Fusiliers from the first wave of attacks. When they eventually got into position, just before 8.00am, they found that the British wire was cut only every forty yards or so and as soldiers grouped around these rare openings waiting to go through, the German machine-gunners made hay. Hundreds of men were cut down before getting through their own wire.

No one from the 16th Middlesex got anywhere near the enemy lines, although a small party of 20 men, led by Captain Frederick Sidney Cockram, did manage to reach the western edge of the crater lip. By this time, Cockram had been wounded three times, but each time he got straight back up and carried the fight to the enemy, urging his men on. When he was hit a fourth time, not even he could continue – by this time he had sustained eight separate bullet wounds. Captain Cockram was recommended for the Victoria Cross for his exploits that morning. He ended up being awarded the Distinguished Service Order.

By now there were about 200 men around the crater, including Lieutenant-Colonel J Hamilton-Hall from 16th Middlesex Regiment:

> *I arrived at the near lip of the crater about 8am and found about 200 dotted about in small partiers of twos and threes, the greater population being on the right half of the crater. These 200 appeared to consist of about 30 to 40 of the Royal Fusiliers, two sections of the Machine-gun Coy, and 3 Stokes mortar guns, the balance of about 120 from my battalion. There were 7 Lewis guns also. Our machine-guns were firing, and most of our Lewis Guns; the Stokes mortar guns soon ran out of ammunition after my arrival. About half the men were firing and some were endeavouring to creep round both lips of the crater. On the further lip of the crater I believe there were either 2 or 3 enemy machine-guns which were firing over the lip of the crater...[3]*

Hamilton-Hall was finding it tricky to consolidate these fragmented outposts, especially without fresh reinforcements or ammunition supplies. He tried to get the message out for the men to dig in as best they could, but by 10:00am it was becoming obvious that British positions around the crater lip were becoming untenable. They had no choice but to run the gauntlet one by one over the bullet-swept grounds of *No Man's Land* to get back to their own lines.

By 10:30am the British grasp on the Hawthorn Ridge crater had all but been lost. Hamilton-Hall now turned his attentions to getting enough men together in the British front-line trenches to fend off any notion of a German counter-attack.

Despite the focus now being on organising and preparing all fit men to ward off any enemy attacks, Brigadier-General Williams, commanding 86th Brigade, sent forward orders for the Royal Fusiliers to renew their own attack on the German lines. It was an order impossible to carry out because of a lack of leadership and the trenches being completely blocked by dead and wounded.

No further attacks were carried out.

In their efforts to take the Hawthorn crater and the village of Beaumont Hamel, the 2nd Battalion Royal Fusiliers suffered 24 officers and 470 other ranks killed, missing or wounded. Of the twenty-three officers and 689 men who entered the battle with the 16th Middlesex Regiment, only a single officer and 196 men survived unscathed.

28

— ● —

1ST JULY: 'TO YOU HAS BEEN SET THE MOST DIFFICULT TASK.' THE SUNKEN LANE

Advancing on the left flank of the 2nd Royal Fusiliers were the 1st Lancashire Fusiliers. The Royal Engineers had been busy in this sector too, building another Russian Sap deep into *No Man's Land*.

This particular sap was called S7 and was dug to connect the British front line (Clive Street Trench – occupied by 1st Lancashire Fusiliers) to a Sunken Lane, which was positioned roughly halfway across *No Man's Land*. S7 was to act as a covered communication trench through which the advanced assault parties could travel in relative safety directly to the Sunken Lane. By using this lane as a jumping off point, the distance to the enemy front line was drastically reduced.

S7 was opened for business just before midnight and by 3.00am 'B' and 'D' Companies from the 1st Lancashire Fusiliers, together with a 100-man special bombing unit complete with Stokes Trench Mortars, moved through Sap S7 and settle into the Sunken Lane.

The orders given to the Lancashire Fusiliers were simple: As soon as the Hawthorn Mine explodes, the trench mortars were to light up and lay fire onto the German front-line positions. At 7.30am, 'B' and 'D' Companies were to advance in extended formation from the Sunken Lane while 'C' and 'A' Companies would provide the second and third waves of attack, launching from the original British positions further back.

It all seemed so straightforward.

At about 6.30am, just an hour before the attack was due to begin, one of the Army's official kinematographers, Lt. Geoffrey Malins, arrived in the Sunken Lane to take some footage of the men who were there. Those images of the Lancashire Fusiliers sitting against the bank of the lane, anxiously waiting for the whistles to blow are some of the most fascinating and haunting images in British military history.

After capturing his film, Malins headed back from the Sunken Lane to take up a new position to film the Hawthorn Mine explosion. Meanwhile, back in the lane, the Germans had spotted the entrance to S7 and subsequently shelled the position with 77mm field guns – causing twenty casualties before they had even started.

When H-Hour did finally arrive, the leading sections of 'B' and 'D' companies, along with the advanced bombers, scrambled up the banks of the Sunken Lane and advanced as per instruction. They were afforded a few moments of grace before the German machine-gunners opened fire, but once they started firing, they caused carnage throughout the British ranks.

Captain E.W. Sheppard recalled what happened to those men who rushed to the advance from the Sunken Lane:

> *A few minutes (not as much, I should have said, as five) after the mine went up, we had seen the battalion on our right, the Royal Fusiliers, start off across No Man's Land, the first wave went forward. The east bank of the lane lay in a slight dip which concealed men getting out of it from the enemy view and fire, but two steps brough them into exposure and the bulk of the first wave got no further than the edge of this dip where they were swept over in swither, and those who were still alive crawled*

> *or were dragged down into the lane which was now full*
> *of wounded.[1]*

Within minutes of H-Hour, many of the men that had nervously looked into Malin's camera lens less than an hour previously were now lying dead or dying just yards from the bank of the Sunken Lane.

It wasn't just the tip of the Lancashire spear that was suffering. To the left rear, 'A' Company suffered huge casualties as they tried to cross *No Man's Land* towards the Sunken Lane. 'C' Company caught machine-gun fire the minute they left their trench line, losing their Company Commander and Company Sergeant Major as they stood on the parapet giving the men the order to advance. One of those men was Corporal George Ashurst:

> *'When I stepped on top of our trench, over the top, it was*
> *badly blown down and there was a corporal lying there*
> *and all his shoulder was gone, blown away. Hit by a*
> *whizz-bang. He looked up at me and he said, 'Go on*
> *Corporal! Get the bastards!' I daren't stop, I just said*
> *'OK' and buggered off as fast as I could run.'[2]*

Just one officer and about 60 men from 'C' Company managed to get to the Sunken Lane safely.

The attack was just minutes old, but was already floundering. The scene in the Sunken Lane was one of chaos, with the entire floor of the lane littered with the bodies of the dead and dying. Some were screaming, some were talking deliriously, others wailing for help and pleading for water. Men who could help were busy bandaging wounds and making the wounded as comfortable as possible. After about thirty minutes of rapid reorganisation the Commanding Officer, Lieutenant-Colonel Magniac, ordered the Stokes mortars to open up rapid fire, under cover of which 2/Lt Caseby led forward about seventy-five men who had been rounded up and were ready to have another go at taking the German positions. It was 08:15am.

> 'All ranks dashed forward bravely, but on topping the crest, just 10 yards from the Sunken Road, they were met by the same heavy M.G. fire and only 2/Lt Caseby and about 10 OR reached the German wire.'[3]

It was practically impossible for progress to be monitored safely from the Sunken Road and with no news coming into the position and no reinforcements being brought up, there was nothing more that could be done for the time being.

At about 10.00am there was a sudden retirement on the right flank by the Royal Fusiliers - possibly the remnants of the detachment clinging on to the crater making a run for it back to their own lines – but this sudden retreat spooked the Lancashire men into thinking the Germans were counter-attacking. This caused a mini stampede in the Sunken Lane as many men made a rush for Sap S7 in a desperate attempt to get back to their lines. After things had calmed down a bit, the men built barricades to the north and south entrances of the lane, just in case the Germans were indeed feeling frisky.

At 11.45am, Brigadier-General Williams of 86th Brigade sent down a message suggesting he had heard rumours of a retirement and ordered Magniac to attack again. Magniac, who had been in the thick of it in the Sunken Lane from the outset strongly refuted any notion of retirement and informed Williams that the attacks had failed because of the men being cut down by machine-gun fire just a few yards beyond the lane.

At 12.30pm, Major Utterson, who had started the day commanding the 10% battle reserve (those men deliberately left out of the fighting to preserve the original unit in the event of a major disaster) was ordered to advance from the British lines with twenty-five men and pick up as many stragglers as possible on his way to the Sunken Lane, once he arrived safely there was to be another advance on the German lines.

Only five men made it to the Sunken Lane. All further planned attacks on the German lines were called off.

Focus now turned back to improving the entrenchments that had already been started and evacuating the wounded back to the front lines via S7. German shells dropped onto the lane sporadically, causing a few more casualties, and enemy snipers caused headaches all day. The Lancashire Fusiliers gamely clung on to the Sunken Lane, but their position was not a good one. That evening, they were forced to retire the bulk of what was left of their manpower, leaving a token defensive unit to hold it as a forward outpost. One of the chosen few to stay behind was Corporal George Ashurst:

> We got twenty-five men and we put about eight men at the bottom end of the road and about eight at the top of the road and about eight or nine in the middle of the road under the oldest soldier because there were no more NCO's. The thing quietened down, the quiet after the storm, we were practically sleeping all night, just lying there. The stretcher bearers were very busy taking a lot out of it – they were cleared by morning. As dawn came, I was against this bit of a barrier we'd built up at the bottom end and I hear some voices the other side of the barrier. I stand up and have a look and there's three Jerries! About 100 yards away stood in a ditch. I said to the lads, 'Jerries!' I took my rifle and fired at the middle one – he went, but whether I hit him or not I don't know. No sooner had he ducked and

the other two followed him out of sight the officer came down to see what the trouble was. I told him. 'Ooooh, we're all right lads, we can dig in now, Jerry will let us bloody well have it!' He was right you know – he did. He started with minenwerfers; you can see them coming. Dropping them here and there, he dropped one right on the body of men in the middle of the road, killed half of them and wounded the other half. One I thought was certainly ours and it was a dud! It dropped about six yards past us towards the far end of the Sunken Road. As soon as it was dark word came, a messenger, 'Evacuate the Sunken Road!' So, we packed in and ran back as fast as we could.[4]

The day had been a disaster for the 1st Lancashire Fusiliers. They had tried to advance multiple times into the face of murderous machine-gun fire, with little or no artillery support. Not surprisingly, casualties were eye-watering, with the battalion diary recording 21 officers and 500 men killed, missing, or wounded.

29

1ST JULY: DEAD MEN CAN ADVANCE NO FURTHER. Y-RAVINE

B y about 8am, news began filtering back to 29th Division headquarters, suggesting that the 87th Brigade had reached their objectives and that the 4th Division advancing on the left and the 36th Division on the right were moving forward nicely with little opposition.

Buoyed by this news, General de Lisle (Commanding Officer of 29th Division) ordered the two lead battalions (1st Essex & 1st Newfoundland Regiments) of his 88th Brigade to put their fighting boots on. They were to attack on a front of around 1,000 yards and occupy the enemy's first line of trenches on the western edge of 'Y' Ravine - perhaps the most impregnable area of the entire front line. And they were to do it with no artillery support.

The order went out at 8.37am but the men from 1st Essex simply could not get into position as they struggled to move through smashed communication trenches that were jam-packed with dead and dying soldiers.

Unperturbed, the Newfoundlanders, keen to get on with the show, clambered out of their second line trench, avoiding the commotions of the communications trenches, and proceeded to advance over open ground in full view of the enemy. It was 9.15am.

'A' and 'B' companies led the charge, with 'C' Company following slowly behind, weighed down by the heavy equipment they were ordered to carry. 'D' Company accompanied them on their right. They had to cover approximately 750 yards of open ground where they were highly vulnerable to enemy fire from their right-hand side because of the lack of flank support from the 1st Essex.

The German machine-gunners did not disappoint.

Those gunners were from the 2nd Machine Gun Company, Regiment 119, and they immediately spotted the movement from their vantage point on the Beaucourt Ridge and pivoted their guns onto the advancing men.

The first obstacle for the advancing Newfoundlanders was their own defensive wire belts, some 250 yards into the advance. Four thick belts of wire that had several pre-cut zig-zag lanes cut into them to allow the men to pass through – every gap had been exactly pinpointed by the German machine-gunners. The results were sadly predictable and described in the Battalion War Diary entry of the day:

> *The enemy's fire was effective from the outset, but the heaviest casualties occurred on passing through the gaps in our front wire where the men were down in heaps. Many more gaps in the wire were required than had been cut.*[1]

Those men who somehow got through those gaps in the wire now faced at least 500 yards of open ground that sloped gently downwards and was horribly exposed to enemy fire coming from the Beaucourt Ridge. One member of the attacking force was 15-year-old Leo O'Neil, who later described the enemy fire as '... *unrelenting, there was no escape from it. Everyone there that day died.*'[2] O'Neil almost died himself as he suffered significant wounds to his left leg, left hand and back.

Halfway across *No Man's Land* was the skeletal remains of a plum tree – known to the Newfoundlanders as the 'Danger Tree'. In this area, the enemy fire was particularly brutal and accurate. Newfound-land bodies quickly piled up. The curtain of fire raining down on to *No Man's Land* was simply too much to bear. The official New-foundland historian described the carnage in exquisite eloquence:

> *Where two men had been advancing side by side, sud-denly there was only one – and a few paces farther on he too would pitch forward on his face. A young subaltern looks around him in vain for men to lead. Defiantly, he brandishes his field telephone at the German trenches; then, putting down his head he charges to his death. The leading man of a pair carrying a ten-foot bridge is hit, and as he falls, he brings down with him bridge and partner. Without hesitation the latter gets up, hoists the bridge on his head and plods grimly forward until machine-gun bullets cut him down.*[3]

Despite everything, a handful of Newfoundlanders were able to get close enough to the German lines to throw over some hand-grenades, but these were only isolated engagements – the vast majority of the attacking force had been cut down long before. In practical terms, the assault had ground to a halt after a matter of minutes.

Back on the Beaucourt Ridge, the German machine-gunners were now taking pot-shots at any attacker trying to make their way back to where they started. But they themselves were running out of ammu-nition – it had been a long morning – and the order came down for them to save their bullets and leave the enemy stragglers to the riflemen of the infantry.

At 9.45am, the Commanding Officer reported personally to Brigade HQ - situated 100 yards behind the front line - that the attack had failed.

Not one member of the Newfoundland Regiment had managed to set foot inside a German trench. Out of 790 men that took part in the attack, 272 were killed and 438 were wounded – a casualty rate of 90%. Only 68 men could answer their name during roll call the following morning.

To all intents and purposes, the 1st Battalion, Newfoundland Regiment, had ceased to exist.

Meanwhile, the men of the 1st Essex were desperately trying to get into position to help their stricken fellows. It had taken them two hours, but they were finally ready. When the orders were given to attack at 10.50am, their leading companies immediately came under intense enemy fire the moment they appeared over the parapet. Getting as far as their own wire, they too found it not cut properly and found it difficult to advance any further. Isolated pockets of men made it halfway across *No Man's Land*, but that was about as far as any of them got – the men from Essex took 229 casualties for absolutely zero gains.

Further attacks were planned, but the British trenches were so congested with casualties it was impossible to get reinforcements anywhere near the front-line. Fresh attacks were delayed numerous times until, eventually at 1.50pm, they were cancelled all together.

The Newfoundlanders' sacrifice did not go unnoticed, and after the dust had settled, General de Lisle informed the Prime Minister of Newfoundland that his countrymen had showed a ...*magnificent display of trained and disciplined valour, and its assault only failed of success because dead men can advance no further.*

The 29th Division had lost 5,240 casualties in one day.

30

FESTE SCHWABEN: THE SCHWERPUNKT OF ALL SCHWERPUNKTS

Like the Hawthorn Ridge to the northwest, the wind swept Thiepval Plateau held significant military value in 1916. Behind the German front line, the ground rose steeply to the top of Thiepval ridge which stood proud, some 250 ft (76 metres) higher than the surrounding landscape.

British X Corps commander, Lieutenant-General Sir Thomas Morland, and his opposite number, *General der Infanterie* Fritz von Below, knew very well that if the British took possession of this high ground, they would have eyes on large swathes of the German defensive network from Beaumont Hamel down to Thiepval village itself – something that would put the whole German held area in jeopardy.

It was not surprising then, that on this particular part of the line the men from X Corps were staring down fortress-like German defences that had been planned, selected, prepared, and further developed with meticulous detail since the initial fighting for the ridge had died down in the autumn of 1914.

As soon as the Germans took up residence, this patch of high ground was instantly covered by significant defensive fire, patrolled constantly, and occupied at night. By 1915 a single trench (known as the *Teufelsgraben* or the Devil's Trench) had been dug around the perimeter of the plateau, protected by belts of wire and many machine-gun nests. Over the coming months, as more and more strong points, dug outs and fortifications were added, the Devil's Trench went through several name changes before finally becoming known as *Feste Schwaben* (the Schwaben Redoubt).

The main defensive structure was centred around a pair of independently wired but linked trenches (*Kampfgrabben* or Battle Trench and *Wohngrabben* or Accommodation Trench) that ran parallel to the second line of German defences, opposite Thiepval Wood.

British aerial photograph of German trenches north
of Thiepval. Schwaben Redoubt is the network
of trenches in the upper right of the photograph.
(Wikipedia)

Kampfgrabben boasted nine dugouts, twenty fire-bays, two heavy machine-gun posts and two teams of *Muskete* light machine-guns. Behind *Kampfgrabben* and linked by five communication trenches, *Wohngrabben* housed a further eight dugouts including a medical aid post and the Company Command Post, as well as further heavy and light machine-gun posts. At the north-west tip of these trenches was *Schlütergrabben* (Splutter Trench) which ran northeast and joined up with *Lachweg* which ran back south to complete the triangle.

It was by no means the largest Redoubt in the area, but such was its strategic importance the German defenders crammed this relatively tiny plateau of land with as much defensive might as they could conjure. Losing it would be catastrophic, which is why the *Feste Schwaben* was treated as the *Schwerpunkt* of all *Schwerpunkts*[1] for the entire Somme region. A point neatly summed up by *Leutnant-der-Reserve* Matthaus Gerster, Reserve Infantry Regiment 119 (RIR119):

> *They (the British) would be sitting on the highest part of the Thiepval Plateau (on the Pozières Ridge), able to observe far into the rear areas and to overlook all the approach routes and battery positions, especially those north of the Ancre. Thiepval itself would have been threatened from the rear (and to the north), St Pierre Division would have fallen, and Beaumont Hamel would have become untenable because it would have been overlooked from three sides.*[2]

Unsurprisingly, the top brass of the German Army was explicit regarding the importance of *Feste Schwaben*:

> *If the enemy gets established there, he is to be ejected at once.*[3]

31

1ST JULY: THIEPVAL. BULLETPROOF
SOLDIERS

Having looked at the defence system around Thiepval Ridge, there was no doubt that the men of X Corps were to have a hot time of it when they eventually went Over the Top. The top man of X Corps and thus the chap in charge of devising the plan to out-smart the German defenders was Lieutenant-General Sir Thomas Morland - a cigar chomping stalwart of the 'Old Army' who had made his name in deepest darkest West Africa.

Morland's master plan to crack open the German defensive safe relied solely on overwhelming numbers of men and shells to force his will upon the enemy. A frontal infantry attack on a two divisional front backed by artillery would be ordered to advance to a depth of 3,000 – 3,500 yards, with various strategic objectives earmarked for completion by mid-morning.

On the left flank of the attack, the 36th (Ulster) Division would attack astride the Ancre River, capturing the north of the plateau and neutralising the small matter of the Schwaben Redoubt on their way.

To their right, the 32nd Division would launch against the village of Thiepval, capturing the Leipzig Redoubt *en route* and finally occupying the southern end of the Thiepval plateau. Once all primary objectives had been taken, there would be a period of consolidation while reserve brigades would make their way through the captured positions and on towards the German second line of defence. According to the divisional timetables, this was to happen at 10.10am – just 2 hours and 40 mins after Zero.

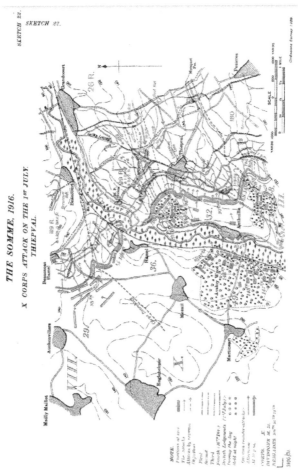

Attack on Thiepval. 1st July 1916

Roughly 21,000 men would be directly involved in the attack. Once again, the demands being placed upon the infantry were significant. This was a bold plan involving the capture of two highly fortified placements. Even Morland himself admitted the objectives represented a bit of a stretch, but he had the upmost faith in his artillery boys to smash open a path for the infantry to exploit and was confident they would come good.

Similar to elsewhere on the attacking front, Morland's field and heavy gunners had three essential jobs: smash the German front-line positions, killing as many German infantrymen as possible; knock out as many enemy artillery guns as possible and sweep away defensive obstacles such as wire and machine-gun nests.

To ensure success, Morland had one heavy gun for every 57 yards of frontline (apart from the Ancre River sector) and one field gun for every 28 yards.[1] During the Great Bombardment, they had fired over 330,000 shells on to enemy positions and on 1st July they were earmarked to chuck over another 56,000. As the final minutes counted down and the fury of the British guns rose to an ear-splitting crescendo, men like 2nd Lieutenant J.L. Stewart-Moore from 107th Trench Mortar Battery were suitably impressed:

> *Before dawn, our artillery stepped up their bombardment to the maximum. It was rapid fire by every gun and the noise was like hell let loose. As the shells passed over our heads, the air hummed like a swarm of a hundred million hornets.*[2]

The pointy end of the 32nd Division's attack comprised two brigades (the 96th and 97th) and they had got themselves ready on the lower slopes of the Thiepval ridge, from Authuille Wood to Thiepval Wood. They had been asked to assault the whole western facing edge of the Thiepval spur – from the Leipzig Salient to Thiepval village. The assembly trenches had only been dug a few days previous and the men who readied themselves for the attack were still recovering from the effort of digging up the chalk and carrying up all the supplies needed for the advance.

The 97th Brigade (led by the 16th and 17th Battalions, Highland Light Infantry) were deployed across a front of about 800 yards right opposite the Leipzig salient. When the whistles blew to mark the start of the attack, the two battalions of the HLI had very different experiences. The chaps from the 16th HLI were hit with intense machine gun fire the second they jumped over the parapet. Despite the withering fire, they advanced in extended order as per their instructions but took huge casualties and were forced to take cover in shell holes.

Leutnant-der-Reserve Friedrich Kassel was part of the German defensive line just north of the Leipzig Redoubt and as he peered over the parapet, he saw waves of 16th HLI bearing down on him:

> *No boys, we are still alive, the moles come out of their holes. Machine gun fire tears holes in their rows. They discover our presence (and) throw themselves on the ground, now a mass of craters, welcomed by hand-grenades and fire.*[3]

Only a handful of men from the 16th HLI made it to the German lines, and they did so by working with their mates from the 17th HLI who had sneaked into *No Man's Land* seven minutes before Zero. When the British artillery barrage lifted at 7.30am, they were in the German trenches before the enemy garrison could react.

By 8am, both Leipzig Trench and the Leipzig Redoubt were controlled by the Highlanders. After a quick round of consolidation, they prepared to move on to the next line of German defence —

Hindenburg Trench. However, the enemy had by this time composed themselves enough to pour down murderous machine-gun fire (from a fortification called the Wonder Work – a key target of the failed attack by the 16th HLI) onto the men crossing over the open ground towards their second objective.

> *Advancing towards the Hun second trench, I felt as if a mule had kicked me above the right eye. Lying prone, I endeavoured to think what had happened. It turned out I had been sniped, the bullet piercing the steel helmet in the front and circling inside three times had cut a furrow above my right eye. I was ordered by Captain Laird, my platoon commander to proceed to the rear. Looking back, I saw him hit by a shell adding another officer casualty to the growing number.*[4]

Private James Jack, 17th Btn., Highland Light Infantry, 97th Brigade, 32nd Division.

By 8.15am, every Highland officer had become a casualty and despite reinforcements from 2nd King's Own Light Infantry and futile attempts to help by 11th Border Regiment, 1st Dorset Regiment and 19th Lancashire Fusiliers, they were unable to advance from their positions in Leipzig Trench.

Elsewhere, the two leading battalions of the 96th Brigade (16th Northumberland Fusiliers and 15th Lancashire Fusiliers) met with disaster from the get-go courtesy of stubborn machine-gun fire emanating from Thiepval fort. The Northumberland's, who were tasked with assaulting the southern and central areas of Thiepval village, were ravaged by bullets almost as soon as they had cleared their own lines. So accurate was the enemy fire that entire lines of men were cut down as they tried to rush the enemy positions.

The fort-based machine gunners also had success cutting down the 15th Lancashire Fusiliers. However, a handful of men from the leading waves entered the German lines before the defenders had organised themselves and emerge from their underground dug-outs. Without stopping to clear these dug-outs, about 100 Fusiliers from this advanced party continued into Thiepval, thus allowing the German defenders the opportunity to swarm out of their shelters and cause havoc with the supporting waves of attackers as they arrived.

These defenders – the 99th Infantry Reserve Regiment – were once more helped by British confusion back at X Corps HQ, who mistakenly thought that Thiepval village was in the hands of the British. As a result, the artillery was ordered not to fire, which left the machine-gun nests and artillery guns in that area completely free to make hay on the subsequent waves of British attacks.

By 9.30am, the 32nd Division's attack had come to a standstill. The *No Man's Land* of Thiepval Spur was a graveyard with wave after wave of follow up battalions being cut to pieces by German machine-gun fire. Writing after the event, Brigadier-General Clement Yatman, commanding officer of 96th Brigade, said that 'only bullet proof soldiers'[6] could have taken Thiepval village that day.

The 1,200 men from the 32nd Division that fell in front of Thiepval would have probably agreed with him.

32

1ST JULY: MORITURITE SALUTANT. THE ULSTERS ATTACK

On the left flank of the 32nd Division, eight battalions from the 36th (Ulster) Division were getting themselves ready for their part in the *Big Push*. They had been tasked with attacking the German front-line positions across a wide-open plateau between Thiepval village and the River Ancre, including clearing out some enemy positions on the edge of the very marshy river valley.

This was part of the line where Field Marshal Haig had somehow convinced Rawlinson to earmark the German second line as the primary objective of the attack. As a result, the lucky Ulstermen would have a very busy day in front of them.

The high-level plan seemed simple enough with two brigades being used to carry the initial fight, with a reserve brigade to be deployed to take advantages of initial successes. On the left flank of the attack, the 108th Brigade was to attack astride the River Ancre - their ultimate objective being the Beaucourt railway station and the surrounding trenches, over a mile away from their starting position.

The right flank of the attack would be carried by the 109th Brigade, who would walk right into the teeth of the Schwaben Redoubt. The Divisional reserve for the show was the 107th Brigade. They had orders to follow in the footsteps of the chaps from the 109th Brigade, pass through the Schwaben Redoubt and onto the German second line of defences.

All in all, six Irish battalions would lead the charge when the bugles were sounded, and they all had very different experiences and outcomes from that initial charge. On the north bank of the Ancre, the men of 12th Royal Irish Rifles and 9th Royal Irish Fusiliers were in trouble before they had even started because of inadequate artillery support in their sector. It was something that Lieutenant-Colonel Stewart Blacker, 9th Royal Irish Fusiliers, had warned the CO of the 36th Division (Major-General Sir Oliver Nugent) about the day before the battle.

> *I remarked to him 'Morituri te Salutant', realising full well the hopelessness of the task allotted to the two battalions.*[1]

Morituro te Salutant. We who are about to die, salute you.

The men had actually climbed up out of their trenches a couple of minutes before Zero to give themselves a head start, but the artillery barrage in this sector (as predicted) wasn't strong enough to keep their German counterparts occupied. As the men picked their way through their own wire, enemy machine guns let rip.

Those that somehow made it through their own wire still had some 600 yards of *No Man's Land* to cross. Men were dropping like flies, with German riflemen with seemingly unlimited ammunition and bristling with stick grenades standing on top of their parapets, wreaking some kind of payback after the week-long hell of the *Great Bombardment*. Very quickly, the assaulting forces had been reduced to random pockets of men inching themselves towards the German positions in the face of seemingly impregnable enemy fire.

Despite the odds, some pockets of the attack made it into the German front-line trench system, and some were even seen making a bee-line towards Beaucourt Station, but such incursions proved ultimately futile. All were either killed, captured, or forced to retreat. By 8am, the Ulsterman's assault north of the Ancre was over.

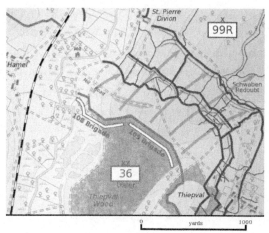

The Ulster attack on the Schwaben Redoubt - 1st July 1916.

The fighting strength of the 9th Royal Irish Fusiliers that morning had been around 600 men; the casualties were so heavy that by the end of the day just 80 rank and file would return unwounded without their officers. It was a similar picture with the 12th Royal Irish Rifles, who suffered 403 casualties in total.

Morituro te Salutant. We who are about to die, salute you.

On the right-hand side of the assault, led by the 109th Brigade (9th and 10th Royal Inniskilling Fusiliers) and the remainder of the 108th (13th Royal Irish Rifles) the results were different. At 7.15am, under cover of the final hurricane bombardment, the leading battalions left their trenches and crept through the gaps in the British wire to take up advanced positions in *No Man's Land*. Some men got to within 100 yards of the German sandbags and many others took up positions in a sunken road that offered decent protection deep *inside No Man's Land*.

When the bugles sounded, the men rushed to the advance. The 13th Royal Irish Rifles suffered a similar fate to the rest of their 108th Brigade colleagues – suffering hugely at the hands of enemy machine-gunners located in St Pierre Divion. However, the 109th Brigade enjoyed genuine success. Within seconds, they were at the German wire, which had been well cut and posed little challenge to the assault.

To help matters even more, the Germans in this sector were slightly slower to emerge from their dugouts and after a brief-but-brutal fight, a long section of what used to be a German front-line trench had been overrun and was in possession of Ulstermen such as Private Lindsay Hall, 10th Royal Inniskilling Fusiliers:

> *All that could be seen was a few twisted iron spikes and splinters of wire lying in the bottom of shell holes.*[2]

Such was the surprise and ferocity of the attack the enemy surrendered in droves. In fact, so many Germans were taken prisoner by the 10th Inniskilling's that when they were moved rearwards, they were at first mistaken for a German counter-attack.

Even before the front-line positions had been consolidated, the leading patrols were making their way towards the Schwaben Redout. This would be an all-together different proposition for the Ulstermen, as the element of surprise was not possible, and the Redoubt was bristling with defensive muscle.

However, during the *Great Bombardment*, the Redoubt had been singled out for 'special attention' - resulting in significant damage to wire obstacles and some of the key trench fortifications being completely smashed to bits. Consequently, the morale of the defending garrison was low. Half of the machine-gun crews had been killed and by the time the first attackers approached the Redoubt, three key machine-gun posts had received direct hits from British artillery. Despite this, the garrison at the Redoubt put up fierce resistance, and the Ulstermen had to fight hard and fight ugly to wrestle control of the Redoubt. The battle took place in narrow, broken trench bays and inside dark, dank dug-outs and progress was made with rifle butts, homemade clubs, bayonets, and pistols.

By 8.50am, the Schwaben Redoubt was in British hands.

When news of the loss of *Feste Schwaben* filtered back through the various German Command Posts, the shock was palpable. Such a setback so early in the day was the stuff of nightmares for German leadership. As far as they were concerned, the British were now in control of the highest parts of the Thiepval Plateau and could now observe far into the German rear positions. They needed to react and react quickly, and *Generalleutnant* von Soden immediately gave orders for the organisation of full-scale counter-attack.

One scenario that particularly worried the Germans was the vulnerability of Beaumont-Hamel, which could now be threatened from the rear and caught up in quite a serious pincer movement. However, the British battle order was not to break out and expand to the left or right, but to continue to plough deep and narrow towards the German second line, and as such it was now time for the support battalions from the 107th Brigade to get in on the action.

As the 11th Royal Inniskilling Fusiliers and the 14th Royal Irish Rifles cleared their own wire and made their way across *No Man's Land*, they were welcomed into the fray by heavy machine-gun fire coming from Thiepval village. Unfortunately for the Ulstermen, the 32nd Division on their right-hand side had failed in their assault, leaving an extensive network of machine-gun nests within the ruins of Thiepval village unmolested. Casualties were unsurprisingly heavy.

Despite this unwanted attention, by about 10am the pointy end of the 107th Brigade had pushed through the Schwaben Redoubt but were now caught in some irritating friendly fire from their own artillery guns that were still smashing up the German second line of defence. Consequently, they were forced to go to ground some 100 yards away from their final objective until the barrage was due to be lifted at 10.10am. This was a pivotal moment in the battle and a huge, missed opportunity, as *Feldwebel* Felix Kircher, 26th Field Artillery Regiment, admitted:

> ... *I rushed up and there, just outside the barbed wire, were ten or twenty English soldiers with flat steel helmets. We had no rifle, no revolver, no grenades, no ammunition, nothing at all; we were purely artillery observers. We would have had to surrender, but then the English artillery began to fire at our trench; but a great deal of the shells were too short and hit the English infantrymen and they began to fall back. If the English would have got through, they would have only met clerks, cooks, orderlies, and such like. For a distance of several hundred metres to right and to left from us there were no German soldiers. It was a decisive moment.*[3]

A decisive moment indeed. The delay had allowed just enough time for the Germans to move a fresh battalion into the line and get another machine-gun into position. It also gave the German artillery guns time to range in on the exposed attackers.

Once the British guns had lifted at 10.10am, the survivors tried their best to capture and occupy the second line of defences. By now, the remnant of the Brigade was decimated, scattered, and desperately trying to hold off organised German counter attacks. Small pockets of men managed to get into enemy trenches, but they were isolated, outnumbered, running low on bombs and ammunition and taking far too many casualties to offer up anything more than a token attack. By midday, what was left of the 107th Brigade had no choice but to retire back to the Schwaben Redoubt.

After a brief respite in the proceedings which allowed both sides to consolidate and reorganise, the Germans launched their first counter-attack shortly after 2pm, working their way inwards slowly from both flanks through trenches and over land. The Ulster's put up stern resistance despite having little to no communication with or support from their own lines. They were reliant on brave runners who continually ran the gauntlet of *No Man's Land* to try to relay messages to and from the besieged defenders. All too many were killed or wounded as they ducked and dodged their way across the battlefield.

At about 4.30pm, aerial reconnaissance reports from the Royal Flying Corps suggested that the British hold on the Schwaben Redout was insecure and despite reinforcements from 146th Brigade (49th Division), resistance within the Redoubt gradually subsided as the evening wore on.

By 10pm, with another German counterattack about to take place from three directions, the decision was made by the most senior surviving member of the British garrison to withdraw to the old German front-line position. Ironically, more reinforcements from 146th Brigade reached the Redoubt, but it was too late to alter the decision to retire. Most survivors eventually made it back to Thiepval Wood under cover of darkness with just a few small parties of men remaining in the original German line including one detachment of around thirty men of 1/7th West Yorkshire Regiment, led by Corporal George Sanders, that were left isolated towards the north-west of the Redoubt. This group in particular would show enormous grit and courage to hang on to their position for thirty-six hours in the face of enormous danger, before being relieved.

The glorious advance of the Ulster Division was over. They were the only men to reach the German second line trench system anywhere on the Somme and they had done this with no 'Regular' battalions to bolster their New Army ranks. But at what cost?

The 36th Division had suffered 4,962 casualties, among them 1,856 dead, 2,728 wounded, 213 missing and 165 taken prisoner.

33

CORPORAL GEORGE SANDERS VC MC

George Sanders was born at 7 Thornton Place, New Wortley, Leeds, Yorkshire on 8th July 1894. His father, Thomas, worked locally as an iron tool maker, and his mother, Amy, worked as a wool filler although she died in 1904.

Young George spent his early years growing up in Leeds and, after leaving the Little Holbeck School, found work as a fitter's apprentice at the Airedale Foundry. Once war was declared in the summer of 1914, it didn't take George long to answer the call of his country, enlisting with the 1/7th West Yorkshire Regiment on 9th November 1914 with the regimental number 3203, just a few months after his twentieth birthday.

After spells of training at York and Gainsborough, the battalion sailed for France and landed in Boulogne in April 1915. In those first few months overseas, he must have impressed his senior officers as he was appointed unpaid Lance Corporal on 4th October and promoted Lance Corporal on 11th November 1915. He was then appointed Acting Corporal on 15th April 1916 after a brief spell in hospital with conjunctivitis.

For the *Big Push* on the Somme in the summer of 1916, the 1/7th West Yorkshires were part of X Corps – their specific role would be that of supporting the 36th (Ulster) Division in their attack against the

Thiepval plateau and the formidable German defensive strongpoint known as the Schwaben Redout. To this end, Sanders' battalion spent the night of 30th June 1916 in support trenches in Aveluy Wood, directly behind the men of the Ulster division who were massed in Thiepval Wood, getting themselves ready for the big attack.

At 7.30am, the Ulstermen rushed forward and took hold of the Schwaben Redout. At 9am the West Yorkshires, as part of 146th Infantry Brigade, were ordered to move up to Assembly trenches in Thiepval Wood and prepare to move forward to support the Ulstermen. This was completed by midday. At 3.30pm, they got the call to move up to the front-line to support the attack, making their way to trenches at *Belfast City* in Thiepval Wood before they were ordered forward once more to reinforce the original British front line. Once this had been carried out, 'C' & 'D' Companies of 1/7th were flung into the crucible of battle to help reinforce the Ulstermen as they fought to hold on to their captured ground.

Amidst the confused scenes on the battlefield, the West Yorkshires were withdrawn late in the day, but a group of around thirty men, including A/Corporal Sanders, were left behind isolated after an assault on a section of the German line. With no officers or NCOs available, he immediately set about organising the defence of their position, all the while reminding the men that it was their duty to hold off the enemy at all costs.

Under Sanders' leadership, the group of men continued to hold the position through the night and on the morning of 2nd July deflected an enemy attack – they even rescued some British prisoners that had previously fallen into German hands.

Throughout this second day, they were subjected to numerous enemy counter-attacks, all of which were fended off despite having no rations, limited ammunition, and a growing casualty list. They were finally relieved early in the morning of 3rd July with Sanders and nineteen survivors returning to the British lines.

George Sanders showed great courage, determination and leadership during this ordeal and was quickly recommended for the Victoria Cross by the Commanding Officer of the Royal Irish Rifles.

He was promoted to full Corporal on 15th July. On 10th August, he was wounded in the face by shrapnel and suffered temporary deafness, but was back at duty just five days later. Promoted once more to Lance Sergeant towards the end of August, he later travelled to England on leave where he received a hero's welcome in his home city of Leeds before being presented with the Victoria Cross by King George V at Buckingham Palace on 18th November 1916. The Official Citation appeared in the London Gazette on 9th September 1916 and read:

> *For most conspicuous bravery. After an advance into the enemy's trenches, he found himself isolated with a party of thirty men. He organised his defences, detailed a bombing party, and impressed on his men that his and their duty was to hold the position at all costs.*

> *Next morning, he drove off an attack by the enemy and rescued some prisoners who had fallen into their hands. Later, two strong bombing attacks were beaten off. On the following day, he was relieved after showing the greatest courage, determination, and good leadership during 36 hours under very trying conditions.*

> *All this time his party was without food and water, having given all their water to the wounded during the first night. After the relieving force was firmly established, he brought his party, nineteen strong, back to our trenches.*

Besides Sanders' VC, the party of men who held out so gallantly was awarded five Military Medals.

George eventually applied for a Commission and left France in January 1917 to enrol with No 8 Officer Cadet Battalion at Lichfield. He was commissioned in 2nd West Yorkshire Regiment on 27th July and was attached to 1/6th Battalion. He was then appointed Acting Captain on 20th December whilst commanding a company.

In command of 'C' Company, 1/6th West Yorkshire Regiment, Sanders was a prominent figure in the hard fighting during the German attack of April 1918. On 25th April, after the enemy had penetrated the front line at Kemmel Hill, he organised his men in support and held the German attack up for some time, inflicting heavy casualties. Although he had suffered gunshot wounds to his leg and right arm, he continued to fight with his revolver in his left hand and was seen at one time on top of a pill box rallying his men and firing into the enemy at point blank range. For his actions at Kemmel Hill, Sanders was awarded the Military Cross, the Citation for which appeared in the London Gazette on 16th September 1918.

> *For conspicuous gallantry and devotion to duty. After the enemy had penetrated the front line, he promptly organised his men in support and effectually held up the enemy for some time, inflicting heavy casualties. He stood on top of a pill-box firing his revolver into the enemy at 20 yards.*
>
> *His splendid example of courage did much to inspire his men at a critical time.*

During the action at Kemmel Hill, he was officially noted as 'wounded and missing' however, he was actually taken prisoner and held by the Germans on Rügen island in the Baltic. It wasn't until July that his parents received a letter from George telling them he was safe, albeit a Prisoner of War.

After the war had ended, Sanders was released from captivity, eventually returning to Britain on Boxing Day 1918, where he was immediately promoted to Lieutenant. He was demobilised in March 1919 before finally relinquishing his Commission in September 1921.

George married Nellie Newby in Leeds on 5th April 1920 and found employment post war as a foreman at Meadow Lane Gas Works in Leeds. During the Second World War, he served as a Major in 8th West Riding (Leeds) Battalion, Home Guard, from February 1941.

George died at St James' Hospital, Leeds on 4th April 1950. He was given a full military funeral before being cremated at Cottingly Crematorium, Leeds, where his ashes were scattered. Besides his family, the service was attended by four Victoria Cross winners (William Butler, Albert Mountain, Wilfred Edwards, and Charles Hull) with Harry Daniels VC sending a wreath as he was too ill to attend in person.

Besides his VC and MC, Lieutenant Sanders was awarded the 1914-15 Star, British War Medal 1914-20, Victory Medal 1914-19, Defence Medal 1939-45 and George VI Coronation Medal 1937. His medals were held privately until they purchased in 2017 by Lord Ashcroft for £288,000. They are now on display in the Ashcroft Gallery, Imperial War Museum, London.

34

— • —

1ST JULY: OVILLERS. SO ENDS THE GOLDEN AGE

T he centre of the great British attack on the Somme belonged to the British III Corps. Sat astride the arrow straight road that links Albert to Bapaume, it was also the place on the battlefield where Haig dreamed of unleashing his cavalry on a magnificent final gallop to victory. His vision was for those mighty chargers to sweep through towards Bapaume, followed by Gough's Reserve Army and protected on either side by the illustrious infantry who would successfully keep at bay the marauding enemy machine-guns.

It was a glorious vision. But it needed the British III Corps to capture their entire sector of the battlefield. And in this particular battle zone, that was going to be a very tall order indeed.

The aforementioned Albert-Bapaume road cut the battlefield of III Corps almost in half. To the south of the road, 34th Division would attack the village of La Boisselle with the help of a couple of cheekily hidden mines excavated directly under the German positions. To the north of the road, the 8th Division would be climbing up the Ovillers spur, to overwhelm the village of the same name and push on deep into enemy territory.

Those enemy positions were a crisscross maze of trenches, strong-points and spurs all of which occupied the high ground of the Ovillers

Spur and overlooked all the British positions, to such an extent that even moving a small group of men towards the front could be met with an avalanche of hostile fire from the Infantry Regiment 180 (IR180) of the 26th Division and the Reserve Infantry Regiment 110 (RIR110) of the 28th Reserve Division who were in situ along this stretch of the line.

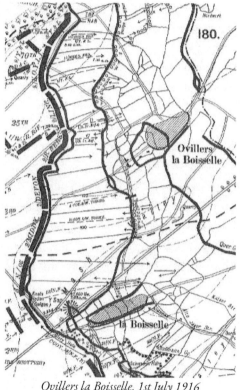

Ovillers la Boisselle. 1st July 1916

On the left (northern) flank of the attack, 70th Brigade was to attack from Authuille Wood through Nab Valley towards the northern end of the Ovillers Spur. Success would only be possible if the 32nd Division on their left flank silenced the Leipzig Redoubt – otherwise they would be exposed to un-interrupted machine-gun fire as they moved across *No Man's Land*.

In the middle of the attacking front, the 25th Brigade would advance directly upon the village of Ovillers. On paper, they had the slightly easier approach as they would be out of sight of the enemy until the final 300-400 yards of their trek across *No Man's Land*. In contrast, the men of the 23rd Brigade had most definitely pulled the shortest straw. They had to advance across a depression in the ground known as Mash Valley, which ran directly alongside the main Albert-Bapaume road. They were to move south of Ovillers and push on over a mile towards their ultimate objective of Pozières village.

The initial stretch of *No Man's Land* across Mash Valley was a murderous 700-800 yards wide and sat at the bottom of a large bowl, which offered absolutely zero natural cover for anyone crossing it. If that wasn't bad enough, the safety of their right flank depended wholly on the success of the neighbouring 34th Division overrunning La Boisselle and silencing the enemy within quickly. If this did not happen, the men of the 25th Brigade would be savaged from enfilade fire from three sides – and that isn't even counting enemy artillery.

All things considered, Mash Valley was quite possibly the single most dangerous and deadly piece of ground on the whole of the Somme battlefront.

The leader of the 8th Division, Major General H Hudson, was understandably nervous of this overreliance on his neighbours and even tried to get his own attack delayed slightly to reduce their exposure. The request was dismissed out of hand by Rawlinson.

As ever, much faith was placed in the pre-assault artillery bombardment, and with the cavalry waiting in the wings, there was even more pressure on the gunners to clear a path for the advance. Not even the most magnificent of mounts could gallop through lines of unbroken enemy wire.

Unfortunately, the artillerymen had stated several times during the preliminary bombardment that they would struggle to be effective against the distant enemy wire and they would even struggle with the closer belts due to a lack of ammunition. These comments either fell on deaf ears or were purposefully not sent up the chain of command as more and more distant objectives were added to the list of artillery targets to aid the much-anticipated breakthrough.

Despite an impressive bombardment that did indeed smash the enemy front-line positions to bits, German morale stood firm as most of the 5,300 men of RIR110 and IR180 waited deep underground for the opportunity to throw some lead of their own back at the British.

With a bombardment of such magnitude, the *Big Push* never pretended to be a surprise attack, however with just hours to go before kick-off, the men holding the high ground on the Ovillers Spur received the news they had been waiting for, courtesy of an intercepted message from deep under La Boisselle:

> *Early in the morning of 1st July word filtered through to us that the enemy would attack that morning... Some of us said that the English would attack at 7.30am. At 5.30am, the Vizefeldwebel stood at the dugout entrance and waited for the enemy's attack while we stood ready with our guns in the dugout. We all looked at the clock and waited anxiously for the enemy attack. We wanted to get back at the Englishmen.*[1]

> *Christian Fischer, machine-gunner, IR180*

In the end, the artillery which was meant to make it all too easy for the infantry ended up being the men's biggest achilles heel.

At 7am, thirty minutes before the whistle, the heavy guns lifted from the German front line to smash the German rear positions, steadily moving onwards towards Pozières in 250-yard movements. This left the much smaller field guns to keep the enemy's head down in the front-line for the half an hour before Zero. These didn't really pack enough punch to deter the German defenders and as a result, the leading assault waves suffered large casualties as they moved into *No Man's Land* early to take up their positions.

The 8th (Service) Battalion King's Own Yorkshire Light Infantry lost 10% of its entire strength *before* the whistles had been blown.

That being said, the 70th Brigade did enjoy initial success. Enemy wire in this section had been cut well and there was a brief moment of distraction for the enemy as the 32nd Division assaulted the Leipzig Salient to the north. In the confusion, the pointy end of the 70th Brigade's assault got into the enemy front-line positions without too much drama. Two leading waves of the 8th KOYLI along with men from the 8th Battalion York and Lancaster Regiment swept straight through the German first line and across almost 400 yards of open grassland to the second line with a handful of men even getting as far as the German third line – but those brave souls were never seen again.

Inevitably, this initial success was short-lived. Despite valiant attempts to consolidate their toe hold, the Germans counter-attacked fanatically with bombs and machine-guns. Meanwhile, the second and third waves of the attack were struggling to get forward to support the breakthrough because of a combination of German re-organisation and the failure of the 32nd Division to keep the machine guns on the Leipzig salient fully occupied. The result was devastating for the men desperately trying to reinforce the initial breakthrough.

> *A very heavy machine-gun fire was brought to bear*
> *on this wave from the left flank and the enemy front*
> *line which had apparently been re-occupied by use of*

> *underground galleries from the enemy 2nd line after the assaulting Battalion had passed over.*

> *...Casualties along the whole line were very heavy, and a general attempt was made to crawl forward under intense machine-gun and shrapnel fire, any available cover being made use of.[2]*

Further attempts to reinforce the assault we made throughout the morning. The 9th Battalion, York and Lancaster Regiment - made up of south Yorkshire miners – were decimated by machine-gun fire from the Thiepval ridge at a range of about 800 yards. Hardly a soul survived long enough to get anywhere near the German lines. Their historian, J.B. Montagu noted with despair: *So ends the Golden Age[3]*.

By late morning, the enemy fire that swept Nab Valley was so intense that all Brigade communication was forced to stop – not even flags could be used. Consequently, no one knew if the men holding enemy ground were alive or dead and no messages could be sent to the artillery to ask them for help. Eventually, those men who had penetrated the enemy lines had either been killed or driven out and by the end of the day, the 70th Brigade was back where they started in their own lines. They had suffered terribly and fought bravely but were unable to hold on to a single scrap of enemy territory.

In the middle of the 8th Divisional assault were 25th Brigade. Here, the two leading battalions (2nd Battalion Royal Berkshire Regiment and 2nd Battalion Lincolnshire Regiment) were to attack the village of Ovillers head on. From around 6.25am, the Germans had begun to retaliate swiftly to British bombardment by chucking over tonnes of high explosive and shrapnel shells of their own – this impeded the first waves as they attempted to move forward to their jumping-off positions out in *No Man's Land*. Both regiments were already suffering, and the attack hadn't even started.

At Zero Hour, the men advanced into a hail of rifle bullets that seemed to come from the German second line. Those pesky machine-gunners perched to the north on the Thiepval Ridge were also adding to the murder and mayhem. As a result, those first waves of men were forced to move forward in quick rushes from shell hole to shell hole until eventually small parties of Lincolns reached the German front-line trench. After a sharp fight with the incumbent defenders, the Lincolns had claimed around 200 yards of enemy trench by about 7:50am, but consolidating their hard-won gains would prove an even tougher test, as the regimental diary of the 2nd Lincolns testifies:

> *The few officers that were left gallantly led their men over the German trench to attack the second line, but owing to the rifle and machine-gun fire could not push on. Attempts were made to consolidate and make blocks, but the trench was so badly knocked about that very little cover was obtainable.*[4]

By 9am, the men holding the position were being exposed to uninterrupted machine-gun fire from the left and the right and were constantly being showered by bombs. It was obvious to all concerned that their position was now untenable.

The 1st Battalion Royal Irish Rifles, who had moved up to support the attack, had been badly maimed in their efforts to reach the isolated position – they just couldn't get enough men across *No Man's Land* in one piece to help out. There was no choice but to withdraw – initially they retreated to shell holes *in No Man's Land*. Their Commanding Officer, Lieutenant Colonel Reginald Bastard, left them there with orders to hold on as best they could while he went back to fetch more men. Bastard managed to get back to his own lines unscathed and rounded up every fit man he could to go back out to reinforce the men he left out near the German wire. Unfortunately, Bastard's band of brave men were cut to pieces as they tried to get back across *No Man's Land* and he was very quickly left with only 30 men.

By now it was obvious to all that any further attempts to attack the enemy was simply suicidal and by 1pm the offensive on the 25th Brigade front was called off. Upon this order, Bastard went across *No Man's Land* again to give the order to his stranded men to head back to their original lines.

By the end of the day, Lieutenant Colonel Reginal Bastard had crossed *No Man's Land* no less than four times and took part in the fighting inside the German trenches. For his gallant actions, he was awarded a Bar to his Distinguished Service Order.

The attack of the 23rd Brigade, on the right flank of the 8th Division's assault on Ovillers, returned depressingly similar results. The leading companies of 2nd Battalion, Middlesex Regiment and 2nd Battalion, Devonshire Regiment began shifting themselves into *No Man's Land* during the final crescendo of the British bombardment – advancing in open order to within 100 yards of the German lines.

According to the diary of the 2nd Devonshires, as soon as the men rose to advance at 7.30am, the enemy quickly got busy:

> *...opened a terrific machine-gun fire from the front and from both flanks, which mowed down our troops, this fire did not deter our men from continuing to advance, but only a very few reached the German lines alive.*[5]

Vizefeldwebel Laasch was one of those deadly machine-gunners firing down Mash Valley from his hidey-hole in the village of La Boiselle:

> *Tightly packed lines poured out of the English trenches, strode across the wide foreground (of Mash Valley) and*

*ended up in the heavy defensive fire of Regiment 180. I
also fired one belt after another into the flank of the ever
advancing English battalions with our machine-gun.
Never in the war have I experienced a more devastating
effect of our fire: the fallen were tightly packed in the
entire hollow up to Ovillers![6]*

A few brave souls did actually make it into the German front-line
trench system, and a handful of men even dared to advance onto the
second line of defences a couple of hundred yards beyond. But these
incursions were quickly dealt with and every attacker that had dared
to breach the German lines was either killed, captured, or forced to
retreat.

The reserve Battalion (2nd West Yorkshire Regiment) was called
forward to help with the attack, but they lost 250 men just getting
into their jumping off position as the German artillery smashed the
British lines in retaliation. Those who had survived the artillery then
had to run the gauntlet of Mash Valley, which was being covered by
machine-gun fire from three sides. Any slight movement was met with
a hailstorm of bullets.

By 9am, the toehold in the German line was collapsing under the
weight of incessant bomb and bayonet raids. The casualties were piling
up, the ammunition was running out, and there was no hope of
getting reinforcements. All that mattered now was getting as many
soldiers back to the British lines as possible.

The attack by 8th Division had been a disaster. It had suffered over
5,000 casualties with almost 2,000 dead. The six leading Battalions
had lost an average of 505 men each with the 2nd Middlesex reporting
623 casualties from of 673 officers and men that went into battle – a
92.6% casualty rate!

35

LIEUTENANT-COLONEL E T F SANDYS, DSO

During the *Great Bombardment*, while many officers and men gazed in wonder at the eye-watering number of shells being thrown at the German lines night and day, Lieutenant Colonel Edwin Thomas Falkiner Sandys was not quite so impressed with the show.

Sandys was Commanding Officer in charge of the 2nd Middlesex Regiment. As one of the lead Battalions of the 23rd Brigade, his men had the dubious honour of having some of the widest stretches of *No Man's Land* to cross throughout the entire assault – 750 yards across Mash Valley to be precise – and he was convinced he and his men were going to walk straight into a bear pit full of uncut wire and enemy soldiers who were ready and waiting for the fight.

Sandys was obsessed with the bombardment and would spend hours at an artillery observation post on Ulna Hill watching the British shells hammer the German lines through his binoculars. It was difficult to see the results of the pounding clearly, but he was convinced the damage being done was minimal. Reports from trench raids along his section of the front didn't help his mood as they told of uncut wire and loud German singing coming from deep dugouts below the enemy's front-line trenches.

In the final run up to the attack, Sandys struggled to sleep and often wandered aimlessly through the temporary camp his men called home. He was convinced the attack would end in failure and raised his concerns to his brigade commander – but his concerns fell on deaf ears. Such vocalisation of doubt was frowned upon by senior officers and was often met with retorts of exaggeration or a general 'windiness' on the part of the man raising such concerns. Rawlinson himself had issued a rather stern warning to his staff, suggesting that *All criticism by subordinates... of orders received from superior authority will, in the end, recoil on the heads of the critics.*[1]

Sandys was 40 years old when he led the 2nd Middlesex over the top on 1st July towards the German lines. The attack saw his worst fears realised, with the Regimental diary recording the results of the carnage:

> *Of the 23 Officers who took part in the assault, only 2/Lt. H.C. Hunt regained our lines unwounded, of the 650 NCO's & men who took part in the assault a bare 50 answered their names in the early hours of July 2nd.*[1]

Lieutenant-Colonel Sandys was shot five times during the attack, and although none of his injuries were life threatening, they were bad enough to force him to return to the rear of the British lines for treatment and eventually back to England for recuperation.

Sandys suffered terribly in the battle's aftermath. He took the huge losses of his Battalion very personally and constantly wallowed in despair that bordered on self-resentment that he never died on that fateful day along with so many of his brave men. Early in September, he wrote to fellow officers in England confessing that he wished he had been killed on 1st July and wanted to end his life.

On 5th September Sandys shot himself in the head with his service revolver whilst residing at the Cavendish hotel in London. He was rushed to St. George's hospital, but died a week later without ever regaining consciousness.

He had finally joined the men he had so intensely mourned since July.

The news of his death made the English press. On 15th September 1916, The Times ran the following piece:

WOUNDED COLONEL'S SUICIDE GRIEF FOR BATTALION'S LOSSES

An inquest was held at Westminster yesterday on the body of LIEUTENANT-COLONEL EDWIN THOMAS FALKNER SANDYS, who was found in bed at the Cavendish Hotel with a revolver in his hand and a bullet wound in his head. He was removed to St. George's Hospital, where he died.

Captain Lloyd Jones, of the same regiment, said Colonel Sandys had been wounded five times and had received the DSO He was very much distressed because of the attack on Jul1 his battalion had suffered severely, and had said he had wished he had been killed with his men. On September 6 the witness received a letter from him saying: "I have come to London to-day to take my life. I have never had a moment's peace since July 1."

Captain R.J. Young said that he was in the attack on July 1, when the battalion suffered severely, and Colonel Sandys was wounded. He had been greatly depressed since, and in a letter which the witness received from

*him on September 6 he wrote: "By the time you receive
this I shall be dead."*

*The Coroner said the case revealed a pathetic tragedy of
a very distinguished soldier, who thought less of his own
wounds than he did at the loss of his men.[2]*

The inquest concluded that he had committed suicide whilst temporarily insane. It was a decision very much of its time that seemed to ignore the humanity, compassion and paternal instinct Sandys obviously held for his men.

There was a lot of insanity flying around the Somme during the summer of 1916, but after more than a century passed, it is difficult to lay much of it, if any, at the feet of Lieutenant-Colonel Sandys.

Sandys was awarded a posthumous Distinguished Service Order for his actions on 1st July. The London Gazette published the announcement of the award on 22nd September 1916:

*For conspicuous gallantry when leading his battalion
and keeping its direction during an attack under very
heavy fire. Although wounded in several places, he continued to lead it until further wounds made it no longer
possible to do so. The fine behaviour of the battalion
was largely due to the Commanding Officer's personal
qualities.*

He was also Mentioned in Haig's Dispatches in January 1917. Lt. Col. Edwin Thomas Falkiner Sandys DSO is buried at West Brompton Cemetery, London.

36

—·—

1ST JULY: THE GLORY HOLE. OVILLERS LA BOISSELLE

On the other side of the Albert-Bapaume Road lay the village of La Boisselle. Thirty-five houses strong, the village had been under German occupation for almost two years – plenty of time for them to construct decent defences – and by the summer of 1916 they had transformed the village into a veritable stronghold, bristling with fortifications and deep dugouts. The outer positions and trenches radiating from La Boisselle pushed towards the Allied lines in such a manner that in places the opposing lines were just metres apart.

Such proximity to the enemy meant that any soldier above ground lived in constant fear of snipers, mortar bombs and grenades. Not surprisingly, the fighting here quickly moved below ground with both sides digging deep under *No Man's Land* to damage enemy positions from underneath and protect their own positions from enemy subterranean activity. In no time at all, *No Man's Land* was transformed into a mass of continual mine craters.

By the time the British arrived in the summer of 1915, La Boisselle had the reputation of being one of the most notorious sectors on the entire Western Front.

It was this dark reputation that gave rise to it being widely known as 'The Glory Hole' by the British troops.

It would be down to the British 34th Division (led by Major-General Ingouville-Williams) to attack and carry the La Boisselle salient and to do so, they would be throwing twelve full battalions at the assault. The plan asked for four columns of advancing infantry, each column being three battalions deep. 101st and 102nd Brigades would make up the initial attack across the four columns, with 103rd Brigade forming the third line and following closely behind.

The one significant difference between the 8th Division attack on Ovillers and what the 34th Division was planning to do at La Boisselle was that there would be no direct attack on the village itself. Instead, shielded by a large smoke screen, the infantry advance would pass either side of the village, sending in small bombing parties backed up by trench mortars and machine gunners to clear La Boisselle from both sides.

This plan raised considerable eyebrows within Brigade and Battalion leadership, but they were repeatedly reminded by their Divisional counterparts that the preliminary bombardment would render the village untenable to the enemy, plus there were the two tiny matters of Y-Sap and Lochnagar mines which would be detonated on either side of the village to eradicate strong points.

Occupying the village would be easy, they said. It would be a walk in the park, they said.

It needed to be a walk in the park given the objectives that had been handed out to the men of the 34th Division. Two brigades would capture the enemy front-line positions either side of La Boisselle: 102nd Brigade (Tyneside Scottish) would move against the north of the village through Mash Valley, whereas the 101st and 103rd Brigades (Tyneside Irish) would attack positions to the south of the village and then move though Sausage Valley. These front-line positions comprised four separate lines of trenches. To get to the fourth line would mean an advance of around 2,000 yards. The 101st and 102nd Brigades were being asked to capture these within forty-eight minutes of Zero (by 8.18am).

After dealing with La Boisselle, they were then expected to capture the German intermediate line known as the *Kaisergraben* which ran in front of Pozières and Contalmaison. This line was to be reached by 8.58am and once in position, the 101st and 102nd Brigades were to stop and consolidate.

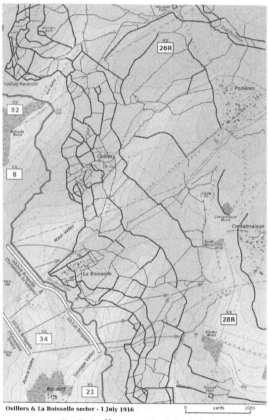

Ovillers & La Boisselle sector - 1 July 1916

La Boisselle sector. 1st July 1916

Next up would be 103rd Brigade who would pass through these captured positions, capture the village of Contalmaison and move to a position on the eastern edge of Pozières. This position was to be reached by 10.10am and then consolidated to become defendable in the event of a German counter-attack from their second line — some 800 yards away.

All in all, the Division was being asked to capture two villages and advance almost two miles in under three hours. Whichever way you looked at it, it was a big ask. They needed to get off to a good start at La Boisselle.

The night before, the big show brought unwelcome news. Raiding parties sent over the parapet to cut paths through the wire were heavily set upon. The German garrison at La Boisselle was very much alive and alert.

So much for the bombardment smashing them to bits.

The 101st Brigade was tasked with capturing the four lines of German trenches to the south of La Boisselle. Their initial success hinged on their ability to occupy and defend the crater left by the Lochnagar mine. This job was given to the 10th Lincolnshire Regiment, also known as The Grimsby Chums. The leading waves of the Grimsby Chums were forced to assemble in reserve trenches as the front-line positions were too close to the mine to be safe. This meant that the men had to travel above ground across 150 yards of smashed earth to even reach their own front-line positions. That's before they could even think of navigating *No Man's Land* towards the crater.

As planned, both Y-Sap and Lochnagar mines were detonated at 7 .28am, two minutes before Zero. Orders had been given to the Grimsby Chums to wait five minutes before attacking, to allow the debris from the massive explosion to settle down. This critical delay gave the German machine-gunners of the 110th RIR plenty of time to clamber out of their dugouts, take up their positions and ready their guns for the attack.

Once the Lincolns eventually started their advance, the results were predictable. The enemy tore into them with devastating machine-gun fire:

> *In our sector opposite La Boisselle it was impossible to advance, the m.g. bullets kicking up the dust like a hailstorm. Only two officers escaped being killed or wounded, while about 70 per cent of the other ranks became casualties.[1]*
>
> *Major Walter Vignoles, DSO & Bar. D Company, 10th Lincolnshire Regt.*

Hot on the heels of the Grimsby men were the 11th Suffolk Regiment on their way to attack Sausage Redoubt to the right of the crater. They also suffered terribly the moment they poked their heads above the parapet, as this excerpt from their battalion diary testifies:

> *In spite of the fact that wave after wave were mown down by machine-gun fire, all pushed on without hesitation, though very few reached the German lines.[2]*

Both leading battalions suffered calamitous casualties, yet the stunning impact of the Lochnagar mine explosion allowed small pockets of men to not only reach the lip of the crater but to infiltrate the German trench system.

Meanwhile, to their right, the fourth column of attack was led by the 15th and 16th Royal Scots. They were tasked to attack across the wide Sausage Valley, but in an effort to minimise the length of travel, the 15th Royal Scots sneaked up to within 200 yards of the enemy lines during the final crescendo of the British barrage.

With bagpipes shrilling, the Scots were up and over the bashed up enemy parapet in no time and moving rapidly towards the Fricourt Spur. Hot on their heels were the 16th Royal Scots – both battalions suffered terribly at the hands of German machine-guns but did push on beyond what became known as Scots Redoubt and into German territory to the right of Sausage Valley.

This success was the exception to the rule, however. The attack was only ten minutes old, and three quarters of the leading British wave had become casualties.

It was all becoming a bit of a nightmare. And then, at 7.35a m the 103rd Brigade (Tyneside Irish) left their positions in the rear and advanced stoically towards the front line – almost a kilometre away across gently downward-sloping ground which included the British support and reserve trenches. They were forced to march above ground to avoid congested trenches - the German machine-gunners had a field day. By the time the men of the Tyneside Irish had reached *their own front line,* they had suffered 70% casualties.

Lieutenant-Colonel Charles Somerset, of 11th Suffolks, summed up the debacle at La Boisselle perfectly when he wrote in the 34th Division war diary:

> *The bombardment had by no means extinguished the*
> *German machine guns which increased their fire as the*
> *waves advanced, and our Artillery barrage moved off*
> *the front line of the German system... They were almost*
> *wiped out and very few reached the German front line.*
> *An artillery smoke screen on La Boisselle was largely*
> *unsuccessful, due to the direction and weakness of the*
> *wind, and failed to obscure German machine-gunners'*
> *views... The Germans put down a terrific barrage on*
> *our front line directly the assault commenced and op-*
> *posite La Boisselle it was doubled...This was the ghastly*

experience of all the follow up battalions, not just 11th Suffolks.[3]

Remarkably, a small mixed group of men managed to fight all the way through to the edge of Contalmaison, some 2,000 yards inside German territory. An even smaller pocket of men from the 16th Royal Scots somehow managed to get inside Contalmaison, but they were quickly captured. These successes were small, isolated, and rare. Overall, the attack on La Boisselle was a disaster.

On the most lethal day in British military history, La Boisselle was the most devastating sliver of the battlefield. More men died and more men were wounded in this area than anywhere else on the Somme.

Major-General Ingouville-Williams had gone forward to watch his men launch their attack. It is likely he witnessed for himself his 103rd Brigade get cut to pieces as they crossed the Tara-Ulsa ridge on their way to their own front line. By 8.30am he was back at his headquarters, anxiously awaiting news of progress. Unfortunately, by about that time, his 34th Division had suffered so terribly it had ceased to exist as an effective fighting force.

The final casualty bill for the 34th Division sailed past 6,000 men. So desperate was the situation that Ingouville-Williams had to ask permission for 19th (Western) Division to be moved in to bolster his position in case the Germans fancied a go themselves at making a move on Albert.

High above the action, Major Lanoe Hawker VC was flying a midday sortie in his DH2 high above the shell ravaged Albert-Bapaume road. Once he had finished his flight, he wrote up his observations in which he noted:

No indication that Ovillers, Contalmaison or La Boisselle had been captured.[4]

37

— • —

1ST JULY: XV CORPS AT FRICOURT

To the south of La Boisselle, the front line veered sharply to the east, skirting around the flattened but fortified villages of Fricourt and Mametz. The villages were nestled either side of Willow Stream with Mametz to the south and Fricourt to the north, just a stone's throw away from the German front line.

If the British could wrestle Fricourt and the surrounding high ground from the Germans, it would open the door for an advance upon Bapaume. It was an exciting thought for the British High Command, and they had high hopes for Lieutenant-General Sir Henry Horne and his XV Corps to whom they had given the task of capturing the two villages on 1st July and pushing on through a multitude of German defensive works.

The problem for Horne was that although Fricourt and Mametz had been reduced to rubble by his artillery, the German defenders had been characteristically diligent in converting the wreckage into a string of strong defensive positions. The enemy defensive system along this part of the line may have lacked the network of carefully positioned redoubts and strongpoints found elsewhere, but it more than made up for it with machine-guns. In this case, there were dozens of machine-gun nests carefully hidden in cellars throughout both villages.

Facing any would-be attackers were the German Reserve Infantry Regiments 111 and 109. RIR 111 was dug in around Fricourt, while most of RIR 109 held positions around Mametz. There were also at least three specialist machine-gun sharp-shooter detachments deployed in this sector. All told, these two villages were defended by about 7,000 men and forty machine guns.

This was not an easy challenge for Horne.

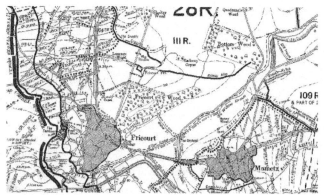

Fricourt and Mametz.

Acknowledging the difficulty of a full-frontal attack on Fricourt and the woods directly to the rear, Horne's final battle plan would see the 21st Division attacking to its north and the 7th Division skirting round the east side to have a go at Hill 110 and Mametz. They would both bypass Fricourt itself with the aid of large smoke screens and link up beyond it. If these flanking attacks were successful, the chaps of 50th Brigade (17th Northern Division) would be asked to have a go at the village directly.

On paper, it seemed a sensible enough plan, although there were genuine concerns among the officers regarding the machine-gun threat emanating from Fricourt village. If these weren't silenced early, there was a real fear they would quickly become a deadly nuisance

– especially for the 50th Brigade. Not for the first time in planning for the Somme operation, all eyes turned to the artillery men – it was going to be down to the big guns to silence the enemy machine-gunner – on top of their other jobs such as destroying enemy artillery and causing mayhem and destruction along the entire enemy front line.

No pressure, then.

To fulfil its objectives, the artillery boys had pulled together an estimated 200 field guns and howitzers and 78 heavy guns across their 5,000-yard divisional front, plus they had scrounged a few French guns to throw into the mix. Despite their numbers, they still had a tough gig to fulfil, and this is the part of the chapter where you might expect me to write something about how, because of a mixture of poor strategy, bad execution and defective shells, the guns yet again failed to live up to the hype bestowed upon them by planners.

But you would be wrong.

On this stretch of the line, the artillery fire was effective for several excellent reasons. First, the geography in this area actually helped the British with many Allied gun positions up on higher ground, giving excellent views of the German positions as far back as Mametz Wood. Also, because of the bend in the line, the British guns enjoyed great broadside angles into which to fire.

Throw into the mix the neighbouring XIII Corps to the south who were nervous about German artillery fire behind Fricourt onto their own front. They took it upon themselves to engage in significant anti-battery activities around Fricourt and Mametz, thus lending Horne's guns a significant helping hand. This extra fire-power, along with the clearer views and the favourable angles of fire, resulted in a more effective bombardment.

In the 65 minutes before zero, the ferocity of XV Corps' artillery barrage was turned up to eleven. An intensive artillery bombardment on all German front-line positions in the area began at 6.25am. An hour later, the Stokes mortars got in on the act, building to a crescendo of noise and destruction. Gas was released around Fricourt at 7.15am with smoke discharged four minutes before Zero to keep those first waves of men away from prying German eyes.

With two minutes to go, several mines were blown at numerous points along the German trench system. Some of the largest mines were detonated in front of Fricourt to distract the enemy from the advance and form crater lips to shield the advance from enemy sight. As all this was kicking off above ground, the German infantry huddled together in their underground shelters, waiting for the inevitable advance. Many of them, such as *Grenadier* Emil Kury of RIR109, had heard the news of the intercepted message at La Boisselle and were ready for a fight:

> *We got our machine-gun ready on the top step of the dug-out and we put all our equipment on; then we waited. We all expected to die.*[1]

On the far left of the advance, men from the 64th and 63rd Brigades of the 21st Division nervously waited opposite Fricourt. Their orders were to advance to the north of Fricourt, capturing the German first intermediate line (Crucifix Trench) before moving through to the second line of defences (Quadrangle Trench) and joining up with their chums from 7th Division in Bottom Wood. 50th Brigade, also of 21st Division, were to wait in front-line positions in case a direct assault on Fricourt was needed later in the day.

While the Stoke Mortars whipped themselves into a frenzy five minutes before Zero, the men of the leading battalions of both Brigades sought to take up their jumping-off positions. Two companies of the 4th Middlesex Regiment (63rd Brigade) crawled forward into No Man's Land but were hit so hard by enemy machine-gun fire they were forced to retreat to their own trench. Those men who had survived the first machine-gun assault had to go back Over the Top for the second time and form up as just a single line – such were the casualties. And it wasn't even Zero Hour.

On their left, the 9th and 10th King's Own Yorkshire Light Infantry (64th Brigade) made good use of a Russian Sap constructed by the Royal Engineers, which meant they could crawl out into *No Man's Land* in slightly safer circumstances – although they too were harassed by enemy machine-gunners who were braving the bombardment.

As the clock ticked towards Zero, the men waited for the barrage to lift and the whistles to blow.

At 07.30am sharp the men launched themselves to the attack in double quick fashion but were met with terrific enemy fire, not only from immediately in front of them but also from Fricourt itself and even from machine-guns situated on the edge of La Boisselle to the north-east. Casualties were high, but the survivors kept going. The enemy wire had been well cut and the supporting battalions were quick to move up and give much needed help. Despite being welcomed by a shower of stick-grenades by the German defenders, enemy front-line positions were captured on a wide front.

> *Left trench 7.30am. Couldn't have faced it unless afraid of funking before the men. Scrambled from shell hole to shell hole, through the wire and craters and awful havoc, terrible sights. Terrible slaughter by the Hun artillery and machine guns, the latter with snipers hurling bullets from every direction. Even behind us, men were mown down right and left. Hun trenches simply a myriad of shell holes. Not so many casualties as expected, as they crowded into deep dugouts and sur-rendered to attackers. Stopped a bullet with my head about 8am – dazed for about an hour or so. My steel helmet saved my life without a doubt...[2]*

Captain Rex Gee, 15th Btn. Durham Light Infantry.
64th Brigade, 21st Division.

Within ten minutes, the chaps from the 21st Division had captured two lines of enemy trenches and over two hundred prisoners had been taken. This success had come at quite a cost – the two leading battalions had lost over half of their men and most of their officers – but there was no doubt about it. Progress was being made.

Once the supporting creeping artillery barrage had moved forward, the advance continued towards a sunken road and Crucifix Trench. A running fight ensued with much work done by bomb and bayonet and by 8am the advance had penetrated almost a mile into German territory.

By mid-morning the British were in control of German trenches from Round Wood, along Crucifix Trench and down to Lozenge Wood, but because the 34th Division was having such a hard time at La Boisselle they were isolated and on the receiving end of enemy fire from all sides.

At around midday, the mini-salient held by the 21st Division was far from secure, and the decision was made to send up some reinforcements to help with the situation. One battalion chosen to help with a breakout from Crucifix Trench was the 10th Battalion Yorkshire Regiment. As they attempted to climb over the parapet, they were met by ferocious machine-gun fire, which temporarily stopped their progress. Major Stewart Loudoun-Shand did what few others would have done in that situation. He immediately leapt on the parapet, helped the men over it and encouraged them in every way until he was shot and mortally wounded. Even then, he insisted on being propped up in the trench and went on encouraging his men until he died. For his actions, he was awarded a posthumous Victoria Cross.

Breakout attempts from Crucifix Trench failed and by early afternoon, the attempted encirclement of Fricourt had run out of steam. It was time for the men to dig in and wait for the relative safety of darkness.

Meanwhile, 50th Brigade was given the nod to begin their direct assault on Fricourt itself. According to the original plan, the attack would be carried out by 7th Green Howards, protected by the 10th West Yorkshire Regiment, who should have been dug in along the northern edge of the village. It was a daunting task, made harder because the 10th West Yorks were not in position and the Green Howards were only three companies strong owing to a devastating error which saw 'A' Company attack the village at 7.45am. Not surprisingly they were cut to pieces in *No Man's Land*. Out of the 140 officers and men who went forward, 108 became casualties.

Despite remonstrations from the Green Howards that the attack would be futile unless the support promised towards the north was in position, the attack was to go ahead at 2.30pm. Orders were orders.

The result was sadly as expected. Despite being covered by friendly Lewis Gun fire, the Green Howards lost fifteen officers and 336 other ranks within three minutes of leaving their own lines. A handful of men reached the village, but they were soon captured or killed. The survivors of the attack were forced to lie low in shell holes until nightfall. Amazingly, the commander of the 7th East Yorkshires, having seen 350 men fall in 180 seconds, decided his men could succeed where the Green Howards had failed. The Yorkshiremen attacked shortly afterwards, but their fate was similar. Five officers and 150 men were knocked out in a matter of yards. Altogether, 50th Brigade's death toll hit 557 with another 565 wounded.

Mercifully, the decision was eventually taken to stop any further attempts at crossing *No Man's Land*.

As night fell on the Fricourt battle ground, the 64th Brigade had made decent progress towards the northeast of the village, the 63rd

Brigade had captured several front-line positions but struggled to get much further and the 50th Brigade had been massacred. All in, the 21st Division had suffered 4,256 casualties (killed/missing/wounded).

Whether the sacrifice was worth it and whether the partial gains could be turned into anything substantial rested upon the shoulders of the men from 7th Division who were attacking Mametz on the other side of the Willow Valley.

38

---·---

1ST JULY: MOSTLY SUCCESSFUL AT MAMETZ

As it turned out, the 7th Division enjoyed considerable success in their attack on the village of Mametz. From a German point of view, this sector of the line was not their most impressive. Trenches and dugouts in this region were not as well made as they were in the north and the seven-day British bombardment had caused significant casualties among those men holding the frontline - forcing several quick rounds of reinforcements, which weakened the garrison.

The bombardment also neutralised a lot of the German battery work, but there were still more than enough active enemy machine-guns to cause considerable pain and heartache for anyone trying to get over *No Man's Land*.

The German front line ran approximately in parallel with the British, and incorporated Bulgar Trench, Mametz Trench, Danube Trench and Kiel Trench; behind it and in front of Mametz was a second line that incorporated Cemetery Trench and a key machine gun post (known as "the Shrine") dug in strongly at the village cemetery. Well behind the village on higher ground ran the third line, incorporating Fritz Trench and Railway Alley.

Attacking initially with two brigades – 20th Brigade on the left flank with 91st Brigade on the right - the 7th Division were to follow a similar strategy to their 21st Division neighbours by driving up either side of the village before attempting a head-on assault. On the left flank of the division front, the 20th Brigade was asked to push north, deep into enemy territory and then pivot to the left to form a defensive flank facing Fricourt from the rear.

It was a complicated task for 20th Brigade. They were being asked to deal with the fortified remains of Mametz on their extreme right, while their left flank had to work their way through 700 yards of mine craters, interconnecting trenches and several miles of subterranean tunnels.

To achieve his objective, Brigadier General Cyril John Deverell deployed three assault battalions to advance side by side; 2nd Battalion Gordon Highlanders on the right, 9th Battalion Devonshire Regiment in the centre and 2nd Battalion Border Regiment on the left, leaving him just the one battalion in reserve (8th Devonshire's) if things got spicy.

Thirty-year-old Captain Duncan Martin was a company commander with the 9th Devon's. During some leave he too the time to make a plasticine scale model of the ground over which he and his men were to attack. Officers were introduced to it in late June with Brigade Major Foss sending a note out to all units of his 20th Brigade and other Brigades from the Division, urging them to come and see it.

> *A Contoured model in placticene has been made by*
> *Captain Mating, 9th Devonshire Regt. showing the*
> *whole area to be attacked by the 20th Infantry Brigade*
> *also Fricourt Wood, Fricourt Farm, Railway Alley,*
> *Fritz Trench, Bright Alley. The model may be seen*
> *at any time on application to 20th Infantry Brigade*
> *HQ Grovetown after 9am on 22nd June. Officers com-*
> *manding Battlaions will arrange for all officers to in-*
> *spect this model. The officers of a Company should all*
> *arrange to see it together.[1]*

Facing the Devonshires in their particular part of the line was a myriad of enemy defences and strongpoints. Starting with Danube Trench – the German front line – which boasted three saps and a machine-gun post jutting out into *No Man's Land* right in front of Mansel Copse. Behind this was Danube Support – the 9th Devons' first objective. Behind that was Shirine Alley, linked to the first two lines by a network of tunnels and dugouts known as the Halt bank. Shrine Alley was a long trench that crossed the road and rail line just behind the Halt – the village station, before extending up the hill towards Mametz, passing just in front of the village cemetery and the notorious Shrine – the focus of many narratives of the Devons' advance from Mansel Copse, but in reality, just one of many dangers that faced the men.

The Germans had concentrated their defences where Shrine Alley crossed the road and railway line. A machine-gun post occupied the Halt and enjoyed uninterrupted views down towards the British lines. The railway embankment housed numerous snipers on one side and the Halt bank on the other. There was another fortified bank just behind the German front line on the Mametz side of the road – again with beautiful views of the British lines. Consequently any advance through Mansel Copse was at risk of being hit from three different positions simultaneously.

Armed with this information, the British did try and do something to nullify the threat. A number of machine-guns were set up behind the British line on the other side of the Albert-Carnoy Road to cover the advance. There was also plans to move up a Livens flame projector- a huge machine housed in tunnels that could fire a massive jet of burning fuel onto enemy positions – but as it was being moved into place an enemy bombardment scuppered any progress, burying and smashing vital parts of the mechanism.

At Zero hour, the first waves of the 9th Devons started their advance on Mametz, with Captain Martin leading from the front. They were forced to begin their attack from the support trenches, some 250 yards to the rear, as the front-line positions had been so badly smashed up by German shellfire. For the first few seconds, the men were sheltered by a small hill, but as they crested the rise and moved downhill, they were in full view of the enemy. The next few minutes were catastrophic.

The men came under immediate heavy fire from the right hand side. Scores of men were hit, including Captain Martin, who was reputedly shot in the head after barely advancing fifteen yards. Despite the grievous losses, the survivors ploughed on unwavering, entered the German front-line trench and began to systematically clear and consolidate their winnings. Small parties of men even pressed on to the German support lines, some 250 yards beyond. However, by about 8am there were no officers left and further progress was impossible. But the actions of the 9th kept the enemy busy and distracted – which helped their fellow attackers.

On the right of the Devons, the 2nd Gordon Highlanders advanced over a 400-yard front, and apart from one section which had un-cut wire, succeeded in overrunning the German front-line positions before the defenders had figured out what was going on. By 8am, they had pushed some 300 yards into enemy territory but were now encountering stiff German resistance, not helped by the fact that the Devons were struggling to keep up and had not cleared a dangerous railway cutting, from which the Germans were pouring down fire.

On the left of the Devons, the 2nd Border Regiment advanced with less German interference and quickly took possession of the German front-line positions on their sector and set off towards their other objectives. With much use of bomb and bayonet, they forced their way forward and by 9.30am they had secured a position deep inside the German support network. Here they came under intense machine gun fire from Mametz and the nearby by Hidden Wood – the wood was eventually cleared following an expensive and bloody attack across open ground.

All being told, the 2nd Border Regiment would achieve something rare and remarkable on this day — their objective. Despite this isolated sliver of success, the struggles of the Devons and the Gordons meant that Deverell's plan of a large defensive flank towards Fricourt would have to wait for another day.

The job of 91st Brigade was to advance across the German front line (Bulgar Trench), past the second line (Cemetery Trench), then capture various strongpoints in Mametz itself and push on past the deep Dantzig Alley communication trench to take the third enemy line, Fritz Trench. The two assaulting battalions for this particular show were the 22nd Manchester Regiment who were assembled astride the Mametz-Montauban track and 1st South Staffordshire Regiment who were pitched up right opposite the Bulgar Point strongpoint which was destroyed as part of a series of mine explosions just before zero. 2nd Queen's and 21st Manchester's were in close support behind the attacking battalions.

To further aid the advance, those friendly chaps from the Royal Engineers had also dug several Russian Saps deep into *No Man's Land* for both sets of attackers, significantly reducing the length of the initial attack.

The mine underneath the Bulgar Point worked a treat and effectively erased it from the map. The first waves of men from both 22nd Manchester and 1st South Staffordshire Regiments made good progress across the narrow *No Man's Land* and into the German first line of trenches but came under heavy machine-gun fire from Dantzig Alley as they approached the edge of Mametz village.

Nevertheless, within half an hour of the whistles being blown, the Stafford's were well inside the village ruins and men from the Manchester's were pressing on towards the German rear positions.

Whisper it, but by 9am it looked like the men of the 91st Brigade might actually meet their objectives for the day.

It wasn't long, however, before these initial successes ran out of steam. Enemy resistance stiffened, and the leading pockets of men were forced back to the German second line of Cemetery Trench. At 9.30am, the support battalions were ordered up to reinforce – but with little effect. The British guns were ordered to fire a few cheeky shells into areas of Dantzig Alley and Fritz Trench that were causing aggravation for the Brits, but it wasn't effective. More shells were slung over just after midday following reports of enemy troops gathering along Dantzig Alley for a counter-attack. This time the bombardment did the trick, and by 1.40pm Dantzig Alley was being systematically cleared by British bombing parties.

At around this time, news came through that the neighbouring 21st Division was planning a fresh attack on Fricourt. To take advantage of this, fresh attacks against Mametz were hurriedly planned. After a brief thirty-minute artillery bombardment, two companies of 2nd Royal Warwickshire Regiment and two companies of the 8th Devonshire's went forward. What was left of the German garrison folded relatively easily, with around 200 men surrendering. By 5pm, Mametz had been taken, and the situation was quiet.

91st Brigade had gained all of its objectives.

Overall, the 7th Division had had a decent day. Progress on the left had been slower than expected and they had not built that defensive flank towards Fricourt, but they had captured and consolidated the village of Mametz. Not surprisingly, the success was costly. 7th Division lost 3,380 officers and men during the fight. The vast majority resulting from machine-gun fire.

39

1ST JULY: KICKING OFF AT MONTAUBAN

The very southernmost tip of the British assault lay in the hands of Lieutenant-General William Congreve's XIII Corps. In this sector, the British enjoyed fantastic visibility deep into enemy territory courtesy of the Maricourt Ridge that ran behind the British lines. This extra visibility, coupled with a significant helping hand from some neighbouring French artillery pieces, meant that for once, the assaulting forces had a fighting chance of a bit of success.

British observers on the Maricourt Ridge could plainly see the chalky zig-zag of the enemy front line along with its support network some 700-1,000 yards beyond. Further back, the German intermediate line (Montauban Alley) ran behind the village of Montauban along a slight dip in the ground called Caterpillar Valley. The German second line, some 3,000 yards distant, was not yet finished.

All told, this was not the strongest German position in the area.

That being said, there was one enemy position that was tough enough to cause Congreve a few sleepless nights. Pommiers Redoubt was situated in-between Montauban and Mametz, about half a mile from the British jumping-off points. It was a formidable circular trench fortress, bristling with machine guns and protected by several thick belts of barbed wire. This position would need some special attention on the day, but apart from Pommiers and a few other smaller redoubts dotted about, the Germans had very little strength in depth on this part of the line, and what they did have had suffered badly at the hands of the Allied big guns.

Oberleutenant Reymann, serving in the 62nd Infantry Regiment, commented on the state of the German position:

> *All three of the front-line trenches were levelled and the whole area formed a large crater field. Where our once broad wire obstacles stood you could only see shattered piles and fragments lying around.*[1]

Congreve – who won the Victoria Cross in South Africa – had set out a typically optimistic plan for his men for the first day of battle: the capture of all the Montauban Spur, including Montauban village itself and pushing on into Montauban Alley beyond. The hope was that this new position would be an ideal starting point for a run on Bernafay and Trônes Woods over the next few days.

To achieve these targets, Congreve organised his men across a two Divisional front with the 18th (Eastern) Division on the left, with the 30th Division on the right being the southernmost Division of the entire British attack. Both Divisions would attack uphill from the low-lying ground in front of Carnoy and Marincourt.

The 18th, commanded by Major-General Sir Ivor Maxse, would head towards the west of Montauban to capture the Mametz-Montauban ridge and then move deep into German-held territory to capture their Intermediate Line, known to the British as Montauban Alley. To gain full control of their sector, the men of the 18th Division would have to deal with Pommiers Redoubt.

The 30th Division, led by Major General Sir John Shea, would advance on the village of Montauban and come up alongside the right flank of the 18th. While its own right flank would press forward towards Dublin Trench while keeping close tabs on their French neighbours.

The Attack on Montauban. 1st July 1916

Both Divisions were throwing all three of their infantry brigades into the fight straight away and would follow tightly behind an artillery barrage that would lift from one German trench line to the next. In reserve, the men of 9th (Scottish) Division were positioned two miles behind the British front line, well away from prying German eyes.

Over 15,000 men would be thrown into the first phase of the assault.

As head of the 18th Division, Major-General Maxse had a reputation as a details man and being a stickler for meticulous training. Several Russian Saps had been dug deep into *No Man's Land* and contained not just the initial attacking waves of men, but also copious machine-guns, trench mortars and a massive fire projection system – the Livens – which could throw out jets of flame up to 90m (300 feet) towards the enemy, incinerating anyone or anything in its way.

If this wasn't enough, a series of mines (the largest being 5,000lbs) were to be blown under the German lines at 7.27am. Three minutes later, the men rose to attack, aided and abetted by a couple of two-ton fire-breathing dragons.

> At zero hour on 1st July the two jets appeared out of the ground to a height of two or three feet above the surface, opposite the German trench lines and well with the range of the machines: the automatic lighters functioned perfectly, and with a roar the streams of oil became ignited and shot forward towards the enemy... No living thing could possibly survive under this visitation...[2]
>
> Colonel C.H. Foulkes. Z Company, Special Brigade, Royal Engineers.

Captain Wilfred (Billie) Nevill's 'B' Company, 8th East Surrey Regiment, was at the very pointy end of the right-hand side of the 18th Division's infantry attack as part of the 55th Brigade. Whilst on leave in

England in May 1916, Captain Nevill purchased a couple of footballs and took them back to the front line with him. His idea was for his men to kick the balls across No Man's Land as they advanced - he even offered a reward for the first member of his company to score a 'goal' in the enemy trenches. On one of the footballs was written:

> *The Great European Cup-Tie Final.*
> *East Surreys vs The Bavarians*
> *Kick off at Zero!*

On the other ball was written 'No Referee' - a signal to his men that, for this particular game, he didn't mind if they got a bit rough and ready with the other side.

One of Nevill's officer mates, Second Lieutenant Charles Alcock, wrote to Nevill's sister after the event to explain the show.

> *Five minutes before zero time he strolled up in his usual calm way and we shared a last joke before going over. The company went Over The Top very well, with Soames and your brother kicking off with the company footballs. We had to face very heavy rifle fire, and nearing the front German trench, the lines slackened pace slightly. Seeing this, Wilfred dashed in front with a bomb in his hand, and was immediately shot through the head, almost side by side with Soames and Sergeant Major Wells.*[3]

Tragedies such as this aside, the initial attack by the 18th Division had started well. The 53rd and 54th Brigades – on the left and in the centre of the Divisional assault – made swift progress, capturing the lightly held German front line within a matter of minutes and moving swiftly through to the support line and rearward trenches of the German forward system. By 8.30am they had covered around 1,000 yards and were closing in on Pommiers Redoubt.

As predicted, the strongpoint was formidable. The wire in front of the position had not been cut properly and slowed progress considerably. Even when a path through the wire was cut, the job was far from complete. The defenders initially put-up stout resistance, but this was a time when the training forced upon the 18th Division by Maxse reaped dividends. The men were familiar with the layout of the position thanks to realistic models used during training – small parties of men swung left and right, enveloping the redoubt. By 9.30am, the position had been nullified. Happy days.

It was not all plain sailing, though. There were some German machine-gunners located in a cratered section of *No Man's Land* that had survived the artillery bombardment, survived the trench mortars and survived the flame thrower to inflict devastating casualties upon the leading waves. Therefore, the leading elements of 55th Brigade had a hot time of it and could not advance at all for several hours until finally, enemy resistance waned.

As the light faded, the survivors of the day got busy reinforcing and consolidating their new positions in Montauban Alley.

On the very right-hand flank of the entire British assault on the Somme, the leading waves of the 30th Division also got off to a tidy start in their attempt to capture Dublin Trench and the village of Montauban. 89th Brigade had the honour of capturing Dublin Trench, a support line position south of Montauban which contained a decent stronghold named Glatz Redoubt. The combined might of British and French artillery had done sterling work on the enemy positions across this part of the line, and they were supplemented by a furious bombardment from six Stokes Mortar batteries hidden inside Russian Saps deep in *No Man's Land*.

The result was a relatively straightforward dash across 400 yards of *No Man's Land* for the men of 89th Brigade, who were there on the right flank of the attack. By the time the German defenders had emerged from their dugouts, it was too late – the front-line position was over-run within minutes of the whistles being blown and within an hour they were sitting pretty in Dublin Trench. Objective achieved. It was now a matter of waiting for the 90th Brigade to leapfrog over them on their way to Montauban.

On the left of 89th Brigade, 21st Brigade also made decent progress, quickly occupying the enemy front-line trench system. However, they were soon caught in enfilade machine-gun fire from the same gunners who had hit Captain Nevill. Such fire slowed progress somewhat and caused heavy casualties, but the men continued to inch forward against an increasingly disorganised enemy. Eventually, they closed in on Glatz Redoubt.

> *We waited outside Glatz Redoubt, all our guns being turned on this ring of trenches which was right on top of the ridge. We got the order, 'Charge!' and away we went at the double, killing all that stayed there. A good many retreated towards Montauban, and we opened rapid fire on them.*[4.]

Private Albert Andres, 19th Battalion, Manchester Regiment, 21st Brigade, 30th Division.

Glatz Redoubt quickly fell and the 21st Brigade eventually linked up with their mates from 89th Brigade. It was now time for the chaps of 90th Brigade to get a piece of the action.

On paper, the orders given to 90th Brigade were tricky. They were being asked to start their approach from way behind their own lines, advance up a hill and capture an enemy held village. Sound familiar? It was exactly what the men of the 34th Division had been ordered to do at La Boisselle, and the men of the 8th Division at Ovillers. And the chaps from 32nd Division at Thiepval.

They had all failed.

But in Montauban, things we different. The entire operation was protected by a dense smokescreen – put down by the two advanced brigades at 8.30am - that actually succeeded in hiding the advance and confusing the defenders. By 9.30am, the leading patrols of 90th Brigade had joined up with 89th and 21st Brigade in their forward positions and an hour later they were ready for the jump on Montauban. Helped by an artillery barrage that smashed what was left of the village to bits, three battalions of 90th Brigade made their move.

It was all over in 10 mins. Montauban had been utterly obliterated by Allied artillery and was completely deserted. Even the many cellars, which in other villages had housed deadly machine guns, had caved in, and been destroyed.

By 11am they had moved further forward and captured their allotted segment of Montauban Alley and then got busy making good their position – but not before some men partook in a spot of light pilfering:

> *Two or three of us went down in a fine German dugout. There were cigars, tinned food, and German helmets. We all took a helmet, cigars and tobacco. Coming out with these German helmets on, we ran straight into our Captain. 'Yes,' he said, 'you all look very nice, but get some fucking digging done!'*

Private Albert Andres, 19th Battalion, Manchester Regiment, 21st Brigade, 30th Division.

Remarkably, given the situation elsewhere on the Somme, XIII Corps had achieved all its objectives for the day, smashing through the German first line of defences with comparative ease. Yet even here casualties were significant, with the 18th Division suffering 3,115 losses (killed, wounded or missing) while the 30th Division lost 3,011 men.

40

— · —

1ST JULY: FRENCH SUCCESS

Responsibility for the French part of the show fell to General Ferdinand Foch – Commander of Northern Army Group. In the early stages of the war, Foch was very much an attack minded leader, but after witnessing catastrophic French casualties during the Battle of the Marne in 1914 he had mellowed somewhat. Gone were his dreams of a rampaging attack sweeping all before it. Now he was all about systematic and methodical efforts that were repeated to slowly suck the life out of the enemy.

As a result, Foch was very much of the mind that his artillery held the key to success and envisioned a lengthy and meticulous artillery operation that had two goals: to smash up the German artillery and then to destroy enemy front-line positions.

> *Our artillery must establish a clear ascendancy over the opposing guns before targeting the front-line trenches and entanglements... Unless completely neutralised before the infantry attacks, the enemy artillery will compromise the advance.*[1]

As he drew up his detailed instructions for both artillery and infantry, he was at pains to impress on his army how he wanted them to behave and interact with the artillery. He wanted a break-in rather than a breakthrough – a series of hammer blows, under protecting a carefully orchestrated creeping barrage that would wear the enemy down. Whilst speed would be important, the attack must not be reckless, and he made it very clear that his infantry should resist all temptations to go running off on un-supported advances deep into enemy territory.

Initially, the French assault was planned to take place across a frontage of 40km, but the shenanigans going on at Verdun meant this had to be reduced to 15km and the number of French armies taking part was cut from three to just one – the French Sixth Army under General Émile Fayolle.

Fayolle's army was split into three Corps. North of the River Somme was XX Corps (led by General Maurice Balfourier) who, it could be argued, had the most difficult assignment. Not only were they reliant on the British on their left to give them support as they advanced, but they also had to advance around a curve in the river which meant by the time they got to the German third line, their attacking frontage would have effectively doubled from 2.6km to over 5km.

South of the river, I Colonial Corps (led by General Pierre Berdoulat) would advance on a front of 1.5km to take the enemy positions between Frise and Dompierre before pushing east towards the German second line between the villages of Herbécourt and As-sevillers. Further south still, XXXV Corps (General Charles Jacquot) were tasked to push through the German lines and capture the open Flaucourt plateau, opposite Péronne, thus denying the high ground to enemy artillery observers. II Corps (led by General Denis Duchêne) would hang back in reserve and await instructions.

Random diversions such as sudden artillery fire, gas attacks and trench raids would be carried out further south by Tenth Army, to divert German attention away from where the main action was taking place.

As the preliminary bombardment began on 24th June, Fayolle was less than optimistic. He was sceptical of what he thought was an over-reliance on the artillery; he didn't enjoy having to depend on the British for French success and he couldn't see any way how his men could score a meaningful breakthrough – regardless of what Foch thought.

When the whistles blew at 07.30am on 1st July, the men from XX Corps obediently left their trenches and began their attack. They had the tricky task of keeping in contact with the British on their left flank who were attacking Montauban, yet within 30 minutes most of the German front-line was in their hands and an hour after that they had successfully captured their preliminary objectives. Despite some resistance in front of the village of Curlu, by evening, French patrols were inside the village.

South of the river, the I Colonial Corps enjoyed similar success. They met very little resistance and the German front-line positions fell with relatively little incident. By 11am, forward patrols had reached the German second line positions and General Berdoulat was keen to press on and take full advantage of the situation. Fayolle disagreed and insisted he wait while the artillery sorted themselves out so they could help. This delayed the next push until 4.30pm, by which time the impetus had been lost. Although they fought their way to the villages of Herbécourt and Assevillers, they could not secure any kind of position and were forced to pull back.

At the most southernly point of the whole assault, XXXV Corps attacked in tandem with their northern neighbours of the Colonial Corps. To protect their right flank (and the right flank of the entire assault) they only attacked with one division which limited their overall impact.

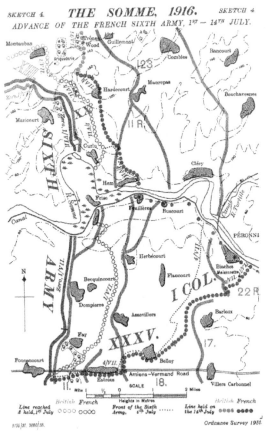

French Advances. 1st-14th July 1916

The success and relative ease of the advance surprised the French and as the sun set on the 1st July, several French generals were making noises about pushing on hard and fast to make the most of the gains. Even Foch agreed and urged Fayolle to press home the advantage. But Fayolle remained resolute in his plans. He would pause, take a breath, consolidate his gains, rotate his men, and resupply his guns before he moved on. Much to Foch's annoyance.

41

**BRAVERY, BULLETS AND BODY BAGS:
REFLECTIONS ON BRITAIN'S BLACKEST DAY**

The cost in terms of lives had been horrific. In one short day, British forces suffered a total of 57,470 casualties, with 19,240 men killed. These numbers were and still are unprecedented. More than a hundred years later, it remains the darkest stain on the record of the British Army.

The conventional and almost universally accepted summary of the day's events suggest that at 7.30am the fully laden British assault troops rose from their forward trenches in unison and walked slowly across *No Man's Land* shoulder to shoulder only to be slaughtered *en masse* as soon as they got in range of the dastardly German machine gunners who were waiting for them.

But this was not quite the case, as hopefully you have discovered by reading the descriptions so far painted in this book. Yes, almost twenty thousand young men were killed in one day, but the vast majority did not meet their maker whilst blindly following an order to walk slowly and steadily towards the enemy.

When it came to specific orders concerning the method of attack, Rawlinson was notably vague. In reality, much of the decision making was left to divisional and regimental leadership, and as we have seen, how individual segments of the line executed their specific attack varied greatly depending on their individual circumstances.

All along the front, these differences are apparent. There were massive mines detonated, such as those at La Boisselle and at Hawthorn Ridge. Attacking the formidable Quadrilateral, the leading waves of 1/8th Warwick's rushed forward like shock-troops with hardly any equipment from Russian Saps cut deep into *No Man's Land*. At Beaumont-Hamel, the Lancashire Fusiliers started their ill-fated attack from the infamous sunken lane deep inside *No Man's Land*. Across the battlefield, 53 out of the 80 leading battalions crept out into *No Man's Land* to start their attack.

Some of the attacking formations did indeed go over at a steady pace, but many of those were following (or trying to follow) a creeping artillery barrage. Ironically, these formations, such as the 21st Division at Fricourt, enjoyed some initial success following this pattern.

These are moot points, though. The fact is that the day was an unmitigated disaster – regardless of how much thought, time and effort went into the tactics. Whether the assaulting troops were trying to rush for a crater lip, or they were starting their advance from the enemy wire, a sunken lane, or their own parapet, success was a rare bird. It seems then that the tactics of the infantry didn't really matter.

The reason for this is brutal in its simplicity; if the German artillery and machine-gun emplacements along the line had escaped the week-long Allied artillery pummelling, they would wreak havoc on any infantry assault, regardless of the tactics employed. A curtain of artillery, meshed together with an interlocking network of machine-guns, each spitting out around 400-500 rounds per minute, would prove fatal against any infantry led attack - whether they walked, ran, or skipped across *No Man's Land*. And you can see this in the results of the day: Those areas of the front that enjoyed more artillery support, especially in the south where British guns were supplemented with French artillery, also enjoyed greater infantry success.

It was not luck that it happened this way. Success on the battlefield was solely down to the effectiveness of the Allied bombardment, not the effectiveness of the infantry.

Historians estimate that approximately 30% of all British casualties on this first day of battle occurred behind the British lines, caused by enemy artillery and machine-guns that could zone in on fresh waves of men coming up to the front line to support the attack. There is something profoundly futile about the thousands of men who were cut down in their own territory without even having the opportunity to sneak across *No Man's Land* and at least try to take the fight to the enemy.

Behind the lines, the general attitude and feeling reverberating within the British High Command ebbed and flowed as the day rumbled on and information found its way to the generals. Initial news was encouraging, but much of it proved to be incorrect and as bad news followed bad news followed bad news, the mood became one of quiet acquiescence.

As the evening approached, the river of information reaching HQ regarding casualties and missed objectives was becoming a torrent. That being said, Rawlinson seemed unmoved when, at about 7.30p m, he became aware that the number of known casualties had topped 16,000.

Throughout the corridors of power, any excited talk of decisive breakthroughs had disappeared. No one dared even mention the word 'cavalry' - they had quietly been given the word to stand down as darkness fell. Staff officers and senior Army leaders alike donned their stiffest of upper lips as they spent the night desperately trying to regroup, calm nerves and fathom out what exactly had happened on the battlefield that day.

It was against this backdrop of stoicism and indifference that Haig and Rawlinson set about planning for the next phase of the battle.

42

—•—

'HOLD OUR CURRENT POSITIONS WITHOUT FAIL.' GERMAN REACTION TO THE 'BIG PUSH'

A part from quickly organising a retaliatory artillery barrage to smash British lines and *No Man's Land* as soon as they got a sniff of the attack, the German defenders in the Somme area were largely content with staying put and defending their positions without launching many counter-attacks of their own. Indeed, the official British history of the attack records just one incident across the entire eighteen-mile front where the Germans ventured beyond their front line to check on a few members of the Leeds Pals who had become entangled on their wire. Witnessing this brief excursion was Pte A. Howard, also of the Leeds Pals:

> *Away on the left, a party of Germans climbed out of the trench. They kicked one or two of the bodies; any showing signs of life were shot or bayoneted.*[1]

As soon as they were done finishing off the men on the wire, the Germans quickly retreated to the relative safety of their own positions.

Up and down the line, the Germans continued to man their positions without feeling the need to venture forward and launch their own attack. Along much of the front the Germans held the higher ground and had a good view of the massed British ranks making their way across No Man's Land. The conditions were practically perfect for defensive machine gunning.

Machine gunners on both sides of the wire saw themselves as something of an elite force compared to the regular rank and file. Often hand-picked and trained specifically in gun handling, maintenance and overall proficiency, machine gun teams led quite a privileged trench life, avoiding many of the heavy carrying duties that burdened the ordinary infantryman. But this day would not be a quiet day. This would be a day when the German machine gun teams needed to earn their money.

It was time to get down to the very serious business of systematic elimination of the enemy.

Unlike riflemen, trained machine gunners did not aim at specific targets. Instead, they worked as a team with other gun crews to create an interlocking network of fire zones. By doing this, machine gun teams could cover a large portion of *No Man's Land* with minimal adjustments to the traverse (horizontal movement) of an individual gun.

Gunners would just tap the side of their gun to move it from one end of its traverse to the other and back again. Tapping was a vital component of being a machine gunner and a gunner would not pass his training unless he had perfected this specific art. A single correct 'two-inch tap' moved the gun about eight degrees of angle, equivalent to two inches at twenty-five yards (hence the name 'two-inch tap') or eight inches per 100 yards. The effect was to spray bullets like a garden sprinkler and creating an almost impenetrable curtain of fire.

It was a skill that demanded continuous precision and accuracy under the most trying of conditions, and it was a skill that the German machine gunners had perfected to a devastating level of competence.

Private Frank Lindley took part in the attack towards Serre with the Barnsley Pals and saw at first hand the deadly effects of enemy machine gun fire as their assault ground to a halt in front of the German wire.

> *Machine-gun bullets were knocking 'em round as if washin' hung on the line. Legs and arms and everything were flying all over.*[2]

Such was their success in cutting down the British advance in those first vital hours of the attack, many German infantrymen felt brave enough to stand on top of their own parapet to goad and torment their attackers, although with thousands of British men taking cover in *No Man's Land* the risk of being hit by a well-aimed rifle shot was still considerable and such acts of machismo were curtailed almost as quickly as they had begun.

Far behind the lines, *General-de-Infanterie* Erich von Falkenhayn, who was a loud proponent of the Verdun battle, was taking stock of the situation.

> *With this superiority [in guns and men] it was inevitable that the enemy, when, on 1st July, the storm at last broke, should score the initial successes. The gains of the English were even less than usual. North of the Bapaume-Albert road they did not advance a yard, south of the road not appreciably beyond the first German line. The French gains were greater; the whole of the German first line from Fay south of Hardecourt, north of the Somme, was lost. In several places, the at-*

> *tack penetrated the second line. Even in this sector, there*
> *was no question of the intended breakthrough having*
> *succeeded.*[3]

Judging by this extract from his memoirs, it would seem he was a touch dismissive of the attack – especially the British effort. Yet his actions in the immediate aftermath belied his apparent nonchalance. No fewer than fifteen full German infantry divisions were routed towards the Somme front within ten days of the initial assault - proof enough that he was worried that the initial assault had at least the *potential* to achieve a breakthrough of some description.

Slightly closer to the action although distracted during the initial assault with a nasty dose of stomach cramps, von Below viewed the situation seriously especially the Anglo – French gains between Fricourt and the Somme river, which in his view put his Second Army under direct threat. He urged his men to hold their positions at all costs.

> *For the time being, we must hold our current positions*
> *without fail and improve on them by means of minor*
> *counterattacks. I forbid the voluntary relinquishment*
> *of positions. Every commander is responsible for mak-*
> *ing each man in the Army aware about this determi-*
> *nation to fight it out. The enemy must be made to pick*
> *his way forward over corpses.*[4]

The fighting on the Somme was about to become yet another battle of attrition.

43

— · —

MEDIC! COPING WITH THE WOUNDED

For many, the original feelings of optimism, patriotism and of doing one's duty that carried them forward in that first attack had quickly worn thin. Any kind of positive thought or emotion were quickly lost amongst the disembowelment of humanity that surrounded the players of 1st July. Such was the opinion of Chaplain Francis Drinkwater, serving with 139th Brigade, 46th Division:

> I shall soon be a pacifist and a conscientious objector – to modern warfare anyhow. It becomes more impossible every month, and the ghastly mangling of human beings 'en masse' seems disproportionate to any conceivable object. 'A bloody mug's game', said one stretcher bearer.[1]

Sadly for the Chaplain, the Stretcher Bearer and the thousands of other men still alive, the Battle of the Somme had only just begun.

Most British soldiers dreamt of getting a 'Blighty wound' - an injury that was non-life threatening but serious enough to warrant their evacuation away from the trenches and back to a nice clean hospital bed in a tranquil English village. Far, far away from the mud, blood, and guns.

However, if they got hit on the battlefield, they still had a lot of work to do to get on that hospital boat back to England. The journey to safety for any wounded soldier was long and tedious, often uncomfortable, and sometimes still pretty perilous.

For many, the most dangerous part of the process would be the very first step – to get off the battlefield safely. Many had to wait until dark to avoid the attention of enemy snipers and machine-gunners, sometimes they left on a stretcher, sometimes on the back of a comrade, or sometimes under their own steam, crawling back a few metres at a time, often in agony, but always desperate to find someone to help them or at least point them in the right direction to the nearest Regimental Aid Post (RAP).

Regimental Aid Posts were set up in spaces such as communication trenches, ruined buildings, dug outs or a deep shell hole, often just a few hundred yards behind the front line. RAPs had no holding capacity and here, often in appalling conditions, wounds would be cleaned and dressed, pain relief administered and basic first aid given. The Regimental Medical Officer (RMO) in charge was supplied with equipment such as anti-tetanus serum, bandages, field dressings, cotton wool, ointments, and blankets, as well as comforts such as brandy, cocoa, and biscuits.

The RMO also completed a Field Medical Card for each patient and fixed it firmly to the patient, often via a tunic button. This card included the soldier's name, rank and unit, a diagnosis, and any special treatments performed. If morphine was given or a tourniquet applied, the soldier's forehead was marked with a "M" or "T". As the patient moved down the evacuation chain, the Field Medical Card remained with him so that information could be added to it and his full treatment could be known.

Where possible, the men were patched up and returned to their duties, but the more seriously wounded were carried by Royal Army Medical Corps (RAMC) stretcher bearers often over muddy and shell-pocked ground, and under shell fire, to an Advanced Dressing Station (ADS).

An ADS was typically set up several hundred yards further behind the lines in amongst ruined buildings or underground bunkers and dugouts. In terms of facilities, the ADS was very similar to the Regimental Aid Post – it could still only offer very basic medical care (although they were generally better equipped that RAPs) and they had no holding capacity. Here the sick and wounded were treated so they could either return to their unit or, if they could not do so, they waited to be picked up by horse or motor-powered transportation and delivered to a Field Ambulance.

During periods of heavy fighting, both RAPs and ADSs could quickly become overwhelmed by the sheer numbers of casualties arriving. Often in these situations, wounded men had no choice but to lie in the open on stretchers until they were seen.

The next step on the journey was to visit a Field Ambulance (FA). Each Army Division would have three FAs, each made up of ten officers and 224 men and divided into three sections which comprised stretcher-bearers, an operating tent, tented wards, nursing orderlies, a cookhouse, washrooms and a horse-drawn or motor ambulance. By mid-1915, trained nurses were also part of the roster of a Field Ambulance.

Next up on the journey of a wounded Tommy was the Casualty Clearing Station (CSS). The CCS would be the first large, well-equipped and static medical facility that the wounded man would visit. Often grouped in clusters of two or three, Casualty Clearing Stations were situated several miles behind the front line – their position dictated by the proximity of railway and/or canal infrastructure. A CCS often had to move at short notice as the front line changed and although some were in permanent buildings such as schools, convents, and factories, many comprised large areas of tents, marquees and wooden huts.

The CCS had three key roles: to retain all serious cases that were unfit for further travel; to treat and return slight cases to their unit; and evacuate all others to Base Hospitals. Facilities included medical and surgical wards, operating theatres, dispensary, medical stores, kitchens, sanitation, incineration plant, a mortuary and sleeping quarters for the nurses, officers and soldiers of the unit.

A typical CCS could hold 1,000 casualties at any time, but even so, they quickly became full to overflowing during times of battle, as seen in this short description of No.44 CCS which was moved into position behind the Somme lines at Puchevillers in mid-June 1916:

> *The first ambulance train arrived on 19th June and, while it wasn't full, the nursing staff were soon busy enough with men injured during the preparations of the battlefield. Then, on 1st July, the battle began... During the first three days of the offensive, 4,500 wounded men were sent to No.44.[2]*

Considering the conditions, the troops were kept in good health at Casualty Clearing Stations, but they were not fully equipped hospitals and often the serious nature of many of the wounds encountered defied the medical facilities and skills of a CCS. Not surprisingly, many CCS positions are today marked by large military cemeteries.

From the CCS, wounded men were transported in ambulance trains, road convoys or by canal barges to the large base hospitals near the French coast or to a hospital ship heading for England.

Ambulance Trains transported the wounded from CCS's to base hospitals situated close to the channel ports. Many trains were French passenger trains which had been converted to run as mobile hospitals with operating theatres, bunk beds and a full complement of nurses, RAMC doctors and surgeons. Emergency operations would be performed despite the movement of the train, the cramped conditions and poor lighting.

On average, a hospital train could take 400-500 patients, with many in a critical way. Throughout the Somme campaign there would be anywhere between four and eight trains leaving the regional CCS's a day, however during the first few days of the battle there were a few more... fifty-one trains departed the Somme area between 2nd-4th July 1916 – that's something like 20-25,000 men evacuated on Ambulance Trains in just four days.

Any thoughts of the train steaming quickly through the French countryside to the coast and a waiting troop ship were quickly dashed. A full train could only travel at 10mph, and Ambulance Trains occupied the lowest rung on the railway priority list, meaning many lengthy stops to let by trains carrying men, ammunition and supplies. Journeys that should have taken a few hours took a couple of days. There were deaths on board all trains.

Under the watch of the RAMC were two categories of base hospital serving the wounded from the Western Front. There were two Stationary Hospitals to every Division - despite their name, they moved about depending on front line movements. Each one held several hundred casualties with many specialising in different types of wounds and sickness, for example gas victims or shell shock cases. These Stationary Hospitals normally occupied civilian hospitals in large towns and cities.

The General Hospitals were located near railway lines to facilitate movement of casualties from the CCS's on to the coastal ports. Large numbers were concentrated in Boulogne and Étaples. Grand hotels and other large buildings were requisitioned where possible, but sometimes these General Hospitals were nothing more than a collection of huts hastily constructed on open ground, with tents added as required. Some of these General Hospitals were run by charitable organisations such as the Red Cross and many were handling the treatment of wounded soldiers long after the war ended.

The last leg of the long journey to Blighty was the Hospital Ship. Most of these were requisitioned and converted passenger liners. It may have been almost the end of the journey, but it was far from being the end of the danger. The risk of torpedoes and mines as they crossed the channel was very real.

On arrival at a British port, the wounded were then transferred to a home service ambulance train and on to various Military and War Hospitals spread all over the country. And so ended the journey from battlefield to Blighty hospital bed.

44

— · —

THE MORNING AFTER THE DAY BEFORE.

B ack in the various British HQ offices dotted around the French countryside, the communications wires were alive with messages hinting of ever-increasing casualty numbers. During the previous evening, reports filtering back to Rawlinson suggested casualty numbers of around 16,000. By the morning of the 2nd this had jumped to 30,000, a number he was prepared to admit was 'heavy' but still he remained unperturbed, commenting that there were 'plenty of fresh divisions behind'[1].

Similarly, Haig made a note in his own diary that day that suggested he too, was not too concerned about the high casualty numbers.

> *The AG reported today that the total casualties are estimated at over 40,000 to date. This cannot be considered severe in view of the numbers engaged, and the length of front attacked...*[2]

Maybe they were concerned about the numbers, but were just too pre-occupied with their next set of decisions to let it show. As leaders of the British Army, they needed to remove themselves from all emotions as much as possible to keep a cool head and concentrate on planning the next stage of the campaign.

The top chaps of the British military machine had a couple of options in front of them when considering stage two: do they continue the attack along the entire Somme battle front (something which Rawlinson was a supporter of) to move the British line within striking distance of the German second line? Should they instead concentrate on the southern battle zone – which was Haig's preference, as it was the only area where there was any inkling of success? Or do they throw their men once more against the Thiepval Ridge to take and hold the high ground?

Oh, the agony of choice.

Rawlinson and Haig met with Joffre to discuss the next steps on 3rd July. It was a bad-tempered affair with Joffre getting very animated, ordering Haig and Rawlinson to attack Thiepval and Pozières.

Eventually, after much heated discussion, Joffre conceded that all the evidence suggested that the ground around Thiepval could not be taken quickly and it would indeed be best to concentrate efforts on securing the southern end of the battle zone, from Ovillers to Bernafay Wood, where progress had been made. Although a diversionary attack would be made at Thiepval to keep the Germans guessing and force them to keep their defences north of the Albert-Peronne road in situ.

45

— · —

MARGINAL GAINS: THE CAPTURE OF FRICOURT AND LA BOISSELLE

In the days immediately following the 1st July assault, there were several small independent missions undertaken intended to push forward the British line to prepare for a larger co-ordinated assault on the German second line, which was pencilled in for the middle of the month.

These actions were not designed to be exhilarating breakthroughs of the enemy defences. Instead, it would be the slow and steady breakdown of enemy manpower, forcing them to continually restructure and reorganise using troops brought in from other areas (such as Verdun).

In front of the village of La Boisselle, men of the 19th Division had attempted to relieve what was left of the shattered 34th Division during the evening of 1st July with a plan to launch their own attack at 10.30pm that night. However, the leading brigades of the 19th Division (57th and 58th) simply could not get into their positions in time, such was the concentration of wounded and dead in the communication trenches and open ground over which they struggled to pass through.

By dawn on 2nd July, the 58th Brigade finally made it to their allotted positions. They were now scheduled to attack alone (the 57th

Brigade was still nowhere to be seen) at 4.30pm that afternoon. A cunning artillery ruse was acted out where a diversionary barrage was sent across to the village of Ovillers from 3.30pm-4pm, followed by a smoke screen released at Zero. It worked. The Germans retaliated with an almighty artillery blitz on Ovillers and even re-routed some of the La Boisselle garrison to Ovillers. As a result, men from 6th Wiltshire Regiment and 9th Royal Welch Fusiliers got across *No Man's Land* relatively unscathed and occupied the edge of the village before the Germans figured out the stunt and put up a bit of resistance.

Regardless, this brief excursion suggested that perhaps the German defences had taken more of a hit on 1st July in this area than originally thought. As a result, the Divisional leaders concluded it would be best to press home any advantage sooner rather than later. La Boisselle was there for the taking and the men of the 19th Division were going to do the honours. To 'help' the attack, those clever staff officers back at HQ had decided that they would learn from the mistakes of 1st July – this time the attack would be at night, under cover of darkness, and in 24 hours' time.

So, to recap, the men from the 19th Division, who had never taken part in a major attack in the daylight before, let alone in the dark, and would have been in situ for less than 48hours with little or no opportunity to reconnoitre the village or surrounding area, would attack at night, across ground littered with the bodies of dead comrades who failed a few days before. Oh, and there would be hardly any artillery support – they would get just an hour's worth of shelling right before zero.

What could possibly go wrong?

The initial skirmishes turned out favourable for our chaps in the 19th Division. Zero was at 03:15am and the first waves of men advanced smartly on the village from the north and the south, bombing their way through the rubble and debris towards its eastern limits. However, this initial success was short-lived. The planning of the assault had been rushed through so quickly that many of the men had no idea what to do once they were in the village.

This confusion, coupled with the small matter of dozens of enemy snipers hidden in basements that had to be individually dealt with via bomb and bayonet, meant that the British attackers chewed through their bomb rations in double quick time. Once the bombs started to run out the 19th Division soon found themselves at the sharp end of a number of enemy counter-attacks.

It wasn't long before the initial attacking force had been pushed back to within 100 yards of where they had started.

Reinforcements from the 10th Royal Warwickshire Regiment and the 8th Gloucestershire Regiment went forward and eventually consolidated the position – but only after a thorough and dangerous search of each and every cellar and strongpoint hidden deep within the piles of rubble in order to snuff out the last of the German resistance.

A new line was established just behind the church in the middle of the village. The British war machine had moved forward 100 yards.

Further south, the situation around Fricourt was slightly more optimistic. The initial assault on 1st July had left the German garrison there in all sorts of trouble, trying to resist British advances from the north and south. Surely it wouldn't take much to kick the Germans out of Fricourt for good?

In the end, the Germans had had the good sense to get out while the going was good and had evacuated Fricourt under cover of darkness. Yet, despite many reports suggesting that the village was free of enemy patrols, there was still a lot of confusion and delay before Fricourt was occupied. If stories are to be believed, it was an adventurous officer from the Royal Engineers that cleared the situation up, just as the artillery began to smash the non-existent defenders to imaginary pieces.

After repeated attacks had failed to capture Fricourt and whilst a bombardment of the village previous to another attack was taking place, the Major got out of our front-line trench and waved his hat. Finding no one shot at him, he walked across, in the open, to a point 200 yards in front of Fricourt Farm, and enemy strong point. Finding no one shot here again on waving his hat, he returned to our line and sent this message to Divisional Headquarters, 'Our artillery barrage is only stopping our infantry entering Fricourt!' This report was considered, and patrols pushed out, who took the village.

Captain A.C. Sparkes, 97th Field Company, Royal Engineers, 21st Division.

Once it had been confirmed that the Germans had indeed evacuated the Fricourt Salient, the British wasted no time in moving through the village and the neighbouring woods, taking up new positions that considerably shortened the British line.

46

—·—

THE UNKILLABLE SOLDIER: LIEUTENANT-COLONEL ADRIAN PAUL GHISLAIN CARTON DE WIART

Adrian Carton de Wiart was born in Belgium on 5th May 1880, but spent much of his time growing up in both Egypt and England, as his father worked as a leading barrister in both countries. Adrian's education began in a day school in Cairo run by French priests, although after subsequent illnesses he moved to England, and was attending the Oratory School, Edgbaston, by 1891.

A natural sportsman, he became the cricket and football school captain and won racquets, tennis, and billiards tournaments. He achieved entry into Balliol College, Oxford at the second attempt and studied law there from 1899. However, his time at Oxford was cut short by the outbreak of the Boer War. Even though he was not a British citizen, was under military age and his parents had no idea what he was up to, Adrian enlisted as a Trooper with the Middlesex Yeomanry on 25th January 1900 under the name of Adrian Carton and headed out to South Africa.

After a quick bout of fever, he joined a local corps but was shot in the stomach and groin while trying to cross a river in full view of a Boer detachment.

It would be the first of many, many wounds he would receive in the crucible of battle during his career.

Whilst in hospital his real identity was discovered. His parents were duly notified, and he was sent packing back to England after being invalided out of the army on 22nd October 1900. He didn't enjoy his time back at Balliol College and after persuading his father to let him return to South Africa, he won a Commission with the 2nd Imperial Light Horse on 23rd February 1901. In September that year, he transferred to the 4th Dragoon Guards and joined them in India in March 1902.

Over the next few years, he enjoyed numerous promotions and by the end of 1905, he found himself as *Aide de Camp* to Lieutenant General Sir Henry Hildyard, General Officer Commanding-in-Chief South Africa. On 25th April 1907, he became a British Citizen and returned to England with his regiment in 1908.

At the outbreak of the First World War, Carton de Wiart was seconded to the Somaliland Camel Corps on operations against Sayyad Mohammad Abdullah (the Mad Mullah). On 19th November, he led an attack against a seemingly impregnable fort at Shimber Berris, Somaliland, held by Dervish forces. During the assault, he was shot twice in the face – damaging his ear and an eye – he was also hit on the elbow. For his troubles, he was awarded the Distinguished Service Order.

Speaking in 1964, Lord Ismay, who served alongside Carton de Wiart in Somaliland, described the incident:

> *He didn't check his stride, but I think the bullet stung him up as his language was awful. The doctor could do nothing for his eye, but we had to keep him with us. He must have been in agony.*[1]

The eye wound was serious, and he was eventually evacuated to Egypt, where he was told he would need to have the eye removed. He refused and returned to England for treatment at King Edward's Hospital in London. However, not even the top eye surgeons in London could save the eye and he was admitted to Sir Douglas Shield's Nursing Home on Park Lane, where his eye was removed on 3rd January 1915.

Not surprisingly, the Army declared him unfit for active service, but Adrian demanded to see a Medical Board to fight the decision. It was agreed that if he could wear a glass eye, his case would be reviewed. He duly went out and got himself a glass eye, went before the board, was declared fit, left the building, got in a taxi, and promptly threw the glass eye out of the window. Instead of a glass eye, he wore a rather fetching black eye-patch - and did so for the rest of his life.

Returning to Lord Ismay, we get a glimpse of Adrian's 'fire-eating' state of mind at that time:

> *I honestly believe that he regarded the loss of an eye as*
> *a blessing as it allowed him to get out of Somaliland to*
> *Europe, where he thought the real action was.*[2]

By March 1915 he had got his wish - he was back with the 4th Dragoon Guards in Flanders on the Western Front. However, the reunion didn't last long. His left hand was shattered during a heavy German artillery bombardment at Zonnebeke on 22nd April and he was evacuated away from the front line. The Belgian doctor who was treating him refused to remove some fingers on his left hand that were hanging on by mere threads of tendons, so Adrian pulled them off himself.

Yes, you read that correctly. He pulled his own fingers off.

He was transferred back to the Sir Douglas Shield's Nursing Home on Park Lane, where his hand was eventually amputated off. While convalescing, he picked up his DSO from the King at Buckingham Palace. He was now *sans* eye and hand, but somehow, he convinced a Medical Board that he was fit to continue on active service and was back in the trenches by early 1916.

By now he was a temporary Lieutenant Colonel with the 4th Dragoons and had been given command of 8th Gloucestershire Regiment in the run up to the *Big Push* on the Somme. Fortunately for the men of the 8th Glosters, they were not involved in the first day of the battle, but they did line up in front of La Boisselle on 3rd July after relieving the men of 34th Division who suffered so much just a couple of days previous.

In the early hours of the morning, an attack was launched on La Boisselle with battalions from 57th and 58th Brigade successfully capturing the village. Shortly afterwards, the Germans launched a formidable counter-attack, regained control of a portion of the village and looked set to push the British back to where they had started. To throw the Germans out of La Boisselle for good, the remaining forces of 57th Brigade – including Adrian and his 8th Glosters – were immediately thrown into the battle.

As the fighting raged on, the commanders of the other three 57th Brigade battalions became casualties, and Carton de Wiart assumed control of their commands and rallied the men. Despite being hit in the back of the head and the ankle, he could always be seen right in the thick of the action, pulling the pins out of grenades with his teeth and throwing them with his one good hand at the enemy. Together, the men clung on to the village and La Boisselle was finally captured on 4th July.

For his actions in averting a serious reverse at La Boisselle, Lieutenant-Colonel de Wiart was awarded the Victoria Cross, the Citation for which was published in the London Gazette on 9th September 1916.

> *For most conspicuous bravery, coolness, and determination during severe operations of a prolonged nature. It was owing in a great measure to his dauntless courage and inspiring example that a serious reverse was averted. He displayed the utmost energy and courage in forcing our attack home. After three other battalion Commanders had become casualties, he controlled their commands, and ensured that the ground won was maintained at all costs. He frequently exposed himself in the organisation of positions and of supplies, passing unflinchingly through fire barrage of the most intense nature. His gallantry was inspiring to all.*

By now he was such a regular visitor at the Sir Douglas Shield's Nursing Home that staff there kept his personal pyjamas ready for his next visit. Those pyjamas continued to be well used – he was wounded through the hip during the battle of Passchendaele, through the leg at Cambrai, and in the ear at Arras.

By the time the war was over, he had been wounded eleven times.

During the inter-war period, Carton de Wiart lived in Poland as a British Military Mission, returning to England soon after the Nazi invasion of the country in 1939. In 1940, aged 60, he led an operation to occupy the Norwegian city of Trondheim and halt the German advance, but unfortunately, the mission failed when the supply lines collapsed.

He also had a brief stint stationed in Northern Ireland until April 1941, whereupon he was appointed as head of the British-Yugoslavian Military Mission. During the journey to Yugoslavia, the Wellington Bomber he was in suffered engine failure and was forced to ditch in the sea off the coast of Libya, an Italian colony. After swimming approximately a mile to shore, Carton de Wiart and his crew were captured by the enemy authorities and sent to a POW camp.

Adrian's time in enemy captivity saw him make five escape attempts in two years. On one attempt, he eluded capture for eight days, despite not speaking Italian and having a rather distinctive appearance. In August 1943, the Italians released him and sent him to Lisbon to assist in the negotiations of their surrender terms. He then returned to London and from October 1943 until his retirement in 1946, he served as the Government's Military Representative with General Chiang Kai-shek in China.

After a long and outstandingly eventful career, Carton de Wiart settled in County Cork, spending his remaining years fishing. When asked about his time in the First World War he famously replied: "Frankly, I enjoyed the war."

The 'unkillable soldier' passed away peacefully in 1963, aged 83.

47

— ∙ —

PRIVATE THOMAS GEORGE TURRALL VC, WORCESTERSHIRE REGIMENT

C arton de Wiart wasn't the only VC winner at La Boisselle that day. Thomas George Turrall wasn't a privately educated fire-breather of a commander. He didn't have an eye patch and as far as we know he didn't cut his own fingers off. Private Turrall was a painter and decorator from Birmingham who, like many in his position, left his wife and baby daughter behind to answer his country's call to arms.

But bravery comes in all shapes and sizes, and Private Turrall's story is equally inspiring.

Thomas George Turrall was born at Speedwell Road, Yardley, Birmingham on 5th July 1886. His father, William, held a variety of jobs such as a labourer in a brickwork, but his mother died when he was just ten. Thomas attended Dixon Road School and subsequently became a painter and decorator; he married Mary Lilian Mansell at Aston in 1913 and their daughter Lilian May was born in May 1914.

In December 1914, Turrall joined the 10th Battalion Worcestershire Regiment and, after a few months of training, moved out to France with his battalion in the summer of 1915. Whilst in France, Turrall was told his wife had suddenly become seriously ill, and he was granted compassionate leave to return to England. When the leave ran out, he was forced to return to his unit but in December 1915 he learned that Mary had died aged just 26. Sadly, he was not granted further leave to attend her funeral and his daughter was taken into the care of the family.

During the first phase of the Battle of the Somme, the 10th Worcester's were part of the 19th Division, who were supporting the attack in the La Boisselle sector of the battlefield. After the disaster of the 1st July, the 19th Division was pushed into the crucible of La Boisselle and quickly prepared their own attempt to take the village.

As part of the attack, Lieutenant Richard William Jennings, who had commanded a Battalion Grenade Squad, led a raiding party, which included Pte Turrall, on an advance beyond the village.

During the raid, the party came under fire from machine guns and Thomas, who had dropped to the ground when the firing started, was the only one of the group to remain uninjured. All others were killed other than Lieutenant Jennings who had a severe wound which had shattered his leg. Thomas pulled Jennings into a shell hole for shelter and bandaged his leg with one of his puttees. He used his entrenching tool as a splint. As this aid was being administered, they were attacked by a group of Germans. Turrall shot two of them dead and the others retired.

The battle for the village raged on around them, with the Germans launching a fierce counter-attack, during which more enemy infantry approached the shell hole occupied by the two men. Jennings had by this time fainted, and Thomas was forced to feign death to survive, albeit he was prodded by German bayonets.

Turrall had to remain until dark in his shell hole and then hoisting up his wounded officer, he dragged him back towards the British lines. Jennings was a very tall man, and his arms were around Turrall's neck, and his feet dragged along behind him. The two men were challenged by British sentries, but were eventually allowed back into their lines.

Lieutenant Jennings gave a full report on Turrall's bravery, but unfortunately his wounds were to prove fatal, and he died a few hours later at Dernancourt field dressing station.

The Regiment notes that Thomas wrote to Jennings' mother recounting his last hours:

> *I hope you will not think me taking a liberty writing to you in this manner, but I feel it my duty to do so, as I was with him the whole time and I think you would like to hear the part we played. I must first of all congratulate you in possessing such a plucky son, for he led our company with unflinching pluck that we were not long in taking the enemy's front line.*

> *I might say that when we reached it we came across a dugout held by the Huns. Here your son remarked: "Give me a bomb I will clear them out". He did so. From there, we went on to the second line. This proved to be an easy thing for we did not find anyone there, so that made us more enterprising. We were not long before we were in the third line. This is, I am sorry to say, the starting of our hard times, for it was here he received his first wound; a rifle shot in the muscle of the left arm.*

> *Nothing daunted him. He kept on until he received another wound, a bomb this time which caught him in the right thigh. I might say that it was from this time that we found ourselves practically cut off from the remainder of the battalion. It was here that a brother officer advised your son to seek medical aid, but he very pluckily refused, although had he chosen to act as advised I am afraid he could not have done so as we two*

were now completely cut off. It was advisable to get what cover we could. So, we retired to a shell hole some distance in the rear. In doing so, your son, I am sorry to say, received two more wounds, one in the right knee, and the other shattered his left leg a little below the knee. As we could get no further I did all I could for him, using my entrenching tool handle and bayonet scabbard as splints, and my puttees as bandages. It is hard to tell you that we were obliged to remain like this for something like three and a half to four hours before I at last carried him in.

How he bore his pain was surprising, for he continually chatted and smoked with me until I at last managed to get him to the dressing station. It was here that we parted, but not without him thanking me for the part I played. I am sure in the success of the Worcester's at (blanked by censor) your son played a very prominent part, although badly handicapped by his wounds. Hoping this little but thrilling account will afford you some small consolation in your great loss and at the same time sending mine and all his comrades' sympathy.[1]

Mrs Jennings wrote to Turrall's mother:

Will you let me know when your brave son is in England? I will go anywhere in England to see him and give him some special thing in memory of Lieutenant Jennings. Your son must be a hero and so strong, for my son was over six feet.[2]

Turrall's VC was published in the London Gazette on 9th September 1916, and he formally received his award in December 1916 at Buckingham Palace.

> *For most conspicuous bravery and devotion to duty (La Boisselle, France). During a bombing attack by a small party against the enemy, the officer in charge was badly wounded, and the party having penetrated the position to a great depth, was compelled eventually to retire. Private Turrall remained with the wounded officer for three hours, under continuous and very heavy fire from machine guns and bombs, and, notwithstanding that both himself and the officer were at one time completely cut off from our troops, he held to his ground with determination, and finally carried the officer into our lines after our counter-attacks had made this possible.*

Thomas returned to active service with the Worcester's, seeing out the rest of the war. After he was demobbed in 1919, he returned to his job as a painter and decorator in Birmingham.

48

— ◆ —

ANOTHER EXPENSIVE DIVERSION: THIEPVAL AND OVILLERS

W hile plans were afoot to exploit the gains in the southern part of the battlefront, it was considered prudent to keep the Germans occupied in the north, so they didn't get a sniff of what was being planned elsewhere.

To do this, not one but two diversionary attacks were scheduled for the morning of 3rd July, targeting Ovillers and Thiepval, just to the north of the action at La Boisselle. Attacking Ovillers would be men of the 12th (Eastern) Division, while the 32nd Division would have a go at Thiepval. Unfortunately for all concerned, these diversions would result in the same grim and futile expenditure of men and resource as the sad affair at Gommecourt not 48 hours past.

Originally, Rawlinson had ordered fresh attacks on Ovillers to happen as soon as was physically possible. When this order was issued (the evening of 1st July) the details of the costly failure on this sector had not yet filtered its way up to HQ. Delays in relief and the subsequent attack on La Boisselle meant that the follow up attack Rawlinson wanted was only penned in for 3.15am on 3rd July after an hour-long artillery bombardment.

The aforementioned artillery show began at 2.15am, targeting the same positions as 1st July, albeit enjoying a bit more firepower, courtesy of the 19th Divisional artillery to the south. Five battalions of the 12th (Eastern) Division attacked from pre-dug assembly trenches at 3.15 a.m., with the left flank covered by a smokescreen.

Initially, it looked like the German positions were only lightly held, and some of the first wave of attackers penetrated into the first and even second line of German defences, but it didn't take long for the Germans to regroup and within minutes they were carpeting *No Man's Land* with machine-gun fire and artillery shells.

Signaller Sidney Kemp of 6th Royal West Kent Regiment was at the very pointy end of the attack:

> *We signallers moved out of the dugout just before 3am. We found that part of B Company was already out in No Man's Land. We got up over the parapet and went towards the German lines. I went over to the German trench and there wasn't anyone else about and it wasn't yet quite light. I went back a bit looking for Webb and the other signaller, when suddenly the German machine guns went into action.*

> *I was suddenly standing alone in No Man's Land, with everyone else either killed, wounded or the few that we left, down on the ground. I could feel the bullets going past me and yet I didn't get hit by any. I then got down on the ground still having my telephone and my rifle.*

> *I saw Captain Harris get up as if he was going to advance again and he toppled over dead. I crawled to where Webb was and together we crawled nearer to the German trench and there we stayed with a few of D Company, who hadn't gone over into the second line of German trenches with Captain Matthews. He was*

killed, as well as Captain Barnett of A Company and
the Captains of both the other companies.[1]

Very quickly, *No Man's Land* became impossible to cross, rendering any hope of reinforcements completely out of the question. Signaller Kemp's Battalion (6th Royal West Kent) lost over 400 casualties in the initial attack and noted with some bitterness in their War Diary that they had received no help from their designated support unit, 6th The East Kent Regiment (Buffs). This wasn't for a lack of trying. The reality was that the Buffs had lost almost 300 men simply trying to get over their own parapet. Mercifully, their commander eventually called off further attempts to cross *No Man's Land*.

By 9am the forward units were running dangerously low on ammunition and were being fiercely counter-attacked – they had no choice but to withdraw as best they could. The attack on Ovillers was over. It had cost the 12th Division 2,375 casualties for zero gains.

The situation wasn't any better at Thiepval - if anything, it was even worse. The proposed assault on Thiepval had been scaled right back at the behest of Haig. Instead of 3 Divisions there would only be two brigades thrown into the breach. On the left was 14th Brigade of 32nd Division and on the right was 75th Brigade of 25th Division. The planning for this part of the show was even more chaotic than usual, which meant that the 75th Brigade had been so delayed in getting to the front line the attack had to be put back three hours.

Unfortunately, no one seemed to have told the artillery boys about the delay and they happily went about their business of smashing Thiepval at 3.15am as originally ordered. By the time the message got through about the delay, they had already fired a good deal of their available shells.

Confusion reigned. 2nd Lieutenant Sydney Stevenson-Jones was with the reserve company of 2nd South Lancashire's when the whistles eventually blew at 6.15am.

Word came down to 'stand to' for the attack. I grabbed my equipment and had hardly got it on when the order came along to 'File out for the charge!' and our guns ceased firing. We, that is B Company, rushed up the communication trench only to find it hopelessly blocked by a company of another battalion coming down. By then there wasn't more than a handful of D Company left, who had gone over first on our right. I just saw Captain Bill Gates lead the head of A Company out under a withering machine-gun and rifle fire and the fag end of C going out on our left, dropping like rabbits. We shunted again to let another company pass and I came up again to see Gates rally the last of A for another rush...

I saw Captain Alexander Blair lead out his company with a cane in his hand as on parade... I saw big Lieutenant Eric Fletcher, his senior subaltern walk on alone right up to the German wire (which was totally uncut, in spite of what we had been told) empty his long nosed Colt into the Germans standing on their parapet firing at him, but they could not bring him down, until one got him and he fell across the wire and hung there all day, the Colt swinging from the lanyard buttoned under his shoulder strap.

I saw big Company Sergeant Major Collins, all 6ft 3 inches of him, walk out under fire and pick up the slightly wounded Second Lieutenant Poundall and carry him. Idiotic – but very brave. Poundall was far better on the ground than being carried shoulder high.

> *I had been watching from a sap that ran forward into*
> *No Man's Land so I kept pace with Gates down it on*
> *the left flank of his company.[2]*

The attack on Thiepval had been nothing short of a slaughter. 2nd Lieutenant Stevenson-Jones had been asked to report on why the attack had failed and why there had been no renewed attempts to take Thiepval while the Colonel had been absent.

His report was brief and to the point.

> *The attack failed because too few men can get across*
> *No Man's Land which is under direct observation from*
> *high ground behind Serre and Beaumont Hamel and*
> *swept by shrapnel and machine-gun fire from behind*
> *the enemy front. Thiepval will never be taken by frontal*
> *attack. A glance at the map will suffice.[3]*

Stevenson-Jones's Battalion had lost 14 officers and over 300 men in this futile attack. Brigadier General N.F. Jenkins was sacked the very next day even though the delay to the attack – which surely affected the chances of success – was beyond his control. The blame for failure must surely lay at the door of more staff officers more senior than Jenkins?

Who in their right mind thought that launching two small-scale independent attacks on Thiepval and Ovillers at different time and with inadequate preparation and planning, with men who were unfamiliar with the ground, would succeed where others had spectacularly failed just 48 hours earlier as part of a much more co-ordinated, well planned and resourced assault?

49

RANDOM ACTS OF WARFARE (PART 1): CONTALMAISON

Despite the mixed results of the actions in the immediate aftermath of the 1st July, Haig and Rawlinson continued with their plan of moving their front-line positions to the south of the Albert-Bapaume Road to within striking distance of the German second line in preparation for another almighty assault.

After finally capturing the villages of La Boisselle and Fricourt, the chaps back at HQ needed another three parts of the jigsaw to fall into place to give this second grand attack a fighting chance of success: the occupation of Contalmaison and the securing of a few key woodland areas - namely Mametz and Trônes Woods.

All three objectives fell under the remit of Rawlinson's Fourth Army and although Rawlinson was quick to repeatedly pass on to his Corps commanders the general view from GHQ that the enemy were on their last legs and that every effort must to expended to allow them no respite, he seems to have forgotten to ensure that any attacks carried out by the three Corps – *his* three Corps - were co-ordinated or simultaneous or joined up in any way at all.

According to the Divisional diary of the time, 23rd Division (III Corps) launched no less than eight individual assaults against Contalmaison and the trenches that guarded its perimeter in the five days between 5-10th July. That's a lot of attacking.

On their immediate right-hand side, during this same time period, the 17th Division (VX Corps) launched at least eleven separate attacks against trenches that ran directly into the sector 23rd Division was trying to overrun.

That's nineteen individual attacks against narrow, neighbouring fronts in five days. Have a guess how many of those attacks (by neighbouring British forces under the same Army Group) were co-ordinated so that the dual forces of 23rd and 17th Divisions attacked together?

The answer is zero.

Not once did they co-ordinate their attacks and deliver them at the same time. Not once. In 19 attacks. Not surprisingly, they didn't make a great deal of headway, but they did manage to rack up around 7,000 casualties between them.

It wasn't much better on the left flank of 23rd Division. Here, they 19th and 34th Divisions only attacked as a joined-up force once.

All of this seems to be a huge missed opportunity and a real shame for the men who had to do the actual fighting. The battle for Contal-maison quickly deteriorated into a confused melee of desperate attacks and counter-attacks as both sides fought over the ruins and rubble of the village.

Inevitably, the casualties quickly mounted up. Sergeant Roland Mountfield of the 10th Royal Fusiliers, 37th Division, was part of the reserves that were pushed up into the breach in an effort to carry the village. As he tried to get rations up a communication trench that linked the front line to an isolated forward bastion, he saw the death and destruction up close and personal:

> *I wonder what the people at home who say, 'We will*
> *fight to our last drop of blood!' would think they were*
> *taken up that trench. For 500 yards it is paved with*

*English dead. I don't know what happened, but there
were evidently caught there by awful shell fire – some
say our own. In places you must walk on them, for they
lie in heaps. I went up with rations and again to help
carry down a casualty on a stretcher. I won't describe
that trench until I have forgotten it a little...[1]*

With little or no co-ordinated instruction, many of the individual
units around Contalmaison continued to busy themselves with isolated bombing operations and attritional local raids.

On the 8th July, the 1st Worcester's of 23rd Division infiltrated as far
as the church before they were forced to retreat under heavy German
fire. Two days later, men of the 8th Green Howards and 11th West
Yorkshire's renewed the attack, and although the Germans put up
stern resistance, they were forced to withdraw from Contalmaison
during the late afternoon. It had cost almost 12,000 casualties, but
Contalmaison was finally in British hands.

50

RANDOM ACTS OF WARFARE (PART 2): MAMETZ WOOD

W hile the British III Corps were banging their heads against the walls of Contalmaison, in the centre of the overall move to inch the British line closer to the German second line, an operation was about to kick off against one of the most formidable defensive positions that stood in Haig's way.

Mametz Wood.

A mile wide and a mile deep, Mametz was the largest parcel of woodland on the Somme battlefield and was in an area where the Germans had really gone to town on their defences. To get anywhere close, any attacking force would have to navigate a complex web of defensive strong points flanking either side of the woodland – these were held by a battalion of the Prussian Guard on the east side and men of the 28th Reserve Division to the west.

If anyone got through that, the woods themselves were held by another section of elite Prussian Guards and presented a nightmare scenario for any would-be attacker. The trees grew very close together, and the undergrowth was thick and difficult to cut through. If this wasn't enough, British artillery was smashing trees left, right and centre, causing chaos in the woods and making it even harder to navigate through.

Any attempt to take the woods would be slow, bloody, and personal.

The task of taking Mametz wood fell upon the shoulders of the 38th (Welsh) Division – a unit of men that had only been in France since the beginning of the year and were yet to see any kind of battle action.

The plan to take Mametz was simple in theory. A two-pronged attack against the woods would start during the morning of 7th July with Major General Thomas David Pilcher's 17th (Northern) Division attacking from the southwest and Major General Ivor Philipps' 38th (Welsh) Division coming up from the southeast. Once they had entered the wood, both Divisions were to advance towards the centre and then swing to the north, clearing the enemy as they advanced. The 38th (Welsh) Division had the added task of sweeping across the southern end of the wood to clear any enemy from that locality.

The 38th (Welsh) Division's part in the planned assault was given to Brigadier-General Horatio J Evans' 115th Brigade.

A preliminary assault by the 17th (Northern) Division was to take place at 2am to help clear the way and the main attack would be preceded by 40 minutes of heavy artillery bombardment which would aim to smash the defenders of Mametz Woods to twigs as well knock out some known enemy machine-gun positions which were hiding in Acid Drop Copse on the left of Mametz Wood and Flatiron Copse and Sabot Copse on the right. Zero for the main assault would be 8am.

The generals thought the woods would be cleared and in British hands within a matter of hours, but as Mike Tyson once said, "Everyone has a plan until they are punched in the face".

The attack started off badly and quickly got worse. The artillery boys failed to silence the machine-gun posts in the surrounding copses, and the smokescreens that had been ordered to at least try to offer a modicum of cover to the advancing Welshmen didn't materialise. As a result, when the whistles blew for Zero, the men of 38th Division advanced over open ground towards the woods in full view of various German machine gunners who were very grateful of the target practice.

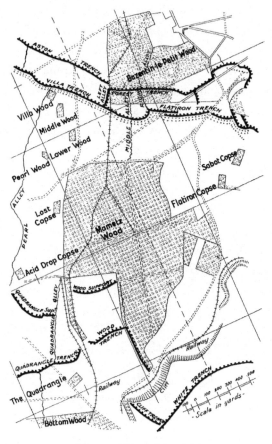

Mametz Wood. July 1916.

Those first waves of Welsh attackers didn't even get close to the woods. Hundreds of men were killed or wounded within the first minutes. It was murder.

Corps commanders insisted throughout the day that the attack be renewed at all costs. Men dug themselves in along a shallow dip in the ground that afforded them some cover from the machine-guns. They were 300 yards from the edge of the woods, but any movement forward was met with an impossible curtain of defensive fire from all angles.

By late afternoon, progress was non-existent, and the casualties were really starting to mount up. Brigadier-General Evans could see that the German defences at the edge of the woods were still intact, and the artillery were firing too deep into the woods to make any difference to his men. If he was to have any chance of success, he needed a tighter co-ordination with the artillery and that would take too long to organise to assist with any further attacks – he instead called it a day and postponed any further assaults from his Brigade.

It was a decision that didn't go down very well back at HQ, but his Brigade had suffered over 400 casualties for precisely zero gain and in Evan's mind there was no point throwing more men into the fray if they had no hope of breaking through.

The next day, Brigadier-General Evans spoke to Captain Wyn Griffiths of his frustration of the previous day. Captain Wyn Griffiths later recalled that Brigadier-General Evans had told him:

> *I spoke my mind about the whole business ... you heard me. They wanted us to press on at all costs, talked about determination, and suggested that I didn't realise the importance of the operation. As good as told me I was tired and didn't want to tackle the job. Difficult to judge on the spot, they said! As if the whole trouble hadn't arisen because someone found it easy to judge when he was six miles away and had never seen the country, and couldn't read a map. You mark my words, they'll send me home for this: they want butchers not brigadiers.*

They'll remember now that I told them before we began that the attack could not succeed unless the machine guns were masked. I shall be in England in a month.[1]

Evans was mistaken regarding his last comment. It would take six weeks, not a month, before he was sent packing.

The 38th Division launched repeated attacks on Mametz Wood over the next 4 days – in total, they assaulted the woods seven times. Only on very rare occasions did they receive any help from either flank. 3rd Division (XIII Corps) on its right-hand side carried out precisely no operations to support the beleaguered Welshmen and the few attacks that were co-ordinated with 17th Division on their left largely failed.

The list of reasons why the Welsh attackers had such a rough time of it at Mametz is long and exasperating. They largely attacked with rushed orders and no flanking support. HQ was badly out of touch with what was happening on the ground – they insisted on more attacks and more attacks and more attacks without trying to understand the actual situation facing the men out there in *No Man's Land*.

And then there was the artillery 'support'.

Preliminary bombardments were too short, accuracy was poor – especially when trying to knock out the numerous machine-gun nests that were hidden in the main woods and the surrounding copses. There was no creeping barrage and if any infantry got anywhere near the woods, there was a large likelihood they would get hit with friendly fire because not enough time had been given to understanding where the troops would be.

Plans were in place for a renewed go at the woods for the early hours of 9th July. However, the attack was put back because of the installation of a new Divisional Commander - Major General Herbert Edward Watts, formerly of 7th Division.

Watts immediately got to work on the plan for the renewed assault on Mametz Woods. He would keep broadly the same plan as his predecessor had knocked up – but with two small amendments. The attack would be *en masse* with two brigades (113th and 114th) and they would attack behind a creeping barrage.

At 3.30am on 10th July, the preliminary artillery bombardment began, and every available 18-pounder gun fired on the wood. Thirty minutes later, the heavier artillery began their creeping barrage that progressed at walking pace through the wood.

As the preliminary bombardment lifted and the creeping barrage began, the men of the Welsh battalions moved forward to begin their steady advance across the open space in front of them. The enemy machine-guns quickly opened fire, laying down a hail of lead that inflicted severe casualties on the Welshmen, but this time they were not to be stopped and the outer edge of the wood was rushed.

During the morning, the fight swayed backward and forwards as the Germans kept counterattacking with reinforcements brought into the wood by a sunken road out of sight of the artillery. Yet by mid-afternoon, both brigades had secured their first objectives some 500 yards inside the woods and were sending out forward patrols to explore deeper.

The day ended with both brigades holding a line roughly 800 yards inside the woods – it was a solid day's work and would provide a decent jumping off point for the next day. But the stress for the infantry was far from over.

> *Our own guns were firing short, and in spite of our attempts to communicate with the rear this continued. The numerous casualties we sustained because of this had the effect of making the men very panicky. Further, the difficulty in seeing more than a few yards in front caused ignorance amongst the men as to where the front*

lay and whether any of our fellows were there; any noise in the bush in front meant a hail of bullets. I, myself, saw an officer of the 15th Royal Welch Fusiliers killed in this way[2]

Captain Glynn Jones, 14th Battalion, Royal Welch Fusiliers, 113th Brigade, 38th Division.

In the morning, both brigades were relieved by a 115th Brigade which had already taken a mauling at Mametz a few days previously. Despite being down on strength, the 115th Brigade captured a few more chunks of the woods and stood its ground in the face of fierce German counter attacks before it too was relieved at dawn on the 12th by elements of the 21st Division. These fresh troops quickly mopped up the remaining areas of the wood and, by midday, the occupation of Mametz Wood was complete.

Mametz Wood was a brutal baptism of fire for the men of the 38th Division. They suffered in the region of 4,000 casualties – around 20% of its pre-battle strength – and took no further part in the Somme campaign.

51
— · —

RANDOM ACTS OF WARFARE (PART 3): TRÔNES WOOD

Trônes Wood was a relatively small pear-shaped piece of wood-land, approximately 1,400 yards long and 400 yards wide at its base. But, with a position just two miles from Combles - a vital German logistics and transportation hub – and with its northern tip tickling the German second line, it was deemed an area of considerable strategic importance for both sides. Haig was keen to get his hands on Trônes Wood before the planned attack against the German second line on 14th July and reminded Rawlinson at every opportunity.

On paper, Trônes Wood was a formidable defensive position. Overlooked on all sides by massed ranks of artillery, it was strongly fortified by the Germans, with a trench system (Trônes Alley) running into nearby Bernafay Woods. A perfect network of wire entanglements and a small arsenal of machine guns covered all approaches. The wood itself had not yet succumbed to the might of the artillery shell and was still a dense thicket which had not been cut back for several years – making it very difficult to force a way through.

As the position of Trônes Wood was on the junction of both British and French positions on the Somme front line, the plan was for the Allies to combine forces and assault the woods together. The date for the show was pencilled in for 7th July. However, a German counter-attack in the French sector succeeded in re-capturing the northern section of Bois Faviere and forced a delay of twenty-four hours.

The initial British attack would be from the south-west and concentrate on capturing the southern tip of Trônes Wood along with Maltz Horn Trench, which ran south from the wood down to Malt Horn Farm. The French, on the right flank of the attack, would take the rest of Maltz Horn Trench, which ran from the farm south to Hardecourt-au- Bois village.

Zero was set for 8.00am on the morning of 8th July.

For some hours prior to the infantry assault, the field guns of both the 18th and 30th Division had rained down shells upon the German positions with little effect. The infantry attack was spearheaded by 2nd Yorkshire Regiment of 21st Brigade (30th Division) who struggled through the smashed trees of the neighbouring Bernafay Wood before they emerged to cross open ground towards Trônes Wood.

As soon as the leading columns came into view, the Germans holed up in Trônes Wood let them have it with machine-guns and a pair of field guns that fired over open sights from the edge of the woodland. Casualties quickly mounted up, and the attack lost all impetus. A renewed effort saw bombing parties attempt to bomb their way in to Trônes Alley, but these also failed. The survivors withdrew back to Bernafay Woods before they were all completely annihilated.

On the right of the British, the French kicked off their assault as planned at 10:05. They had a much better time of it and captured their allotted section of Maltz Horn Trench up to a position right opposite Maltz Horn Farm. However, because of the failure of the 21st Brigade to get anywhere near Trônes Wood, their left flank was completely exposed to enemy machine-gun fire.

The 30th Division was ordered to assault Trônes Wood once more – even if it meant throwing the entire division into the fight. Shortly after midday men of the 2nd Wiltshire Regiment sneaked up a sunken road and got into the Maltz Horn Trench, they were followed by a company of the 19th Manchester Regiment who then linked up with the French and forced the Germans in situ to retreat. This was partial success, but someone still had to deal with Trônes Wood.

At about 1pm, the rest of the 2nd Wiltshire's launched another attack against the southern end of Trônes Wood. Like the 2nd Yorkshire's before them, they suffered heavy casualties, but a few groups of men reached the south-east edge of Trônes Wood, where they immediately set about digging in.

It was barely a toe-hold, but it was at least something.

In the early hours of the following morning, the 2nd Royal Scots Fusiliers of 90th Brigade captured the ruins of Maltz Horn Farm and then bombed their way up Maltz Horn Trench to the edge of Trônes Wood itself. At about the same time, another attack on the woods was being prepared. The 17th Manchester's were due to attack from Bernafay Woods at 3am but were badly disrupted by enemy gas shells and their assault took place three hours late. Nevertheless, they managed to get into Trônes Wood and by 8am they had reached the eastern edge of the woods. Soon after, they had linked up with Royal Scots Fusiliers and were sending out patrols into the northern sectors of the woods.

It was still early on 9th July, but Trônes Wood was in British hands.

This success, however, was to be short-lived. Within hours, the Germans were smashing Trônes Wood to bits using every single working artillery gun from Bazentin to Maurepas. And with the Germans massing on the eastern side of the woods for a serious counter-attack, the British units pulled back towards their own lines.

By 4pm the woods were back in German hands.

A British counter-attack to the German counter-attack was ordered for the evening, despite the dominance of the German artillery. The 16th Manchester Regiment launched their attack from the sunken lane towards the south of the woods, which caught the German defenders slightly off guard. The objective was to re-take the southern portion of the woods and cover the left flank of the Royal Scots who were bravely hanging on to Maltz Horn Trench.

The Manchester's succeeded in linking up with the Royal Scots, but could not make any headway towards the woods, courtesy of numerous and persistent enemy snipers. Consequently, they were forced to dig in some 60 yards short of the woods, where they spent an uncomfortable and very exposed night.

After two costly days of fighting, the Allies had launched four separate attacks on Trônes Wood and had failed four separate times. But the mighty moustaches back at HQ did not defer or falter. After some night patrols seemed to suggest the enemy were not holding their positions in large numbers, it was decided a fresh advance at dawn would be the best thing to do. After a short preliminary bombardment, the 16th Manchester's, backed up by a Company of the 4th South African Regiment, advanced slowly in sections through the wood. It proved to be quite the impossible task, and many men became lost and disorientated. Reports were sent back that the woods were clear of the enemy, but this was not the case, and the Germans were soon busying themselves to rid the woods of the Allies. By 8am they had been pushed all the way back, just about clinging on to their original conquest of the south-eastern corner.

The rest of the day was relatively quiet, giving the British the opportunity to swap out the 90th Brigade with the 89th Brigade and swap the Royal Scots Fusiliers in Maltz Horn Trench with the 20th Battalion King's Regiment.

Whilst the change in personnel was taking place, the staff officers conducting this show had a brainwave – they would now use overwhelming artillery force to flatten Trônes Wood completely. The plan was that as soon as the bombardment had ended, the 20th King's would bomb their way into the southern area of the wood and link up with the 2nd Bedfordshire's, who would advance up from the sunken lane to the south.

At 2:40am, all available artillery guns were spitting fire directly onto Trônes Wood. Forty-five minutes later, the men of the King's Regiment bombed their way up the Maltz Horn Trench, but despite capturing two enemy machine-guns and killing dozens of Germans, they couldn't quite reach the woods. Meanwhile, the men of the 2nd Bedfordshire Regiment were having a grim time getting across *No Man's Land* into the southern edge of the woods. Machine-gun fire was decimating their ranks, but two companies of men made it across, moving along north and east before running into German defences built upon an impassable concoction of shattered timber, torn tree roots and twisted barbed wire. By lunchtime, the Germans were back in control of the woods.

The battle for Trônes Wood had been raging for four days, and the wreckage of the fight was getting out of hand. Corpses and wounded men littered the floor and swarms of flies were a constant companion to anyone trying to make their way through the battered tree stumps and smashed undergrowth. When Lieutenant William Bloor was sent to have a look as an artillery forward observation officer, he was appalled at what he found.

> *The place beggars description quite – there has been the fiercest fighting here for four days, and both sides have taken and lost the wood several times. Wounded have not been cleared away, and there are some who have been all that time without food or any attention.*[1]

The battle had taken a massive toll on the men of the 30th Division that had tried so desperately to capture Trônes Wood. In the five days from 8th-12th July, the Division had suffered 1,934 casualties - killed, wounded and missing. It was time to give the survivors a bit of a rest. They were replaced by Major General Ivor Maxse's 18th (Eastern

Division) who had been in the thick of it on 1st July but were now back in the front line.

By now, the decision had been taken at High Command that the assault on the German second line was definitely going to take place at first light on 14th July. For this attack to stand any chance of success, it was imperative that Trônes Wood was in British hands.

Major General Maxse had just forty-eight hours to capture the woods.

His 55th Brigade quickly took up their new positions intending to attack at 7pm that night following a two-hour bombardment. Unfortunately, all did not go well. The 7th Battalion, Royal West Kent Regiment struggled to navigate their way through the woods in the dark whilst the 7th Queen's Regiment were stopped 100 yards from the woods' edge by determined enemy rifle, artillery and machine gun fire before they were forced to return to their original positions.

It was midnight on the 13th/14th July. Yet another attack on Trônes Wood had failed and the big offensive on the German Second Line was due to start in three hours' time – indeed less than 300 yards away from Trônes Wood the men who would take part in that offensive were already getting themselves silently organised in the dark.

Time was running out – again the orders came down from HQ – The 54th Brigade – commanded by Brigadier General Shoubridge - was required to have the wood under their control before dawn. The success of the 9th Division's attack on Longueval in a few hours' time depended on it.

No pressure then.

Because of the tight time schedule, Shoubridge knew his attack would have to be as simple as possible if it was to have any chance of success. His men would advance from south to north, establishing an eastern defensive flank as they progressed. The 12th Middlesex would lead the way with the 6th Northamptonshire's right behind them and maintaining the defensive flank.

It had to work. He had no choice. But it started off badly. The Middlesex chaps were slow to get into position and Lt-Colonel Francis Aylmer Maxwell VC, in charge of the operation on the ground, was forced to switch the battalions around. It would now be the Northampton's leading the charge.

At 3am, the first waves of men headed out across *No Man's Land* from the sunken lane at the southern edge of the woods. Just like their predecessors, they had over 1,000 yards of open ground to cover and, just like their predecessors, they had to endure a firestorm of bullets and shells as they made their way across. Casualties were high, but by 4.30am the survivors had gained control of the southern perimeter and despite being severely down on numbers and becoming increasingly disorientated, they were doing their best to move north through the shattered remains of the woods.

At 8am, the 12th Bn. Middlesex Regiment was sent forward in support, with Lt-Colonel Maxwell VC moving forward into the wood with his men. There he found that fighting had stopped, and that there was a mix of men from different units who had either already been there from previous attacks to men lost in the current assault.

To reorganise and co-ordinate the flagging attack, he rounded up as many men as he could find, and ordered an officer to take a compass and walk from the southeastern corner of the woods to the western edge. The men followed him in a long queue, once the officer got to the edge, the order was given to face right and with Maxwell himself in the line, every man was told to advance shoulder to shoulder, firing at the hip into the undergrowth and tangled mess in front of them as they progressed.

It was an extraordinary example of leadership and organisation. And it worked. By 9:30am, the Germans had been completely driven out of Trônes Wood, forced to flee towards Guillemont, and the right flank of the 9th Division had been secured for their advance on Longueval.

Map IX.

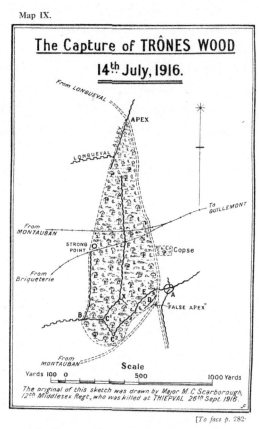

The Capture of Trones Wood. 14th July 1916

But should it have taken so long and cost so many casualties to capture Trônes Wood? Each attack by 30th Division was made by a few isolated companies or a single battalion, with sub-standard artillery support. It was no surprise little progress was made – and even if they made some gains, the might of the German artillery machine in this area made quick work of any incursions. Ultimately, Rawlinson's hands off approach to leading this phase of the programme resulted in a glut of random acts of warfare (there were forty-six separate attacks against enemy positions between 2-13th July) that badly underperformed and proved costly in terms of men and resources – all of which may have been prevented if he would have insisted on greater co-ordination and co-operation between his Corps Commanders.

That being said, these 'random acts of warfare' secured 20 square miles of enemy territory, compared to just three-square miles captured on 1st July. In addition, they forced the German army into a costly piecemeal defence that it could ill afford.

Maybe these random acts of warfare weren't quite so random after all?

52

14TH JULY: THE DAWN ATTACK

T he British strategists had been mulling over a new and improved attack in the Somme area since 2nd July. General feeling was if a small advance in the south could be achieved it would act as a great springboard for a large-scale march upon the German second line. As such, on 8th July, Rawlinson issued his first set of operational orders for just such an attack – sketching out a four-division assault on the German second line between Longueval and Bazentin-le-Petit.

In general, this line was a slightly easier proposition than the first line, which was attacked on 1st July. The dug outs were not as frequent or as deep and the trench system was nowhere near as extensive. There was, however, copious amounts of wire to contend with. And machine guns. Lots of those. And bombs. And artillery. The term 'slightly easier' is relative.

The key design feature of this attack was that it would take place at dawn, in an effort to save the men from crossing a 1,500 yard wide *No Man's Land* devoid of any cover in bright sunlight. It was this kind of scenario that cost Rawlinson's III Corp so dearly on 1st July, and he was quite keen to avoid a repeat performance.

By starting the attack at dawn, he reckoned he could get his men to form up undetected, under cover of darkness, close to the German front line - therefore minimising the open ground they would need to cross. As soon as dawn broke, the show would begin, and his boys would rush the German positions before the enemy realised what way was up.

Haig hated the idea. He didn't think the officers and men on the ground had the experience or know-how to move two infantry divisions over large distances and get them into the correct positions at night without being rumbled. He instead offered his own idea, which involved XV Corps attacking from Mametz Wood before undertaking a complicated manoeuvre which saw them pivot sharply east and head towards Longueval.

Not only did Rawlinson hate Haig's plan, so too did his Corps commanders, and after much lobbying, Haig finally agreed to go along with Rawlinson's original plan for a dawn attack. By now, there were just 48 hours to go before Zero and much to do.

In some aspects of the planning, it was clear to see that some lessons from 1st July had been taken on board by the chaps at HQ. Take the artillery bombardment for example. The Great Bombardment that preceded the initial assault was an artillery show of epic proportions, however, the intensity of shelling planned for the dawn attack was five times greater and with one important difference: All the shells were earmarked for the enemy's forward positions, not shared between the entirety of the German defensive setup.

Yet not every lesson dished out on 1st July was being taken to heart. For example, that of mission creep: otherwise known as continually adding to the objectives of the advance until they became wildly optimistic and risky.

Rawlinson's plan started off sensibly enough, concentrating on capturing a sizeable chunk of the German second line with a handful of horses from the 2nd Indian Cavalry Division on hand to have a go at High Wood if the opportunity presented itself. Yet, within a couple of days, the role of the cavalry had grown exponentially.

The Cavalry would no longer only be released if the infantry had made progress. Now the 2nd Indian Cavalry would rush to capture High Wood, and then push on to Flers and Le Sars, some three miles beyond. At the same time, both 1st and 3rd Cavalry Divisions would get a piece of the action with their own distant objectives. Suddenly, the shape of the offensive had shifted significantly. It was no longer a highly concentrated effort on the German Second Line, which asked for an advance of a few hundred yards. Now it was a wide-ranging affair extending to the enemy third line and beyond – an advance of roughly four miles across a 10,000 yard front.

That right there is the very definition of 'mission creep', yet this time it was not Haig doing the meddling but Rawlinson himself. Despite Haig making numerous requests for Rawlinson to limit the Cavalry to just a few elements to take High Wood, Rawlinson carried on with his grand plans. His view was based on his belief that all serious German resistance would be silenced by the devastating bombardment and, once his men were through the initial front line, the ground beyond would be at their mercy for a rapid and swashbuckling advance on horseback.

Sound familiar?

In the early hours of 14th July, the four divisions involved in the initial assault moved into position with the 21st and 7th Divisions from XV Corps on the left and 3rd and 9th Divisions of XIII Corps on the right. This was trickier for the men of XIII Corps as they had to cross over 1000 yards of *No Man's Land*. They went across in small groups, crawling the last 50-100 yards carefully so as not to be detected. By 3.15am, all men were in position – it was a remarkable piece of organisation.

The Germans had no clue what was about to hit them.

The artillery of Fourth Army had been pounding the German second line along the attacking front for 3 days solid. At 3.20am a hurricane bombardment, supplemented by machine-guns worked to-

gether to build to the final crescendo. At 3.25am the whistles blew, and
the leading British infantry units duly stood up and moved forward
through a mist, with just enough light to recognise where they were
going.

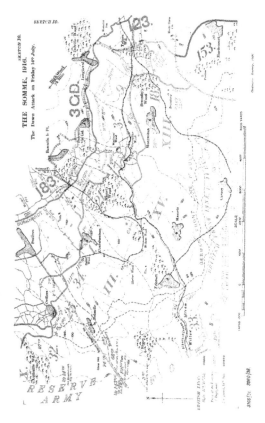

The Dawn Attack. 14th July 1916

Yet again, the results of the artillery bombardment were patchy.
The extreme flanks of the attack seemed to enjoy cut wire and badly
smashed up enemy positions, but towards the centre the results were
more variable with some units of 8th Brigade (3rd Division) running

straight into thick belts of uncut wire and strong defensive positions which had seemingly been missed altogether by the British guns.

That being said, it wasn't long before the entire German second line system – except that area in front of 8th Brigade - had succumbed to the attack and by early afternoon the entire line was in British hands. It was a remarkable start to the day, but thanks to the substantial mission creep covered earlier, there was still much work to be done.

Specifically, that work took the shape of three villages and three woods behind the German lines. These were Bazentin-le-Petit village and woods, Bazentin-le-Grand village and woods, the village of Longueval and Delville Wood. All were deep inside enemy held territory and all were strongly fortified. But they had to be captured to pave the way for the cavalry charge the British High Command so desperately wanted.

If Rawlinson's predictions were correct, German morale would be shot to bits and this next phase of the battle would be a walk in the park.

Alas, this was not the case. German morale was far from broken. Also, because the artillery bombardment had almost exclusively concentrated on the German second line positions, the areas beyond had largely avoided any serious shelling. The German defensive positions here were still intact and very much alive with well supplied, well concealed and highly motivated defenders.

What started off as a swift, sharp and successful attack had become a slow and bloody struggle against fierce and fanatical resistance. Both Bazentins (woods and villages) were eventually captured by late afternoon, but on the right flank, the men of XIII Corps only succeeded in occupying the southern sector of Longueval and a tiny slice of Delville Wood.

Notwithstanding the lack of progress during the afternoon, Rawlinson still clung on to the dream of unleashing his cavalry upon those highly cherished long-distance objectives. When news trickled through to HQ that enemy resistance in Longeuval could be on the verge of collapsing, Rawlinson immediately ordered units of 2nd Indian Cavalry Division forward. By the time he had sent Haig the optimistic message 'Indian Cavalry sharpening their swords', the horses were already charging through the fields between Longeuval and High Wood.

Despite being hit by a double whammy of machine gun fire from High Wood and Delville Wood and artillery fire from Flers, they still speared 16 enemy soldiers before being forced to dismount and take up defensive positions.

This little episode cost the Indian Cavalry 138 horses and 10 men either killed or wounded and closed off what was a frustrating day for the British. It was a day that proved that if you threw enough artillery power at a single objective, that objective could be carried relatively quickly. However, it also proved that fanciful ideas of rapid advances by foot and by hoof deep into enemy territory without such artillery back up were still unrealistic – especially when the entire strategy of such breakthroughs were based on enemy morale and resistance suddenly disappearing into thin air.

That said, compared to the 1st July, this attack was a success and did wonders for British optimism along the corridors of power. Haig described it as 'the best day we have had in this war'. In just two weeks, he had captured the German first and second lines along a front of 6,000 yards. Yes, the costs in terms of killed, missing and wounded had been brutal, (around 9,000 men) but the German Second Army defending the area had also taken a beating. What's more, Haig was now within touching distance of the fabled Thiepval Ridge.

Maybe, just maybe, the British could now use these new positions as a springboard to even greater advances over the coming weeks...

53

— • —

THE HORROR OF HIGH WOOD

Haig and Rawlinson could have been forgiven if they had woken up on the 15th July with a cognac induced headache after the relative success of the previous day. The men of the 7th Division and their cavalry comrades who spent the night in and around High Wood also had a headache that morning. Theirs was not cognac induced but was wholly a result of their current predicament which, if being generous, could be described as 'precarious'.

The cavalry charge had taken the German defenders, situated in Wood Lane – a trench/sunken lane running from the eastern edge of High Wood down towards Longueval – by surprise. The subsequent infantry advance – despite not being able to keep up with the charge - took portions of the Wood and by 8.45pm on the 14th July, men of the 2nd Queen's (Royal West Surrey) had reached and secured the north-east corner of the woods and were busy digging in. The cavalry men dismounted and took up holding positions along Wood Lane until reinforcements came.

Those reinforcements didn't come. But German reinforcements did arrive, courtesy of the Switch Line - a long defensive line that ran through the northern fringes of High Wood and allowed the German defenders to move troops along the battlefield with relative ease.

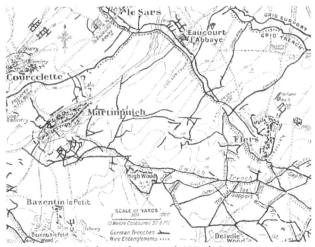

German defensive lines, High Wood, Somme 1916.

At midnight, the Germans launched a counter-attack that forced the British back. The order to retreat out of the woods was given at 3.30am. With High Wood, Wood Lane and Delville Wood to the south-east all still in German hands, the men of 91st, 98th and 100th Brigades who were lining up to the south of High Wood in readiness for another attack on the morning of 15th July were now under fire from three sides.

Precarious, to say the least.

To make matters worse, the 33rd Division was planning a big assault on the Switch Line in front of Martinpuich. However, to get there, the infantry would be strolling across *No Man's Land* in full view of High Wood. For this attack to be successful, High Wood had to be completely clear of the enemy. No pressure then.

After a short, sharp artillery bombardment, the first waves of the 91st Brigade set off for over open ground towards High Wood. Men from the 1st Queen's and 9th Highland Light Infantry (Glasgow Highlanders) had to pass over the bodies of their own comrades –

casualties of the previous night's fighting - as they made their way up the slope towards High Wood and the invisible Switch Line.

The Glasgow Highlanders suffered terribly. Their numbers were steadily whittled down by incessant machine-gun fire. They tried to rush forward in groups and then crawl forwards slowly individually. Nothing worked – only a handful of men survived. The Queen's fared slightly better, and their leading formations got within forty yards of the Switch Line before discovering that a waist-high belt of barbed wire had not been touched by the artillery bombardment and formed an impossible barrier. Meanwhile, more and more defenders were flooding into the Switch Line and pouring fire mercilessly onto the first line of the Queen's. The bodies were piling up. The second line of men was sent forward, but they met an identical fate. It was becoming a bloodbath.

Somehow, small pockets of Highlanders sneaked into the wood, but inside was no less confusing or dangerous. The Highlanders attempted to spread out and make an orderly advance, but they got less than thirty yards before running into the enemy, who greeted them cheerily with rifle fire and stick grenades. Private F. Middleton was on the receiving end.

> *We immediately took ground cover. George Cunning-*
> *ham on my left had a knee shattered. My other*
> *two buddies, Johnnie Aitken and Willie Walker were*
> *killed. Another lad close by dropped with a bullet*
> *through his stomach and was crying out in agony. It*
> *was only then that I realised we were in a clearing. A*
> *few yards to my left there was a shell hole, and another*
> *lad and myself managed to pull George Cunningham*
> *along to it. We were loosening his equipment when word*
> *was passed along to retire left out of the wood. We had to*

> *crawl on all fours for perhaps 100 to 150 yards amidst*
> *a hail of bullets. It took all our strength to do it.[1]*

The leading company of the 16th King's Royal Rifle Corps was sent up to try to help out, but as soon as they crossed the open glade they were hit with machine-gun fire. A second company was sent up after them at 10.30am, but they suffered a similar fate.

It was obvious to all involved that the attack on High Wood was going horribly wrong. And it got worse. A hastily arranged artillery bombardment on the fabled Switch Line was arranged for 11.45am after which, men of the 2nd Worcestershire Regiment would attack the woods' southern edge, following in the footsteps of the High-landers. But the bombardment fell short and only succeeded in hitting portions of the 1st Queen's who were desperately clinging on to their forward positions. To add insult to injury, the Germans let loose with an artillery barrage of their own, which really didn't help matters. Under increasing pressure and totally exhausted, the few survivors of the 1st Queen's were forced to fall back.

Throughout the afternoon there were repeated attempts to get close to the woods, but all failed and by early evening the combined efforts of 91st and 100th Brigades had bled dry to the tune of over 2,500 casualties. It was clear that High Wood would not succumb to infantry assaults anytime soon, so the clever chaps back at XV Corps HQ came up with an alternative cunning plan.

The order went out to completely evacuate High Wood and its immediate surrounding areas to prepare for the artillery boys to shatter it with shells.

Even before the evacuation was complete, Rawlinson had issued fresh new orders demanding that High Wood be completely captured the following day. Fortunately for the planners, the weather took a turn for the worse. Low cloud, mist and rain meant that registering artillery targets was nigh on impossible. Rawlinson was forced to delay the attack until 20th July.

The plan for this fresh attack was simple on paper. A forty-minute bombardment would start at 2.55am, followed by an infantry attack. The infantry in question was the 19th Brigade of 33rd Division. They would capture the whole of the wood and the Switch Line to a distance of 50 yards on either side of the wood. They would be assisted by 11th Field Company, Royal Engineers, and a Pioneer Company from 18th Middlesex Regiment to help consolidate positions and construct strong points. On their right flank, 7th Division's 20th Brigade would attack towards the eastern edge of the Wood, capturing Wood Lane as they went.

The bombardment was timed to lift at 3.35am to allow the infantry access to the woods. Advancing into the gloom, the initial stages of the attack went according to plan. The forward ranks of 19th Brigade found the southern areas of the wood practically empty of enemy and made steady progress. On their right-hand side, the 20th Brigade had made it to the Martinpuich-Longueval Road with little drama and was also making decent headway.

Then it all started to go horribly wrong.

Inside the woods, the Cameronians walked into a strong machine-gun position in the west corner of the wood. The ensuing fight alerted the defenders in the Switch Line, who also got in on the action. Meanwhile, as the men from 20th Brigade moved through the cornfields of the old cavalry charge, they walked right into hidden bands of enemy riflemen and machine gunners and enfilade machine-gun fire from the edges of High Wood itself.

Very few men got within 50 yards of Wood Lane. Those who did manage somehow to prevail found themselves isolated and were soon overrun. It was obvious that they would never make progress unless High Wood was captured, and those machine-guns silenced.

Although a significant portion of the woods had been cleared, there were still several enemy machine-gun posts that were causing havoc, and the casualties were piling high.

And then the Germans launched a counter-attack.

Charging with fixed bayonets from the direction of their strong point, they threatened to overwhelm what was left of the 19th Brigade's attacking force. They needed reinforcements, and they needed them quickly. Enter the 2nd Royal Welsh Fusiliers, led by Major Crawshay.

Crawshay and his men had been waiting impatiently for the nod to get going for hours, but he had received no news, no updates and, more importantly, no orders. By the time he was given the green light to move on up, the battle had been raging for over seven hours and he had lost almost a third of his men because of enemy artillery. Despite all that, he had his men get in position and by 2pm they were lined up opposite the woods, ready to go.

Through sheer determination and bloody-mindedness, they entered the woods and silenced the enemy strongpoint in the western corner. Once that nuisance had been silenced, they completed the capture of the wood. The whole thing was done within an hour. Major Crawshay instructed a signaller to send a message back to HQ with the good news. However, in his message, he clearly stated he would not be responsible for holding the wood. He had taken too many casualties, as had the rest of the 19th Brigade's battalions. There was no way the woods could be held and consolidated without an influx of fresh men.

Those reinforcements didn't arrive.

What did arrive, however, was another massive German artillery barrage followed by the obligatory infantry counterattack which saw them re-take the Switch Line and the western corner of the wood. The British were pushed back to the southern edges, meaning the middle of the wood effectively became a *No Man's Land* of sorts. What was left of the 19th Brigade desperately set about consolidating their positions, hoping for some kind of relief.

That relief finally arrived at 1am but it was too little too late. The Germans were back in control of High Wood.

Almost immediately, the Germans got busy on a new defensive position to the west of High Wood, in front of the Switch Line, known as the Intermediate Trench, which meant that taking control of the wood would now be harder than ever.

Another bid to capture High Wood was attempted during the night of 22nd/23rd July by two battalions of 154th Brigade, 51st (Highland) Division. A preliminary bombardment began at 7pm on 22nd which caused the Germans problems but one of the attacking battalions lost direction within the wood and became food and drink for the machine-guns while the other battalion was caught by machine-gun fire from the new Intermediate Trench system. By 3am, the attack was over with nothing to show for it apart from another 450 casualties.

As July gave way to August, German casualty figures were approaching five figures with the German 7th and 8th Divisions suffering 9,498 casualties (killed/wounded/missing) from 15th-27th July at High Wood. British numbers are more difficult to ascertain because of the heavy rotation of units, but they are most likely very similar.

Perhaps other tactics were needed to carry High Wood rather than repeated frontal infantry assaults?

54

— ⋅ —

'AT ALL COSTS!' DELVILLE WOOD

D espite the British throwing the kitchen sink at Longueval, the
Germans defenders not only clung on to remnants of the village, they managed to move in re-enforcements that became quite the
nuisance to the British attacking force. So much so, that Rawlinson
was forced to throw extra men into the fight in the shape of the 27th
Brigade, who had originally been pencilled into storm and occupy
Delville Wood.

At about 1pm on the 14th the message went out to the 1st South
African Brigade – they had now been chosen to attack Delville Wood
at 5pm.

Not surprisingly, that deadline was missed. It was nigh-on impossible to organise the men in such a short period of time, especially with
the unstable situation around Longueval. The attack was postponed
until 7pm but when that deadline came and went peacefully, Zero was
eventually scheduled in for early morning on 15th July. The orders for
South African Brigadier-General Henry Lukin were simple:

Take the wood at all costs – even if the village of Longueval had not
been fully captured.

Lukin sent three battalions of the 1st South African Brigade into the
firing line at Delville Wood. He planned to approach the woods from
the south-west on a single battalion front with the 2nd Battalion at the

sharp end, the 3rd Battalion in close support, and the 4th Battalion in reserve. The men moved into position from Montauban during the night, under the watchful command of Lieutenant-Colonel W.E.C. Tanner of 2nd Battalion.

At 6.15am the assault on the woods began with Private Hugh Mallet of 2nd Battalion, South African Regiment, right in the thick of it.

> *We arrived at the edge of the wood at about dawn,*
> *everybody on tenterhooks and just as the last man got*
> *in, old Fritz opened fire with big and little guns, rifle*
> *and machine-gun fire. What a time we had!^{1}*

The woods themselves were relatively small - barely covering a square mile - and initial progress was relatively smooth, if a little slow, due to the tangle of trees destroyed in the previous shelling of the area.

Despite the difficult nature of the ground, the South Africans met little resistance and captured the southern part of the wood with minimal fuss. Tanner sent a couple of companies out to secure the northern perimeter and by early afternoon all but a strongly held German position in the north-western corner of the wood (which adjoined Longueval) was in South African hands. Happy days.

It was all looking pretty good for Tanner and his Springboks, but their good fortune was about to run out. Rather than securing most of the woods, they were now in a trap. Their advance had actually created a bulge in the German lines, and they were now surrounded on three sides with only a slender safety route back to 26th Brigade in Longueval.

It was time to consolidate and dig in. All the men were equipped with spades, but digging in the woods was practically impossible with all the smashed tree trunks and thick roots. The South Africans had to do with shallow scrapes in the ground that would offer scant protection from the whirlwind that was about to hit them.

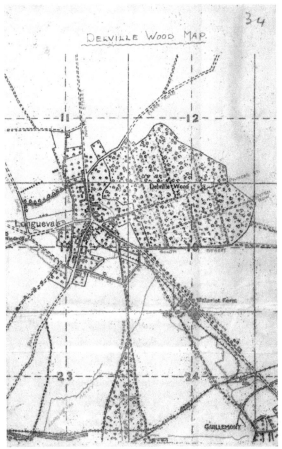

Delville Wood. From the War Diary of 63 Field Company RE (9th Div). The National Archives WO95/1754

What did hit the scrambling Springboks was not one, but three German counter attacks backed up by a ferocious artillery barrage that threatened to vaporise every living thing inside those woods. Lieutenant-Colonel Tanner was wounded during this episode, replaced by Lieutenant-Colonel Thackery.

The enemy counter-attacks were heroically dealt with. The South Africans were showing themselves as not just superhumanly tough, but they possessed more than enough field craft and marksmanship skills to hold their own – even in such a fiery crucible as Delville Wood.

More inspirational orders were received, which urged the men to not only hold on to their positions 'at all costs' but to press on towards the German garrison and push them out of the woods. Easier said than done, but eventually, during the early hours of the 18th the surviving South Africans not only repelled a significant German attack that at one point threatened to push them out of the woods entirely, but counter-attacked the enemy and succeeded in taking the northern edge of the woods that had thus far eluded them.

Happy days. Again.

Yet, it was a hollow victory. The German defenders had been ordered to retreat out of the woods to give their artillery the space and freedom to smash the woods with unprecedented severity. Which they duly did. It has been estimated that on the 18th July the German artillery threw 20,000 shells into Delville Woods, often reaching a rate of fire of around four hundred shells per minute.

To repeat: Four. Hundred. Shells. Per. Minute.

To save you reaching for your calculator, I can tell you that's around seven shells a second. Remember those shallow scrapes in the ground that the South Africans had struggled to dig out? Against this kind of next-level artillery barrage, they were practically useless. The result was unsurprising. It was utter carnage, as a desperate message sent by Lieutenant Owen Hubert de Burgh Thomas of 3rd Battalion clearly shows:

I am now the only officer left in A Coy. One Lewis Gun crew have been blown up. Can you send another crew? I have wounded men lying all along my front and have no stretchers left, and they are dying for want of treatment... Can you obtain stretcher bearers. Urgent. I consider the position is now untenable, and have had my breastworks all blown in... Most of the men are suffering from shell shock and I do not consider we are fit to hold the position in the event of an enemy attack.[2]

It was rapidly approaching crisis point – not only for the beleaguered South Africans inside the woods but also for the men of 3rd Division who were still scrapping for possession of Longueval. They had been kicked out of the village and this allowed fresh German troops to close in on the woods from all sides. From their point of view, it was only a matter of time before they were back in control of Delville Wood.

But no one seemed to have passed that memo onto the South Africans, who fought back fanatically, causing many a German casualty. The fighting was fluid, with no actual front-line. Pockets of men were committed to close quarter fighting and hand to hand combat. It was brutal. It was deadly. Eventually the Springboks were driven back to the southwestern edges of the woods, but, assisted by a group of Highlanders, they held firm.

By now, the men had been in the woods for four days under constant sniper attack and artillery bombardment. They were desperate for relief, but the truth was there just wasn't anyone to relieve them. The entire area surrounding the woods had been hammered with gas and high explosive artillery – smashing supply routes and keeping any hint of supporting troops well out of the way.

Back inside Delville Wood, the Germans sent a fresh detachment in order to kick the South Africans out once and for all. They failed to do so. Thackery's small band of men held on grimly to their positions, with the Colonel himself getting in the thick of the action, fighting hard with rifle and Mills bomb. After finally being relieved by the Norfolk Regiment on the 20th July, Lieutenant-Colonel Thackery marched out of Delville Wood with just two wounded officers and 140 other ranks.

Out of the 121 officers and 3 032 other ranks who formed the Brigade on 14th July in morning, only 29 officers and 751 other ranks were present at roll call when the unit was gathered some days after the battle. They had fought heroically against all odds and had most definitely held their position 'at all costs.'

The fighting for control of Delville Wood carried on for over a month with the British sending in units from seven different Divisions. It was eventually fully captured on 14th August but continued to be in the thick of the Somme front-line action until the middle of September.

55

— · —

GIDDY'S DELVILLE WOOD DIARY

W alter Giddy was born at Barkly East, Cape Province, South Africa, in 1895. He was the third son of Henry and Catherine Giddy and schooled at Dale's College in King Williamstown. He volunteered, together with friends, for overseas military service in 1915. He served in the 2nd S.A. Infantry Regiment and kept a small diary where he recorded his time at the front.

His diary was copied and transcribed by his younger sister, Kate. Below is an excerpt covering his time in Delville Wood. It has been copied here as it has been transcribed/written. To retain its authentic voice, it has not been edited.

> *14th July 1916*
> *News very good this morning. Our troops driving the Huns back, and the cavalry have just passed, they look so fine. The Bengal Lancers were among them, so I was told. We're under orders to shift at a moment notice. It rained heavily this morning. I hope it does not hamper the movements of the cavalry. If this move ends as successfully as it has begun, it will mean such a lot to the bringing of the war to an end. Our chaps are getting so tired of the mud and damp. There's such a change in*

the sunburnt faces of Egypt, and this inactivity makes one as weak as a rat. The cavalry have done excellent work, now it remains to us infantry to consolidate the positions. We're just ready to move forward...

15th/16th July 1916

We (South African Brigade) went into Delville Wood and drove the Huns out of it, and entrenched ourselves on the edge, losing many men, but we drove them off... Then snipers were knocking our fellows over wholesale while we were digging trenches, but our chaps kept them off. I got behind a tree, just with my right eye and shoulder showing, and blazed away.

We held the trench, and on the night of the 16th July they made a hot attack on our left, 16 of them breaking through, and a bombing party was called to go and bomb them out (I was one of the men picked). We got four and the rest of them cleared out. It rained all night, and we were ankle deep in mud, rifles covered with mud, try as we would, to keep them clean.

17th-20th July 1916

The Huns started shelling us, and it was just murder from then until 2 o'clock of the afternoon of the 18th, when we got the order to get out as best you can. I came out with Corporal Farrow, but how we managed it, goodness knows, men lying all over shattered to pieces, by shell fire, and the wood was raked by machine guns and rifle fire.

Major McLeod of the Scottish was splendid. I have

never seen a pluckier man, he tried his level best to get as many out as possible. We fall back to the valley below, and formed up again. I came on to camp and was ordered by the Doctor to remain here, having a slight attack of shell shock. I believe the 9th took the wood again, and were immediately relieved, but the lads are turning up again in camp, the few lucky ones. If it was not for a hole in my steel helmet, and a bruise on the tip, I would think it was an awful nightmare...The lads stuck it well, but the wood was absolutely flattened, no human being could live in it.

Major McLeod was wounded, and I gave him a hand to get out, but he would have I was to push on, as I would be killed. Many a silent prayer did I sent up, for strength to bring me through safely. I found a Sergeant of the 1st all of a shake, suffering from shell shock, so I took his arm and managed to get him to the dressing station. Just shaken hands with my old pal John Forbes. He is wounded in the arm and is off to Blighty. I quite envy him.

A sad day for S.A... They say we made a name for ourselves but at what a cost. All the 9th are resting on a hillside. Small parties of 25 to 40 men form the companies, which were 200 strong a short two weeks ago. We have taken back several miles...

21st July 1916
Had a bathe in the Somme, and a change of underwear, now lying on the green hillside listening to our Division band, a happy day for the lads that were lucky enough

to come through.

22ⁿᵈ July
General Lukin had us gathered round him and thanked us for the splendid way in which we fought in Delville and Bernafay Woods. He said we got orders to take and hold the woods, at all costs, and we did for four days and four nights, and when told to fall back on the trench, we did it in a soldier like way. He knew his boys would, and he was prouder of us now, than even before, if he possibly could be, as he always was proud of South Africans. All he regretted was the great loss of gallant comrades and thanked us from the bottom of his heart for what we had done.

Having survived the battle of Delville Wood, Lance Corporal Giddy was killed by shrapnel on the 12th April 1917 near Fampoux. He was 22 years old.

56

FROMELLES: THE WORST 24 HOURS IN AUSTRALIA'S ENTIRE HISTORY

An attack in and around the villages of Fleurbaix and Fromelles, some 50 miles north of Albert, had been mulled over by British GHQ for some time as a way of taking the German eye off the Somme sector. However, by mid-July, it was clear that the situation on the Somme was such that a diversion of this nature was no longer needed. Yet Lieutenant-General Sir Richard Haking (GOC XI Corps), the local commander of the area, was still keen to press ahead with the operation, despite no clear objective or plan.

The original idea was to put up a diversionary attack in the Fromelles region to stop the Germans from moving troops from this sector further south to re-enforce the Somme area. This attack would also be the first to involve the Australians on the Western Front. Their 5th Division had landed in France just days before and would be thrown in right at the deep end, assisted by the British 61st Division.

This attack would see the ANZAC and British attackers travel across a low, wet *No Man's Land* towards a strongly fortified salient nicknamed 'Sugar Loaf' due to its size and shape. Taking the Loaf would not be easy, and would need some clever tactics, perhaps a surprise attack under darkness using a small number of elite troops.

After careful consideration, the clever chaps of the Army High Command decided that a huge artillery bombardment, followed by a full-frontal mass infantry attack in broad daylight, would be the best way to go. The artillery bombardment would definitely smash the defenders to little pieces, and the infantry would be able to amble up the hill, cigars on the go, and take the positions.

Sound familiar? Unfortunately, it seems that the lessons of The Somme were not being fully heeded.

The attack was pencilled in for the afternoon of 19th July. On the eve of the battle, General H.E. Elliott, the senior Australian officer at Fromelles, asked British Staff Officer Major H.C.L. Howard how he thought the Aussies would get on, especially as it was becoming clear that the German defences were way more substantial than first thought. Howard replied bluntly:

> *If you put it to me like that Sir, I must answer you in the same way as a man to man. It is going to be a bloody holocaust.*[1]

For seven hours before zero, the German lines were shelled to bits. The German trench system in this part of the line was made up of breastworks (trenches built up from the ground using wood and sandbags) due to the high water table in the area. Entrances/exits to trenches were via 'Sally Ports' – rough doorways built into the trench walls. Not surprisingly, every local German machine-gun had each and every 'Sally Port' well within their sights and completely zeroed-in.

That seven hour artillery bombardment consisted of around 200,000 shells. That amount of hardware smashing into ground with a high water table meant that *No Man's Land* was quickly reduced to a muddy bog, devoid of cover – which would prove disastrous for the attacking infantry.

The whistles blew in the late afternoon of 19th July. On the British front, the initial results were mixed. Some elements of the 182nd Brigade got into the German front-line trench relatively easily, but uncut wire held up the advance to the enemy second line and German machine gunners enjoyed some easy work. This was an isolated 'success' as most of the British first wave barely managed to get over their own parapet before being shot up by shrapnel shells and machine-gun fire.

On the Australian front, the initial results showed some promise. The 15th (Victoria) Brigade attacked immediately next to the British and suffered badly at the hands of German machine-guns some 300 yards short of Sugar Loaf. Yet in the middle of the Australian battle front, the 14th (NSW) Brigade reached the enemy front line relatively unscathed and even took several prisoners.

Reinforcements, including ten machine-gun crews, were sent forward to help consolidate the position while others tried to advance further. The terrain was terrible: flat muddy fields devoid of any cover and littered with deep ditches full of water. They didn't stand a chance.

Later in the evening, the British asked the Australian 15th Brigade to join up with a renewed assault on the German lines at 9pm. At 8.20pm the attack was suddenly cancelled, and all men were ordered back to their own lines, but those men already in enemy positions were overwhelmed and suffered terribly.

After more high-level chin wagging, it was decided that 184th Brigade, which had already failed to get across *No Man's Land* once, was to attack Sugar Loaf overnight. After a short, sharp hurricane bombardment, the men got ready to go, but the enemy retaliated with an artillery bombardment of their own of such ferocity the attack was cancelled. The orders to stand down didn't reach part of the assault group – the 58th Australian Battalion attacked on their own. Unsurprisingly, they never made it through *No Man's Land*.

Meanwhile, the situation for the remnants of the 14th Australian Brigade that were still clinging on to their gains inside enemy territory was becoming desperate. Enemy artillery was hindering any thought of an orderly retirement. Despite all available men being thrown in to reinforce the position, a German counter-attack at 3.15am forced them back to the German first line.

By now, the Australian forces were split into two, each side becoming increasingly isolated and vulnerable to complete encirclement. The order to retreat at daybreak was given, however, by the time the retreat had begun; there were even more enemy machine-gun posts in position, inflicting devastating casualties on the retreating Australian troops.

It was not a pleasant introduction to battle for the Australians. After a little over twenty-four hours of fighting, they had suffered 5,513 casualties. The British had fared slightly better, nevertheless, 1,547 casualties were not insignificant. Not one inch of ground had been won. It was a complete disaster.

The Australian War Memorial describes the battle as "the worst 24 hours in Australia's entire history."

57

— • —

23RD JULY: AN ORGANISED ATTACK ON A BROAD FRONT. OR NOT.

B ack on the Somme, the recent progress around Delville Wood caused Rawlinson a bit of a tactical headache. The wood split the battlefield – to the left of the wood the British faced north, but to the right they faced east. This meant that any subsequent push towards the next set of objectives – Pozieres, High Wood, Longueval, and the German positions beyond – would see two attacking groups move further away from each other as they made progress. Which was not ideal.

On 16th July, Rawlinson brought his Corps Commanders together for a high-level strategy briefing to discuss this particular conundrum and announced to the group a distinct (and timely) change in strategic direction:

> *The time for isolated attacks had now finished and an*
> *organised attack on a broad front was now necessary.*[1]

Given the carnage that had beset the British army on the Somme since 1st July, this change in tack must have been music to the ears of the senior commanders present. The continued insistence on narrow, independent attacks had exposed their men to concentrated enemy artillery and murderous flanking machine-gun fire time and time again – with obvious consequences.

All was rosy then, in the Fourth Army garden. A new plan, a new strategy. A new hope. Alas, there were still one or two (or three) tiny little 'challenges' to overcome before the party poppers could be released...

First off, Rawlinson told his commanders they had just 24 hours to sort out this new offensive plan and get it going because he wanted to hit the Hun on 17th July. He later backed down and gave them an extra day, but even so, 48 hours to develop and issue orders, organise the men, and draw up an appropriate artillery bombardment was hugely optimistic.

The weather wasn't helping. It was heavily overcast, which made artillery spotting next to impossible. Finally, there was the French. Rawlinson was keen to combine his attack with the French VI army, but any kind of attempt to co-ordinate dissolved into a comedy of errors and mis-timings. Initially, the French postponed their part of the attack because of the weather, thus the joint assault was moved to the 20th. Even with this delay, the British were not ready and, on the 19th, had to admit to the French that their preparations would not be finished until the 22nd.

Fed up with waiting for the British, the French went ahead with an attack on the 20th anyway, but this failed dismally. Foch then suggested a renewed joint assault should be tried on the 23rd. Rawlinson agreed, but shortly afterwards the French admitted they would not be ready again until the 24th. This time it was the British who lost patience, announcing they would go Over the Top, with or without the French, on the 23rd as planned. Eventually, the French agreed to a small contingent being ready to help out on the British right flank.

I hope you followed all of that.

Final orders were issued by Rawlinson on 21st. It would be a substantial night attack carried out on a six Divisional front with 1st Division on the left flank, then 19th, 51st, 5th, 3rd and finally 30th Division taking up position on the right flank. The main thrust of the attack would kick off at 1.30am on 23rd. Apart from the group of British and French attacking together on the far right of the attack, who launched their attack at 3.40am – some two hours and ten minutes later.

What could possibly go wrong? Quite a lot, as it happens...

The preliminary bombardment was due to start at 7pm on 22nd July, but before the guns got into action, there were a couple of 'interesting' developments that considerably darkened Rawlinson's mood.

Alarmingly, aerial spotters had discovered a brand-new German trench that ran right across the line of advance for both 19th and 51st Divisions, on the western flank of High Wood. To counter this piece of unwelcome news, Rawlinson decided that these two Divisions should deal with this new trench first – attacking it at 12.30am – before moving on to their main objective at 1.30am – a local 'Switch Line' - an important communication trench which ran parallel to the front line and enabled the German army to move men and resources quickly to and from different sectors of the battlefield.

Then there was the French. Again. They had now decided that they would not be ready until the 24th so had pulled out of the show altogether. All things considered; this was not a major blow – the French contingent was only a small fraction of the overall assaulting group. – so Rawlinson kept to his original plan and went ahead without French help. Yet he didn't change the Zero time for 3rd and 30th Divisions who were pencilled into attack later at 3.40am but only because of their link up with the French.

As a result of all this time-foolery, only 1st and 50th Divisions would attack at the original Zero hour of 1.30am. 19th and 51st Divisions were to go forward at 12.30am and 3rd and 30th Divisions still had their alarms set for 3.40am.

The fragmentation of start times didn't stop there. 5th Division also discovered a shiny new enemy trench line in the way of their advance towards their section of the Switch Line to the east of High Wood. Divisional leaders took it upon themselves to move their attack time forward to allow them to take care of the new obstacle in their way. But not at 12.30am as per 19th and 51st Divisions who found themselves in the same predicament on the other side of High Wood. No, the boys from 5th Division decided it would be better to attack at 10pm the night before. But only their left-hand brigade would do this. The right side of their attacking front would set their clocks in accordance with the Divisions on their right flank (3rd and 30th) which was 3.40am.

Then, on the left side of the whole attack, 1st Division conferred with the Australians of the Reserve Army who were attacking Pozieres at 12.30am. As 1st Division's advance would see them skirt the right-hand edge of the village, they moved the timing of their attack to match that of the Australians.

In summary, not one single Division of Rawlinson's Fourth Army attack was adhering to his original start time of the assault. Actually, that isn't true. No one had told the men of the 51st Division about the new German Trench in their sector of *No Man's Land* and no one had bothered to tell them about the new Zero hour of 12.30am. So, they would go over the top at 1.30am as originally planned, but against a surprise objective they knew nothing about and with no support on either side.

Rawlinson's concerted and co-ordinated attack had disintegrated into four disparate strikes with Zero spread over five hours. Those early attacks would alert and prepare the German defenders for the subsequent fights no doubt – but Rawlinson continued on.

The crazy timings weren't the only defects in Rawlinson's plan. He had given his artillerymen a complicated and challenging task regarding supporting the attack. The Switch Line and the two new trench lines were all situated on reverse slopes out of sight of the guns.

The gunners therefore relied on aerial observation to ensure accurate shelling, but the weather in the run up to the attack was rainy and overcast, making this task very difficult. Then there was the actual timing of the bombardment. Starting at 7pm the night before gave them only a few hours of daylight – which was simply not enough time for them to make any kind of impact.

As a result, when the left-hand brigade of the 5th Division went 'Over the Bags' at 10pm, the German defenders were ready and waiting and only a handful of men got anywhere near the enemy trenches. By 2am, those men who had survived were back inside their own lines.

Next up were the 1st and 19th Divisions who were due to set about the enemy at 12.30am. However, the enemy were by now on high alert and even as the men were assembling at their jumping-off positions, they were treated to a torrent of artillery and machine-gun fire. The enemy fire was so intense they simply couldn't mount the attack and were forced to fall back. They tried again at 1.30am but suffered a similar fate. On their right, the 19th Division fared no better.

An hour later, the 51st Division attacked to the west of High Wood, blissfully ignorant of the presence of the new German trench. They got hit hard, not only from this new position, but also from the woods itself. The 51st Division achieved nothing except to add to the casualty tally of the attack so far.

Five hours and 40 minutes after the first whistles blew, the last act of this bizarre attack got under way on the right flank. Around Longueval and Delville Wood, the men of 3rd Division were not organised properly, they had hardly any map reading equipment and, as a result, quickly became lost and isolated. The German defenders had a simple time of it, picking off small groups of attackers, stumbling along blindly in the dim pre-dawn light. That particular attack ground to a halt quickly, with not a single yard of ground gained.

On the very right of the attack, the 30th Division had some initial success, but it was short-lived. The objective here was the village of Guillemont and in this sector the British artillery had decent positions with good views of the enemy lines, which meant they were much better equipped to smash seven bells out of them. Which they duly did.

However, the German defenders in this area switched up their tactics slightly. Instead of housing their machine-gunners in the trench system at the mercy of the British guns, they repositioned them well away from the danger zone in shell holes. This meant it was significantly more difficult for the British artillery to find and destroy them, unless they systematically smashed every inch of ground – which they had neither the time nor the ammunition to do so.

It was a clever piece of thinking from the German side. When Guillemont was attacked, the British made decent initial progress, penetrating a good way inside the village. Then the Germans hit them from three sides with machine-gun fire. Suddenly, it wasn't quite so rosy for the attackers.

> *We attacked before dawn, I being told off to carry a coil of barbed wire on a stake. We had 1,000 yards to go over the open. I soon dropped the barbed wire and lost the spade off my back – the Germans were waiting for us![2]*

> *Private Albert Andrews, 19th Battalion, Manchester Regiment, 21st Brigade, 30th Division.*

The Germans were indeed waiting for them. The Manchester's were practically surrounded and cut off from their own lines by artillery and machine-guns and then hounded by relentless counter-attacks. It was impossible for them to hold on to the village and by the early afternoon those who could had returned to their original lines.

Rawlinson's attack had failed miserably. A calamitous array of start times had reduced his 'organised attack on a broad front' to another collection of random acts of warfare backed up by inadequate artillery support. And yet again, it was the ordinary soldier in the trenches that had to pay the price for such foolhardiness.

58

— · —

Pozières: ANZACS Attack

P ozières is an unremarkable village nestled either side of the infamous Roman road that runs from Albert to Bapaume. Sitting on the highest point of the Somme battlefield it was one of the key objectives for Haig's *Big Push* of 1st July and although the disaster of that day meant he got nowhere near it, the strategic importance of the village meant it was never far away from his thoughts.

On 11th July, Rawlinson and Haig met to discuss the planning of the coming dawn attack. During those conversations, Rawlinson expressed his concern regarding the serious German defensive positions in and around Pozières, which, in his opinion, threatened the continuation of the entire show. Haig obviously agreed and shortly afterwards got on the blower to General Gough to give him two pieces of 'good' news.

First, thanks to a slight reshuffle of Army boundaries, Pozières was now Gough's problem and second, he was to capture the village at the soonest opportunity.

To help, Haig allocated I ANZAC (Australian New Zealand Army Corps) comprising the 1st, 2nd and 4th Australian Divisions, to Gough's Reserve Army on 17th July.

For Gough and the ANZACs, it was time to get busy.

The Australian units in question had been in northern France for about three months following on from their exploits at Gallipoli. They were moved further south to the Somme sector in July and were rumoured to be part of the 'dawn raid' action before Haig pointed them at Pozières instead.

After a quick recce from 1st Divisional leader, Lieutenant-General Sir H.B. Walker, it was decided to attack the village from the south-west on a mile-wide front. A couple of key enemy positions were earmarked as primary objectives: Pozières Trench which ran in front of the south-west side of the village almost as an outer perimeter, and the two main trenches of the German Second Line in this sector – known as OG1 and OG2. These two lines ran practically parallel to each other and were almost perpendicular to the Albert-Bapaume road to the north of Pozières, continuing down the village's eastern side.

The attack would be carried out by three brigades; 1st Brigade (1st Division) would line up on the left flank and concentrate on capturing Pozières Trench, whereas 3rd Brigade would have a go at the OG lines. 2nd Brigade would be in reserve, ready to dive in wherever needed. On the night of 19th/20th July, the Australians made their way from Albert to take over the British positions in front of Pozières. This was easier said than done as the German artillery was especially active at that time, smashing the ground with an incessant bombardment that included copious amounts of gas shells.

Zero was pencilled in for the night of 20th July, but General Walker was not happy with the position his men had been given. He wanted more forward trenches dug to reduce the amount of *No Man's Land* his chaps had to cross. It was a sensible ask and Reserve Army HQ agreed to put back the attack 24 hours to accommodate the request. However, in exchange, they casually extended his objectives. Instead of just attacking Pozières Trench and OG1 / OG2, he was told he needed to push on towards the orchards in front of the village and then to the southern edge of the Albert-Bapaume Road to the southwest of the village.

Meanwhile, the artillery boys had been hard at it with their preliminary bombardment since 19th July – they had a set of structured targets and timetables they needed to follow in accordance with the objectives. But these objectives had now changed. As a result, the attack was again postponed, allowing for artillery modifications. The new Zero was now 12.30am on Sunday 23rd July.

In the last minutes before the whistles were readied, every gun from the batteries of four separate divisions hit Pozières and the surrounding area with everything they had. When the whistles blew, and the leading waves set off from their jumping-off positions, they had difficulties in recognising any kind of enemy position or trench – such was the ferocity of the bombardment.

On the left side of the advance, 1st Brigade met with little resistance and was quickly in possession of Pozières Trench. The following waves of men passed through and made their way on to further objectives, including the orchard. On the right side of the attack, things weren't so rosy, with events quickly descending into brutal hand to hand combat.

During the advance, the junction of Pozières Trench and OG1 became impassable due to machine-gun fire and bombs coming from a German strong point positioned elsewhere in OG1. Before the officers in situ could put together the relevant orders to take out the strong point, Private John Leak took matters into his own hands. He ran forward, bombing the position until he arrived at the scene and finished the job with his bayonet. By the time Lieutenant Monteath had followed him into the strong point, Leak was calmly wiping off blood from his bayonet with his felt hat.

For this little episode, Private Leak was awarded the Victoria Cross.

Despite Leak's heroics, it quickly became clear that without fresh supplies of bombs and manpower, Monteath would struggle to hold on to his position in OG1 for long. At 1.30am a relief was attempted but was held up by another strongpoint at the junction of OG1 and another communication trench named Munster Alley.

As dawn broke, more reinforcements were on their way to help. Among them were Lieutenant Arthur Blackburn, who had been sent forward with 50 men and two teams of bombers with orders to silence the strong point and finally secure OG1. He quickly proceeded to within 100 yards of the trench until he came across a barricade blocking the trench. Breaking it down, they bombed their way forward, pushing the Germans back. Beyond the barricade, the trench was so badly damaged by artillery fire it was practically non-existent, as such, any more forward movement was exposed to heavy enemy machine gun fire.

Blackburn, along with a group of four men, crawled forward to establish the source of the German machine-gun fire, but all four of the men were killed, so he returned to his detachment, organised some trench mortar support and had another go with a fresh set of men. Another four were killed by machine-gun fire.

He returned, spoke to the Commanding Officer and secured artillery support for another attempt at silencing the enemy machine guns. This time, Blackburn was able to push forward another 30 yards before being held up again, this time by German bombers. After a perilous survey of the situation, Blackburn established the Germans were holding a trench that ran at right angles to the one they were in. Blackburn then led his troops in the clearing of this trench and had another go at capturing the strong point - the source of the machine-gun fire - but lost another five men. Not wanting to lose any more men, he stayed where he was until relieved.

For his dogged determination and persistence, Lieutenant Arthur Blackburn won Australia's second Victoria Cross of the battle.

Meanwhile, back at HQ, Gough was getting reports that the Germans had all but fled the village itself, leaving only the odd sniper. As such, he ordered the artillery to stop firing on Pozières itself to the let the men investigate.

As those orders were being filtered through the correct channels, men of the 2nd Battalion (1st Division) were moving forward on their own volition to investigate a curious concrete structure on the western edge of the village by the side of the Roman road. It turned out to be a large, fortified observation and machine-gun post, which they managed to overrun and take three officers and twenty-three men captive in the process. The official name for this structure was *Panzerturm* (armoured turret) but the Aussies nicknamed it Gibraltar, which is easier to say.

By the end of the 23rd, the Australians had occupied the majority (but not all) of the village of Pozières but were struggling to make much progress on the right-hand side of the attack in OG1 and OG2. Gough urged his ANZACs to complete the possession of Pozières and drive forward to Mouquet Farm – cutting off Thiepval in the process and ordered two combined attacks for the night of 24/25 July – another assault on OG1 and OG2 at 2am followed by a final sweep of the village at 3.30am.

The move against the OG lines laboured again. The assaulting troops struggled to find their way in the dark, and only a small portion of the fighting men got where they needed to be. Despite this, they succeed in entering OG1 and then into OG2 before they were hit by an energetic German counter-attack. Meanwhile, back in the village, the Australian 8th Battalion completed the sweep up. Pozières was finally Australian.

News didn't filter through to German Command that they had lost Pozières until about 7am. The village was a critical part of their defensive structure and the order to retake at all costs was quickly issued. Several attempts were made to take it back immediately, but these were batted away pretty easily.

It was then decided that a more co-ordinated and organised counter-attack was needed, and to give the German decision makers time to chew over their options, they let loose their artillery.

The German barrage started off methodical and relentless, covering all areas of the Pozières battleground – especially the western approach which was re-named Dead Man's Road by the incumbent Aussies. On the 25th, the bombardment intensified to levels rarely seen on the Western Front. A rare lull in the fighting in other areas of the Somme meant the Germans could point rather a lot of guns at Pozières at that present time. Which they duly did. From the Australian point of view, they girded themselves as best they could against what they thought would be an inevitable counter-attack.

But the counter-attack never came. It was called off by General von Boehm at the last minute. He could not put together what he thought he needed for a winning push and had decided not to risk losing more men and materiel.

As the bombardment finally eased off, news came through that the Australian 1st Division was to be replaced in the line by the Australian 2nd Division. The Australian 1st Division had suffered 5,285 casualties on its first tour of Pozières. When the last of the survivors were relieved on 27th July, one observer said:

> *They looked like men who had been in Hell... drawn and haggard and so dazed that they appeared to be walking in a dream and their eyes looked glassy and starey.*[1]

The Australian 2nd Division had barely taken up their new positions before Gough was in their ear declaring the need for urgent and immediate action. The Divisional Commander, General Gordon Legge was pretty inexperienced and caved in to this pressure, proposing an attack on the night of 28th/29th July, even though he could not carry out two vital actions that would make any kind of attack much, much easier.

All the artillery action had created enormous dust clouds, making it impossible to see if the two large wire belts in front of OG1 and OG2 had been cut. Nor could he dig new jumping-off points closer to the objectives in time. All he could do was extend an existing trench slightly closer to OG1.

The fresh attack was a disaster. The Germans had detected the movement of men in the build up to the attack and were ready and waiting. Much of the wire was indeed still intact, and any kind of gain was swiftly dealt with by determined German defenders. The 2nd Division suffered 3,500 casualties.

British Army seniors were less than impressed. Haig noted in his diary for 29th July:

> *The attack by the 2nd Australian Division upon the enemy's position between Pozières and the windmill was not successful last night. From several reports I think the cause was due to want of thorough preparation.[2]*

He wasn't wrong, but to be fair to Legge, he hadn't been given enough time to undertake any kind of thorough preparation.

Legge was keen to have another go and at a conference on 29th July, orders were drawn up for the failed attack to be repeated during the night of 30/31st July. This time, Legge would be given some extra tactical help from British HQ. More thorough artillery planning, a Zero hour in the light, more shells would be fed to the guns and a brand-new system of jumping-off points and communication trenches were worked on.

In the end, the date of the attack had to be put back to 9.15pm on the 4th August to allow for the completion of all the pre-fight arrangements. At 6pm on 4th August, the preliminary bombardment started in earnest, following a pattern and rate of fire that had been used for the past few days, so as not to alert the enemy.

This careful planning and preparation delivered. When the 2nd Division went in, OG1 was captured with little fuss, and quick progress was also made towards OG2. Despite the usual navigational challenges, the attack was a resounding success, with both OG lines on the eastern stretch of Pozières Ridge falling into Australian hands. From their vantage point on top of the ridge, the Aussie victors could see deep into German-held territory. This got the German High Command very nervous indeed, and they quickly issued a familiar-sounding order.

Pozières Ridge must be recovered at all costs.

The inevitable retaliation came during the night of 5th August just as the 2nd Australian Division were being relieved by their 4th Division counterparts. The new Australian positions meant they could be shelled from all directions, including from Thiepval – and it seemed that every available gun was aiming at them that night.

The following day, an initial enemy surge towards the OG lines was met by Australian machine-gun fire and was forced to retreat slightly and dig in.

The bombardment continued, which made the process of relief a very tricky and dangerous one indeed. At 4am on the 7th August, the Germans launched their final attempt at recapturing the ridge – and they almost succeeded. On a 400-yard front, they quickly occupied the thinly held OG lines to the northeast of the village and advanced on Pozières itself.

It was at this moment that Lieutenant Albert Jacka, who had won the Victoria Cross at Gallipoli, emerged from a dugout and attacked the German line from the rear. This sparked a chain reaction of Australian fight-backs and very soon a vicious hand-to-hand struggle had erupted. As more Aussie support flooded into to the area, they eventually overpowered the enemy attackers. Any surviving German was taken prisoner.

By 2.30pm, the whole of the front line was reoccupied. The Germans made no more attempts to retake Pozières Ridge.

The 2nd Australian Division was completely removed from the front line by 7th August. It had been in the line for twelve days, had endured an almost continuous enemy bombardment during that time, and had suffered over 6,830 casualties.

In less than seven weeks in the fighting at Pozières and Mouquet Farm, three Australian divisions suffered 23,000 casualties. Of these, 6,800 men were killed. It was a loss comparable with the casualties sustained by the Australians over eight months at Gallipoli in 1915.

59

— • —

OHL: TROUBLE AT THE TOP

By mid July 1916, the pressure on General Falkenhayn and the German General Staff was really piling up. The continued bloody stalemate at Verdun was not going down too well at home and now, with the Allies making progress on the Somme, this part of the Western Front could collapse all together.

The situation on the Somme was so alarming, reinforcements had to be pulled in from Verdun and other fronts, but this influx of fresh manpower was causing organisational headaches all its own. The German Second Army was now in charge of over twenty Divisions and was struggling to cope.

Falkenhayn needed a new plan. Fast.

To fix matters on the Somme, he lifted *General der Artillerie* Max von Gallwitz from his current position at Verdun and moved him, along with his entire headquarters structure, to the Somme area where he was asked to take charge of all German operations south of the river. Gallwitz was a seasoned campaigner who had previously had success against the Russians in 1915 and followed that up in the same year with a significant role in smashing the Serbian army.

Gallwitz and his structure would be put under the temporary command of General von Below, even though Gallwitz was technically superior in rank. This was because of von Below's local knowledge and was part of standard Germany army policy to have all reinforcements report to the local commander.

It was a fine plan. At least on paper.

Unfortunately for Falkenhayn, paper plans are unable to account for egos and politics. And in this situation, there were some big egos and plenty of politics at play. Gallwitz basically refused to go along with the plan as soon as he found out he would be reporting to Below, telling Falkenhayn that unless he had the power to run his own show, he would rather stay where he was in Verdun.

By this time, Falkenhayn was desperate, so that very same evening he made a new plan. He would split his Second Army into two: First Army, commanded by von Below, would take charge of all operations and manpower north of the river Somme. Second Army, commanded by von Gallwitz, would operate in a similar fashion south of the river. Both armies would subsequently be placed inside the newly formed Army Group Gallwitz, with Gallwitz given ultimate operational control over this new Army Group and, hence, both armies.

Gallwitz was appeased, Falkenhayn was relieved, but, not surprisingly, von Below was livid. He saw this move as an affront to his leadership abilities and had to be talked out of resigning there and then.

Army Group Gallwitz was a bold, controversial decision and one that Falkenhayn badly needed to succeed. Putting egos aside, both von Below and von Gallwitz appreciated the fact that a shortage of manpower was the critical factor inhibiting success on the Somme.

The German army in this sector had taken such a pounding that all reinforcements were being immediately drafted in to plug gaps in the line. The need for local firefighting was such that there was no opportunity for any strategic operational thinking. The two leaders were also in agreement that they needed to take a more proactive stance on the Somme. Indeed, Below had recently suggested to Falkenhayn that they should seriously consider a large-scale attack of their own. It was rejected out of hand.

On 17th July, von Gallwitz met with Falkenhayn and presented his ideas for a major offensive targeting the right flank of the French Army, which he believed stood a chance of causing great stress to the French and would relieve some of the pressure on the Somme.

Falkenhayn listened but dismissed the idea, telling Gallwitz he should focus on holding on to the line instead of fancy ideas of pushing forward.

With the new command structure in place, it didn't take long for mis-communications, disputes, and difference of opinion to build up, and within days there were rows breaking out between senior commanders concerning all manner of items, including the deployment of reserves for a counter-attack at Pozières:

> *A very carefully planned counter-attack on Pozières to be conducted by 18th Reserve Division was scheduled for 25 July, but due to heavy British superiority it did not achieve its objectives. This caused General von Gallwitz, whose own Second Army also failed in an attack near Estrées, to issue an order to First Army that in future only places of tactical importance were to be recaptured. This order, not without reason, irritated General von Below.[1]*

Things went from bad to worse over the coming weeks and came to a head in mid-August amidst a particularly brutal French attack near Maurepas. The attack was so severe and casualties so devastating that von Below was forced to replace the 1st Bavarian Reserve Division even though they had only been in the front line for less than a week. When news of this filtered back to von Gallwitz, he was less than impressed and despatched a strong reprimand to von Below for sending in relief far too early. Below was livid (again) and once again had to be talked out of making a rash career decision.

It must have been obvious to Falkenhayn that his experiment on the Somme wasn't working. On 25th August, he issued orders stating that Army Group Gallwitz would cease to exist. It was a bitter blow personally to Falkenhayn and the rumour mill amongst the corridors of power at OHL went into overdrive. There were many critics of Falkenhayn's cautious and defensive strategies and there was growing frustration and disillusionment at some of his decisions, especially his unhealthy obsession with Verdun and now the likely defeat of the Second Army on the Somme. It was not looking great for the General once held in such high esteem.

The final act played out on 27th August when Romania declared war on Austria-Hungary. Senior German figures had been watching the Romanian situation closely for a long while, but Falkenhayn had convinced anyone who would listen (including the Kaiser) that there was no immediate risk and they (Germany) had several weeks at least in which to plan and execute a pre-emptive strike.

The Kaiser dismissed Falkenhayn that same day and appointed two national heroes in his place. *Generalfeldmarschall* von Hindenburg was appointed as Chief of the General Staff and *General* Ludendorff was appointed as First Quartermaster General.

In his diary for 29th August, Crown Prince Rupprecht noted the new appointments with much excitement:

At long last![2]

His sentiment was widely shared across the entire German military machine.

TENSION AT HOME: A BLIGHTY BACK AND FORTH

G ermany didn't have a monopoly on doom and gloom during the summer of 1916. By the end of July, several politicians and senior leaders back in London were also feeling decided uneasy about the whole Somme show.

Since the encouraging gains of the dawn attack, the fight seemed to have bogged down into a series of loosely connected bloodbaths that had resulted in little or no tactical or territorial gain.

Isolated battles such as Fromelles, Pozieres, Delville Wood and High Wood had resulted in eye watering casualty lists, but for what? The people at home needed something a bit more tangible than the 'we are helping to relieve pressure on Verdun' line, that was continually trotted out by the men at the top of the British military tree.

Despite not covering himself with glory at Gallipoli, a certain Winston Churchill was one of the more vocal critics of the current Western Front strategy and argued his case in a memo circulated within the War Cabinet.

The month that has passed has enabled the enemy to make whatever preparations behind his original lines he may think necessary. He is already defending a 500 mile front in France alone, and the construction of extra lines about 10 miles long to loop in the small sector now under attack is no appreciable strain on his labour or trench stores. He could quite easily by now have converted the whole countryside in front of our attack into successive lines of defence and fortified posts. What should we have done in the same time in similar circumstances?

Anything he has left undone in this respect is due only to his confidence. A very powerful hostile artillery has now been assembled against us and this will greatly aggravate the difficulties of further advance. Nor are we making for any point of strategic or political consequence. Verdun at least would be a trophy – to which sentiment on both sides has become mistakenly attached. But what are Péronne and Bapaume, even if we can take them?[1]

This kind of criticism riled Haig to no end, and he quickly responded in typical Haig fashion.

1. *Pressure on Verdun relieved. Not less than six enemy Divisions besides heavy guns have been withdrawn.*

2. *Success achieved by Russia last month would certainly have been stopped had enemy been free to transfer troops from here to the Eastern Theatre.*

3. *Proof given to the world that Allies are capable of making and maintaining a vigorous offensive and of driving enemy's best troops from the strongest positions has shaken faith of Germans, of their friends, of doubting neutrals in the invincibility*

*of Germany. Also impressed on the world, England's strength
and determination, and the fighting power of the British race.*

4. *We have inflicted very heavy losses on the enemy. In one month,
30 of his Divisions have been used up, as against 35 at Verdun
in 5 months! In another 6 weeks, the enemy should be hard put
to it to find men.*

5. *The maintenance of a steady offensive pressure will result
eventually in his complete overthrow.*

*Principle on which we should act. Maintain our offen-
sive. Our losses in July's fighting totalled about 120,000
more than they would have been, had we not attacked.
They cannot be regarded as sufficient to justify anxiety
as to our ability to continue the offensive. It is my intention:*

To maintain a steady pressure etc.

1. *To push my attack strongly whenever and wherever the state of
my preparations and the general situation make success sufficiently probable to justify me in doing so, but not otherwise.*

2. *To secure against counter-attacks each advantage gained and
prepare for each fresh advance.*

3. *Proceeding thus, I expect to be able to maintain the offensive
well into the autumn. It would not be justifiable to calculate on
the enemy's resistance being completely broken without another
campaign next year.*[2]

It was a robust retort, but deep-down even Haig was feeling a bit frustrated with recent progress on the Somme. He didn't like the way Rawlinson was going about things by insisting on lots of small-scale tactical battles. He didn't like the fact they were uncoordinated; he didn't like the fact they were poorly planned; he didn't like the fact they were not focussed, and he didn't like the fact there didn't seem to be much in the way of high-level strategic thinking to the whole episode.

In his mind, Rawlinson and his Fourth Army should be putting all their efforts into breaking down the German positions that threatened the extreme right flank where it joined with the French.

Over the next couple of days, Haig clarified that the only attacks he wanted to see from his Fourth Army were to be aimed squarely at Ginchy and Guillemont, situated just to the east of Trônes Wood.

61

GRINDING IT OUT AT GUILLEMONT

By the time Rawlinson had gathered his senior commanders to-gether on 31st July to discuss the next steps, the British had already tried – and failed - to capture the village of Guillemont twice.

The first attempt was made on 23rd July when men of the 19th Manchester Regiment and the 2nd Yorkshire Regiment attacked from Trônes Wood across a *No Man's Land* that was around a thousand yards wide and totally devoid of any cover. They were let down by poor artillery support and were forced to withdraw. Many casualties were suffered, especially from within the ranks of the Manchesters.

A second attempt was made during the night of 29th/30th July using a substantially larger body of men - including part of the French Sixth Army - the bulk of which would again attack across the same wide and exposed *No Man's Land*.

On the right flank, 89th Brigade (30th Division) was to advance on Falfemont Farm and the German second position to the south of Guillemont. The village itself was to be hit by 90th Brigade (30th Division) and to the north, Guillemont station and trenches to the north-west were to be attacked by the 5th Brigade of the 2nd Division.

Zero was pencilled in for 4.45am.

Initial progress was encouraging with men of the 2nd Royal Scots Fusiliers entering Guillemont from the south-west before moving northwards through the village to link up with the 18th Manchesters. Uncut wire around the station meant that the machine-gun nests located there were free to wreak havoc on much of the attack before the German defenders launched an energetic counter-attack. British artillery were powerless to help because of many Manchesters and Royal Scots Fusiliers being still inside the village – they were eventually surrounded and either taken prisoner or wiped out. Guillemont remained in German hands.

When approaching the planning for Act 3 at Guillemont, Rawlinson initially seemed to have taken on board Haig's demands. The enemy had fortified Guillemont to within an inch of its life, with multiple machine-gun nests providing a deadly welcome to any invading infantry, along with dozens of deep dugouts and tunnels that defied even the heaviest of heavy artillery.

Faced with this particular puzzle, all necessary arrangements were to be carried out to ensure the required level of artillery support was in place to be successful. But the reality was Rawlinson wasn't about to change his approach and he continued to oversee small-scale attacks at High Wood, and Delville Wood. At Guillemont, the attack was launched on 8th August, but yet again, the resources thrown at it were woefully inadequate.

Rawlinson called off the attack the following day to allow for more thorough preparations. Looking at his diary entry for the 8th August, it is pretty clear where he thought blame for yet another failure at the steps of Guillemont lie:

> *... failure was mainly due to the want of go and inferior training of the infantry.*[1]

Harsh. And in Haig's eyes, not particularly fair. He thought the blame lay not with the men on the ground, but with the plan they were being asked to follow. He insisted Rawlinson widen out his advance from the River Somme to High Wood in order to have a better chance of success and to meticulously plan every detail.

Haig was not the only senior Allied General to have concerns as to how the Fourth Army was going about its work. General Joffre was not particularly impressed either and proposed that the French army should be included in whatever plan Rawlinson cooked up.

Rawlinson seemed to have taken this advice to heart and got busy on an extended attack. Although the small scall skirmishes continued including one on 11th August with the French aimed at capturing the spur to the south of Guillemont. After some initial progress was made, neither French nor British troops could hold on to their gains in the face of yet another impressive German counter-attack.

Rawlinson's large-scale offensive was planned for 18th August, but things started to go wrong early. The commander of the French Sixth Army declared his men were too exhausted to commit to a large offensive and thus reduced French participation to just one division. As a result, the attack would be made by five divisions across a 12,000-yard attacking front from Intermediate Trench (High Wood) on the left down to Guillemont on the right.

The last time Rawlinson put his mind to an attack on this kind of scale, he was successful. However, there are some important comparisons to be had when looking back at the Dawn Attack of 14th July. That attack was across a front of just 6,000 yards and was made with four divisions. Using some basic presumptions, that equates to 1,500 yards per division compared to 5 divisions attacking across 12,000 yards (to save you grabbing your calculator, that's 2,400 yards per division – a 60% increase).

From an artillery point of view, the guns chucked over 491,000 shells in the run up to the 14th July. For this fresh attack they had just shy of 400,000 - that's fewer shells to cover twice the frontage. Plus, with German machine-gunners now not limiting themselves to front-line positions and taking up refuge in random shell holes all over the place, the artillery saturation required to nullify their threat had gone through the roof.

It doesn't take a genius to see where this is going...

The attack went in – from High Wood to Guillemont - at 2.45pm on 18th August. Results across the board were disappointing, but it wasn't for the want of trying or for trying new things.

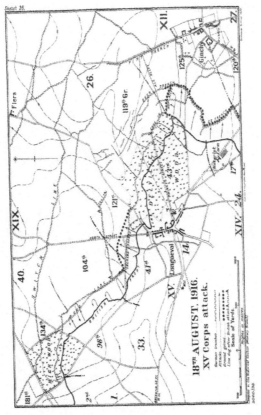

Battle dispositions on 18th August 1916. High Wood to Guillemont.

At High Wood, the attacking forces tried desperately to innovate their way to success. They manoeuvred huge flamethrowers up to the front line to wreak havoc on the enemy and engineered pipes full of explosives pushed deep under enemy territory, ready to blow the German positions to bits. Unfortunately, the pipes failed to explode, and the British artillery fell short of its targets but did manage to destroy both flame throwers before they could be brought into action.

Right in the thick of the action at High Wood was Private Arthur Russell and his Vickers machine-gun team. They were attached to the 4th King's Liverpool Regiment in their attack on Wood Lane Trench, which ran from High Wood down towards Longueval.

> *The infantry commenced to scramble over the parapets and our crews of Vickers machine gunners to move up the saps in No Man's Land. Almost the same moment the German front which for several hours had been uncannily quiet, broke into violent action with a great crash of artillery, trench mortars, field guns, howitzers and siege guns – everything they had. At the same time their trench garrisons let off into the ranks of the attacking British troops a blaze of rifle and machine gun fire, and a shower of stick bombs.*[2]

The attack on Wood Lane, and on High Wood itself, failed. It was a similar story up and down the attacking front, but yet again, the way it was organised didn't offer the greatest chance of success. Although everyone went over the top at the same time, they did so in isolated pockets with many battalions only sending forward a couple of companies of men at a time.

This meant that those that tried to get across *No Man's Land* were at risk of flanking fire from all angles as there was no co-ordinated attack on either side to keep the enemy busy. As there should have been in such a large-scale offensive.

There was a modicum of success to the north of Guillemont where 24th Division seemed to have caught the Germans by surprise and advanced the British line some 500 yards. But these gains, along with other small wins around Delville Wood, were the exceptions. Everywhere else – the Switch Line, the Intermediate Line, High Wood, Wood Lane, and Guillemont - remained in German hands.

The prize for the 24th Division – the only Division to make any kind of progress on this tortuous day – was to be chosen for yet another go at Guillemont village on 21st August. Unfortunately, yet again, the attack lacked the manpower and firepower to do any real damage. Despite everything that had been thrown at them over the last few weeks, the German defenders of Guillemont stood firm.

For Haig, these latest failures were simply not acceptable.

He was expecting at any moment the delivery of what he thought would be the game changer of the war – Tanks – and he was determined to throw them into battle in September. But to deploy them properly, he needed to straighten out the front line, and that meant capturing High Wood, Ginchy and Guillemont. To his mind, Rawlinson had been chasing failure after failure since mid-July and was getting nowhere with these vital objectives. On 24th August, he sent Rawlinson his strongest dressing down to date:

> *The only conclusion that can be drawn from the repeated failure of attacks on Guillemont is that something is wanting in the methods employed. The next attack must be thoroughly prepared for in accordance with the principles which have been successful in previous attacks, and which are, or should be, well known to commanders*

of all ranks. The attack must be a general one, engaging the enemy simultaneously along the whole front to be captured, and a sufficient force must be employed, in proper proportion to the extent of the front, to beat down all opposition. The necessary time for preparation must be allowed, but not a moment must be lost on carrying it out[3]

Harsh, again. But fair.

The weather then intervened. Steady rain meant no attack could be implemented, and this gave Rawlinson plenty of time to ponder over his current predicament and to plan his shiny new attack. However, a very large German shaped spanner was thrown into the works on 31st August when the 4th Bavarian and the 56th Infantry Divisions launched the mother of all counter-attacks across the Delville Wood salient, pushing the British back into what was left of the woods. In just two hours, the British had lost all the ground they had fought so hard for over the last two weeks.

Such inconveniences didn't stop Rawlinson. He continued to push ahead with preparations for his own attack, now pencilled in for 3rd September. It was going to be a grandiose affair, with five divisions attacking from Guillemont up to High Wood and another four Divisions from the Reserve Army going in from Pozières to the Ancre Valley. Besides that little lot, the French would also get in on the action, attacking north and south of the Somme river.

There could be no doubt there was a lot more manpower involved this time round plus there were some tactical changes: trenches were dug in *No Man's Land* to the northwest of Guillemont to give the attacking troops more of a chance to get to the flank of the village. Also, the problematic strong point to the southeast of the village – Falfemont Farm – would be attacked in a preliminary engagement.

The attack was to go in on 3rd September, with the preliminary charge at Falfemont Farm kicking off proceedings at 9am sharp.

That preliminary attack was an utter shambles. The artillery missed its target completely, and on seeing this, the French contingent refused to attack. Ignoring the lack of French help and the poor artillery shoot, the 2nd King's Own Scottish Borderers went over as planned. The results were predictably disastrous. The Borderers didn't stand a chance. All this attack did was to give the enemy advanced warning of what was to come.

All that being said, the main attack, especially around Guillemont, fared pretty well. The new trenches that were dug meant that the attacking forces approached the village from a different direction than the previous attempts, catching the German defenders off guard.

Also, all that previous hammering of the village had actually destroyed the vast majority of the underground bunkers and fortifications, meaning progress was a bit easier, especially as there were three full brigades of men swarming through. Success wasn't just limited to Guillemont; Falfemont Farm fell too. Altogether, the men in this area advanced 4,500 yards along a 2,000 yard front.

Nice work.

The news in other parts of the line was less favourable. To the north of Guillemont, the 7th Division had been given the job of capturing the village of Ginchy. Smaller in stature than Guillemont, but still highly fortified. The tactics used here were reminiscent of early attacks on Guillemont – and the results were the same. German machine-gunners ruled the battlefield, and the attack failed. As did the 1st Division's attempt to grab hold of High Wood.

Haig decided to make no further attempts to take High Wood until his new wonder weapons (Tanks) had arrived. Ginchy, however, was another matter. He was determined to claim victory here and sent in the 16th (Irish) Division to do the job. On 9th September the Irish captured the village in two hours. Assaulting directly from Guillemont (a new direction to what the defenders were used to) and benefiting from a very splendid creeping barrage seemed to do the trick. Ginchy was now Irish.

This success made an enormous difference to the state of the British line. The dog leg around Delville Wood had now been straightened out, which meant the German artillery and machine guns could no longer fire upon the British forces from three sides. Also, any further British attacks would now be in the same general direction (rather than moving away from each other with such a kink in the line) which made it much easier to give artillery support.

Haig was happier, and maybe Rawlinson had just dodged a bullet.

62

THE LAST VC: CSM GEORGE EVANS

William John George Evans (1876-1937) was born in Kensington and educated within various city schools during his childhood. Upon leaving education, he found work as a general labourer before signing up with the 1st Scots Guards on 5th March 1894. In late 1899, he moved out with his regiment to serve in the South African War where he served for six months in the Orange Free State, seeing action at Belmont and Modder River before returning to Britain in April 1900.

Once home, he was subsequently seconded to the Imperial Representative Corps, accompanying the Duke and Duchess of Cornwall and York (later King George V, and Queen Mary) on their tour of Australia during the Commonwealth Celebrations.

After this royal tour, he returned briefly to South Africa and then served as an instructor back in Britain, before leaving the Scots Guards in 1902 to join the police force, first in Derby, and then Manchester, where he married Clara Bates, a tobacconist's assistant from Derby on 21st September 1903 – they went on to have four children.

In 1910, George joined the National Society for the Prevention of Cruelty to Children (NSPCC) as an inspector in the Manchester region. Shortly after war broke out, he swapped his work with children for another stint with the rifle, enlisting with the 18th Manchester

Regiment as a Sergeant on 4th January 1915. Two months later, he was appointed Company Sergeant Major (B Coy).

After intensive training in Manchester, Grantham and Salisbury Plain, the Battalion left for France on 8th November. While he was away, his wife carried on his work with the NSPCC.

More training in France followed, before the Battalion was moved out to the Somme area in January 1916. 'B' Company's initial duties were to guard the village of Vaux by occupying a series of posts on the edge of a maze of tributaries of the River Somme. One of the most important fortified posts in the area was known as Knowles Point and on 27th February 'B' Company faced its first big test in the shape of a powerful enemy attack, which they repulsed using grenades and machine guns.

The battalion stayed in the Somme area throughout the spring and was very much a part of Haig's *Big Push*. On 1st July 'B' Coy were part of the assault on Montauban and all members of the Battalion were called upon to face up to a big German counter-attack that took place the following day and night. A week later, they were back in the fight at Trônes Wood, being ordered to rush the woods at around 3pm after earlier attacks had failed.

Two days later Evans and his 'B' Coy were ordered to follow the 17th Manchester's through the shattered wood to its eastern edge. They were met by a hurricane bombardment and copious amounts of machine-gun fire, and were forced to collect bullets from their dead comrades, but the advance was quickly called off because of the high volume of casualties. By the end of the day, there were only around 100 men left from the entire battalion.

After a brief rest and an influx of around 470 new faces to freshen up the battalion, they were ordered to move out to Mansel Copse to prepare for an attack on the village of Guillemont.

At 11pm on 29th July, the Battalion left their assembly trenches to start the three-mile march to Trônes Wood (captured a couple of days earlier) where they would start their advance on Guillemont. The Germans were actively shelling the area with both shrapnel and gas shells, forcing the men to march with gas masks on. It was a difficult march in the dead of night and many men were lost in the deep shell holes. They only just managed to get to their jumping-off positions in time for the 5am whistle.

Despite a heavy mist which made maintaining the correct direction tough, initial progress in the attack was positive with the men gaining an early entry to Guillemont and establishing themselves in the western suburbs of the village while they waited for the Royal Scots Fusiliers to link up with them as per instructions.

Very soon, however, the enemy retaliated with an impressive artillery barrage that was falling on and behind the men, effectively cutting them off from their own positions and meaning no reinforcements could get through to help them.

It was in this crucible that Company Sergeant Major Evans won his Victoria Cross by getting an important message back to British lines. This meant not only defying the German artillery barrage but also resisting the attention of enemy machine-gunners and riflemen who could track and cover his every move back across a *No Man's Land* that was devoid of protection. By the time Evans had the message in his hands, five men had already tried to deliver it. All five had been killed.

His citation was published in the London Gazette on 30th January, 1920:

> For most conspicuous bravery and devotion to duty during the attack at Guillemont on the 30th July 1916, when under heavy rifle and machine-gun fire he volunteered to take back an important message after 5 runners had been killed in attempting to do so. He had to cover about 700 yards, the whole of which was

under observation from the enemy. Company Sergeant Major Evans, however, succeeded in delivering the message and although wounded, re-joined his company although advised to go to the dressing station. The return journey to the company again meant a journey of 700 yards under severe rifle and machine-gun fire, but by dodging from shell-hole to shell-hole he was able to do so, and was taken prisoner some hours later. On previous occasions at Montauban and Trônes Wood this gallant warrant officer displayed great bravery and devotion to duty and has always been a splendid example to his men.

Despite his efforts, the men continued to be cut off and the survivors, including CSM Evans, were taken prisoner. During this Guillemont operation, the 18th Manchester's suffered 470 casualties (killed, wounded, missing and captured). Out of sixteen officers who took part in the battle, only one returned.

As a POW, Evans was held in various camps across Germany, where he was reputed to have lost six stones (38.1KG) in weight due to poor diet. He was finally exchanged via Holland on 6th June 1918 and stayed there until he was finally repatriated in mid-November.

Because of these delays, Evans was the last VC to be Gazetted for the First World War (30th January, 1920) and he didn't receive his award from King George V until 12th March the same year.

Once back home and settled, George resumed his work for the NSPCC before dying suddenly on 28th September 1937, aged 61. During his time with the Society, it is estimated he helped over 12,500 children.

In addition to the VC, Evans was awarded the Queen's South Africa Medal 1899-1902 with four clasps (Belmont, Modder River, Orange Free State, South Africa 1902), plus the 1914-15 Star, British

War Medal, Victory Medal, and the George VI Coronation Medal 1937. In 2002, his family loaned the medals to the Imperial War Museum, where they are on display in the Ashcroft Gallery.

63

— · —

SIT REP GERMANY: LURCHING FROM ONE CRISIS TO ANOTHER.

B ack within the German corridors of power, it hadn't taken *Field Marshal* von Hindenburg long to figure out the scope of the challenge that lay before him on the Western Front.

> *The situation on the Western Front was not lacking in food for thought. Verdun had not fallen into our hands and the hope that the strength of the French army would be worn down by the gigantic wall of fire which had been brought down on the north and northeast fronts of the fortress had not been realised. The prospect of our success for our offensive there had become ever more hopeless, but the operation had not been halted. On the Somme, the battle had now been raging for almost two months. There we lurched from one crisis to another. Our lines were permanently under the most extreme strain.[1]*

Both he and Ludendorff had three immediate challenges they needed to overcome sharpish: In no particular order, these were to figure out how to deal with Romania who had just thrown their hat into the ring on the side of the Allies; how to convince the *Kaiser* that the whole Verdun show needed to be called off once and for all; and the very real need to shore up the defences in the Somme sector of the Western Front, in terms of organisation and extra manpower and resources.

In early September, they travelled west to chair a critical high-level conference in Cambrai at the HQ of Army Group Prince Rupprecht. They summoned every Army Group leader and chief of staff to the conference and on 8th September, they all sat down to discuss the current situation and figure out the grand plan going forward. Everyone present was given their chance to air their feelings, share their ideas and recommendations and suggest what help was needed from OHL.

It was a tense affair, but in the end, most of the army leadership present went home more hopeful about the future. This hope was fuelled by the fact that both Hindenburg and Ludendorff patiently listened to all their challenges, ideas, and grievances, and gave assurances that the fighting at Verdun would be stopped soon.

There was also the small matter of raising eight new infantry divisions, five of which were to go to the Western Front, and over ten trainloads of ammunition were promised per day. There was also an urgent demand for more aircraft and balloons, which were promised just as soon as they were available.

A week after the conference, Ludendorff began to distribute an avalanche of orders, directives, and instructions to all field headquarters. It was a detailed level of direction that covered the use of ammunition, replacing equipment, placement of reserves, mine warfare, front line garrison organisation and air spotting for the artillery. It was in complete contrast to how Falkenhayn had run the show, but it was very necessary.

64

— · —

METAL MONSTERS: TANKS

I n among the Flanders fields of autumn 1914, the landscape hadn't yet succumbed to the merciless pounding of the guns, and farmers still harvested their crops and went about their normal business. It was, among other things, the sight of some of this agricultural machinery that got a few of the clever chaps from the BEF thinking. Wouldn't it be a great idea if they could have an armoured, motorised gun to support the infantry when things got a bit frantic in the field? It would be even better if the aforementioned armoured mobile gun could be loaded onto caterpillar tracks like some farm equipment, meaning easier movement across a wider variety of terrain.

A formal memorandum on 'special devices' was compiled in December 1914, in which such equipment was officially mentioned for the first time. Simultaneously, the Royal Navy was working on similar ideas. The naval minister, a certain Winston Churchill, having read the army report and being involved in the Navy ideas, put together a Technical Landship Committee (taken from the Navy's code-name for some of their ideas) in February 1915.

By June that year, the committee had formulated their technical want list. They demanded a land speed of 4mph, 'rapid' all round manoeuvrability, a range of twelve miles, and some big guns, all bolted to a caterpillar track. On the basis of seeing a wooden mock up in

September, Sir Douglas Haig, Commander-in-Chief of the BEF, was impressed enough to order forty and went off dreaming of these new machines ripping through the German defences with ease, scattering the enemy and destroying their positions. Prime Minister Lloyd George approved the project and production started in April 1916.

Imaginatively named after their coded transportation name of 'water tanks', the first batch of Mk I tanks entered service with the Heavy Section of the Machine Gun Corps, later to become the Tank Corps, in June 1916.

The tank was designed to overcome the problems faced by infantry in crossing trenches and barbed wire whilst under fire from machine guns. The vehicle had a crew of six, was armed with either two 6-pounder guns and machine guns (the male), or just machine guns (the female). The vehicle was armoured against rifle and machine-gun fire and operated on tracks that could cope with uneven ground, crush barbed wire, and could cross trenches.

However, conditions for the crew inside the vehicle, with an exposed engine and uncertain ventilation, were far from glamorous and the Mark I tanks were slow and mechanically unreliable. Yet, they offered significant mobile firepower; they had the capability to destroy strongpoints and could advance protected from virtually all enemy small arms fire.

British High Command thought the war was as good as won.

The day when the tank was to make its operational debut was pencilled in to be the 15th September, 1916. Tactics and strategy were mulled over for months and months. In the end, Haig, going against the advice of his field officers, decided to mass all 49 serviceable tanks in an attack on a limited objective during the Battle of Flers-Courcelette.

65

'AS STRONG AND AS VIOLENT AS POSSIBLE'. THE BATTLE OF FLERS-COURCELETTE

Haig had been mulling over a decisive mid- September battle since early August. He knew that by then the first batch of tanks would be delivered – it was just a matter of how best to deploy them for maximum effect.

On 16th August Haig told Rawlinson the good news – he would definitely get tank shaped presents for his next big charge - and three days later he was asked to submit his plans that, in Haig's mind, should be a sweeping attack on all three German lines that faced them, ultimately enabling his beloved cavalry to penetrate deep into the soft underbelly of German-held territory.

The trouble was, Rawlinson had until then never laid eyes on a tank and although he was intrigued about what these new wonder weapons could offer him, he didn't possess the childlike excitement of Haig. His demeanour didn't improve when he accompanied Haig, Gough, and other frightfully important senior officials to a showcase of tank manoeuvres where they saw first-hand some tanks crossing trenches, climbing parapets, and running over obstacles such as wire, ditches and trees.

Two out of the six tanks broke down and one officer was rendered unconscious whilst driving his metal charge because of the fumes inside the tank.

Rawlinson left the show thinking there was a definite use for tanks on the Western Front, but they should be used sparingly. This was clear in the plan he submitted to GHQ on the 29th August.

He had decided that trying to capture all three German defensive lines would be too much for one attack. Instead, he wanted to target a few strategic positions, such as the fortified villages of Flers and Martinpuich, which would then provide a springboard from which to consolidate the rest of the German line over the following 24 hours. There was no mention of the German third line, there was no mention of conquering a demoralised enemy and there was absolutely no mention of the cavalry.

Haig hated it. And he told his diary exactly what he thought.

> I studied Rawlinson's proposal for the September attack and for the use of the 'Tanks'. In my opinion he is not making enough of the situation and the deterioration of the Enemy's troops. I think we should make our attack as strong and as violent as possible and go as far as possible.[1]

Haig didn't just direct his disappointment at his diary. Oh no. He sent his Chief of Staff to Rawlinson's HQ with a similarly worded note and followed that up with a much more verbose memorandum which included detailed instructions including a strong desire for five divisions of Cavalry which were to cut through the enemy's gun line and rush on towards Bapaume.

Rawlinson eventually gave in and drew up a new plan – but not before holding a conference with his Corps Commanders where he told them that Haig was insistent that they should really go for it on this attack and that the cavalry boys should prepare to saddle up once more to push deep into enemy territory.

The outcome of the conference was a meatier and more expansive plan that boasted four primary objectives for the infantry: The first was the German front line, the second objective concerned the defensive systems covering the village of Flers. Third on the list was Flers village itself, along with the surrounding ground to the east and west of it. Finally, the fourth objective included the capture of a number of other villages in the immediate vicinity: Gueudecourt, Lesboeufs, and Morval. Liberating these areas would provide the ideal launchpad for the cavalry to do their thing.

The maximum depth of advance would be 5,000 yards. The infantry would move forward in four distinct stages over a 4.5 hour period. Then it would be the cavalry's turn to get in on the action – its objective being the high ground in front of Bapaume.

Recognising what was now being asked of the infantry, Rawlinson increased the divisional strength of the attack from six divisions to nine. The cavalry had been expanded too, and there were some special tactics saved for the tanks and the artillery.

Rawlinson planned to deploy the tanks in groups and pitch them against various enemy strong points. Importantly, he designed the creeping artillery barrage in such a way that it would not fire in the areas where the tanks would operate. In essence, he was specifying artillery free 'lanes' of about 100 yards wide, in which he wanted his tanks (and accompanying infantry) to operate.

It was an interesting tactical decision. The tanks were being pointed at known enemy strongpoints with no artillery support. Normally, these strongpoints were the primary targets for artillery, hoping they would be destroyed so they couldn't annihilate the infantry advance.

The tanks could not engage with any strongpoint until they were pretty close to it and travelling across the smashed battlefield at around

2mph, they could well be slower than the infantry they were meant to support. With Rawlinson's plan, there was a real probability that the infantry would be advancing on to these strong points in front of the tanks and with no artillery backup.

Haig loved the new plan.

The early tanks were slow, cumbersome, primitive machines that weighed 27-28 tonnes (depending on its configuration) and travelled at a walking pace over typical battlefield terrain. Even at such slow speed, these metal monsters required a great deal of effort to manoeuvre into position and an enormous amount of maintenance to keep them moving.

> *We moved off from our camp behind the lines at 5pm on the thirteenth. We went in a long procession and progress was slow, as corners take some time in manipulating. Troops rushed to the side of our route and stood, open-eyed, thousands swarmed round us and we seemed to cheer people up as we went. At about 8pm we got onto the main road. We covered about one and a half miles in eight hours. To add to the joy, it was pouring with rain. The number of trees I broke, motor lorries I damaged and ammunition wagons I jammed was high.[1]*

Zero was pencilled in for 6.20am on 15th September.

In Haig's mind, the most critical area of the attack was the right flank. Here, the 56th Division were tasked with providing a defensive flank against the village of Combles, which would allow both the 6th and Guards Divisions to concentrate on their tasks of capturing the villages of Moral, Lesboeufs and Gueudecourt. If these villages were not in British hands quickly, the cavalry could not be deployed.

56th Division failed in all of its objectives.

Two out of its three allotted tanks broke down before reaching their own lines. This meant that the enemy machine-gun posts that had been the intended target of the tanks – situated inside the artillery-free tank lanes were completely untroubled and enjoyed free-rein to cut down the advancing infantry. The troops near these tank lanes were devastated – losing up to 90% of their attacking force.

The neighbouring 6th Division faced the formidable German position called the Quadrilateral. In Rawlinson's plan, the heavy artillery was meant to smash this area to bits and neutralise the threat before three tanks would go forward in front of the main infantry rush to quell any lasting resistance. It was a sound plan on paper. But the artillery boys completely missed their target, and two tanks broke down far behind the British front line. The one tank left made its lonely journey forward and engaged the strong point with significant fire, but was forced to retire after the Germans used armour piercing rounds in retaliation.

By the time the 6th Divisional infantry launched their attack, their tank's role in the battle was already over. They were on their own. Not only did they have no tank support, they also had no artillery creeping barrage either. Some bright spark back at HQ had decided that the preliminary bombardment and the tank surprise would be enough, and no more shelling would be required on the German front line for the initial phase. This was less than useful for the men rushing across *No Man's Land* straight into a string of enemy machine-gunners who were completely un-touched.

The 6th Division attack was annihilated within ten minutes – taking 3,000 casualties. Even though the Guards Division somehow occupied 2,000 yards of enemy territory across a 1,500 yard front, Haig's cavalry dream was in tatters.

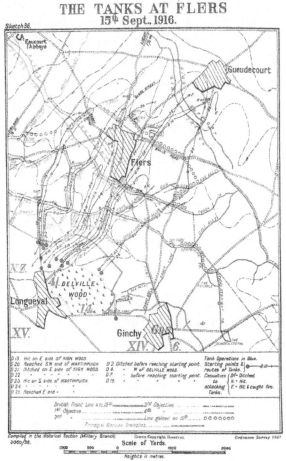

Tanks at Flers. 15th September 1916.

On the left-hand side of the attack, the aim was to afford the important right flank some defensive cover as it motored forward hand in hand and hoof to hoof with the cavalry. Ironically, in the face of the utter failure on the right, the men on the left had a much more successful time of it.

Here we find the 2nd Canadian Division from the Reserve Army positioned astride the Albert-Bapaume road with the 15th (Scottish) Division from Fourth Army on its right flank. On paper, they had a stern task ahead of them. The Canadians were to occupy the fortified village of Courcelette while the Scots were to knock over Martinpuich.

The Canadians had decided to deploy their tanks in a mopping up capacity only, leaving the infantry to lead the attack. This meant no special tank lanes and, more importantly, no artillery gaps in the line. They were also helped by the Germans, who launched their own attack just before Zero.

Not only did the Canadians deal with the attack effectively, it meant that the German front-line positions in and around Courcelette were jam-packed with would be attacking infantry – many of whom got badly caught up in the British preliminary bombardment.

As a result, the first Canadian waves met little resistance. By 7.30am the entire village was in Canadian hands with tentative patrols sneaking out beyond to see what was occurring.

At Martinpuich, the 15th (Scottish) Division enjoyed equal success. Here occurred a rare thing – the state and morale of the enemy troops actually matched the prediction of GHQ. They seemed to be caught by surprise, and didn't put up too much of a fight. Even though the attack went ahead with no tank support (they arrived too late to take part) the German garrison was happy to surrender. Over 700 prisoners were taken without too much fuss.

In the middle of overall attack were men from the 50th, 47th, 41st, New Zeland and 14th Divisions – they had the toughest gig on paper. First, they had to capture the formidable Switch Line, then the German second line along with the heavily fortified village of Flers, and then move onto the German third line around Gueudecourt.

On the right flank, the 14th Division suffered badly thanks to the same bunch of enemy machine-guns that wrought havoc amongst the Guards Division. Once they eventually located the Switch Line, they were forced to dig in and consolidate their positions despite being nowhere near the German Second line.

For both the 41st and New Zealand Divisions the effectiveness of their artillery barrages made the initial phase of the advance relatively straight forward. Which was a good thing, because only a fraction of the available tanks could advance any meaningful distance as *Leutenant* Oeller, commanding 1st Company, Infantry Regiment 14 witnessed:

> *About 6.45am the British moved to occupy trenches and pushed forward from the edge of Delville Wood astride the Longueval-Flers road. Our machine gun and rifle fire forced them one by one to jump back into the trenches. About 7am the British launched forward out of Delville Wood and along the low ground to the left of the Flers-Longueval road in four or five columns, each eighty men strong and ten paces between columns. The thrust was accompanied by three armoured vehicles, of which one ditched as it attempted to cross the road.[1]*

Despite not having a full complement of tanks, the Switch Line was captured within thirty minutes. The attack then made a bee-line for objective number two – a line of trenches just to the south of Flers. When approached, these were found to be practically deserted and were captured with little incident.

By 7.20am, forward detachments from both Divisions were bearing down on Flers. This was the opportunity for the remaining tanks to prove they were a weapon worthy of all the hype... There were still four machines operational within the 41st Divisional sector. They got into position and moved steadily towards Flers behind a creeping barrage.

By 8.30am they were on the outskirts of the village with the infantry in close support. Three machines fanned out to the left and right of the village, knocking out any remaining machine-gun nests they encountered. The fourth machine rumbled down the main high street and dealt with another machine gun post that was causing a nuisance.

The presence of the tanks at Flers really shook up the German defenders. Many of the defenders simply abandoned their positions, seeking the safety of the rear. This panic facilitated the capture of the entire village of Flers in pretty short order.

At this moment, the British and New Zealand attack was enjoying fantastic momentum. A good chunk of the German second line had been captured, and Gueudecourt wasn't too far away. Was this the moment Haig had been waiting for? That decisive breakthrough of the enemy lines with the infantry overwhelming a demoralised enemy as they rampaged onwards to a full and decisive victory?

Alas, no.

By mid-afternoon, all tanks had been put out of action. Casualties were piling up, and confusion abounded in the face of heavy German counter-attacks. At 4.30pm, the orders were given to dig in and consolidate the new positions.

The attack was over.

Back home, the British press had a field day with wild reports of masses of Germans soldiers running for their lives at the sight of these metal monsters, of them being squashed by the huge metal tracks (remember the top speed of these beauties) and general mass hysteria in the enemy ranks as the gallant and noble British Tommy rode atop his iron horse tearing an unstoppable march towards the German lines. Towards victory. Towards freedom.

Those men that were in the thick of it had a slightly different opinion. They generally agreed the tanks had been thrown in too early and poor deployment had meant the British had wasted a golden opportunity. Writing after the war, correspondent Philip Gibbs summed up this view nicely:

> *Individual tank crews commanded by gallant young officers and served by brave crews did astounding feats, and some of these men came back dazed and deaf and dumb after forty hours or more of fighting and manoeuvring within steel walls, intensely hot, filled with fumes of their engines, jolted and banged about over rough ground, and steering an uncertain course... But three had not been anything like enough tanks to achieve an annihilating surprise over the enemy as afterwards was attained in the first battle of Cambrai; and troops who had been buoyed up with the hope that at last the machine-gun evil was going to be scotched, were disillusioned and dejected when they saw tanks ditched behind the lines or nowhere in sight when once again they had to trudge forward under a flail of machine-gun bullets from earthwork redoubts. It was a failure in generalship to give away our secret before it could be made effective.*

Despite all this, the British High Command loved them and ordered more, and to be fair to the manufacturers, the subsequent versions were much improved. Yet throughout the rest of the war, partly due to design weaknesses and reliability issues, and partly because of poor tactics, the tank was reduced to being only a bit-part player in the Allied victory. Their subsequent reputation as the fire-breathing monster that dashed the enemy – a narrative perhaps evident more in Britain than anywhere else - was largely created by post-war writers and commentary, often with their own agenda.

66

---·---

A WANTON WASTE OF MEN. 47TH DIVISION AT HIGH WOOD

I n the centre of the overall Flers battle front, the 47th (London) Division were given the task of collecting up High Wood on their way to their ultimate objective of the Flers Line, which they were expected to occupy via a German Switch Line, which ran right behind the wood as they looked at it, and the Starfish line some 700 yards beyond that.

As part of Rawlinson's overall plan, they were given four tanks to help them carry High Wood, but after a reconnaissance of the ground with some of the tank commanders, Divisional big-wig, Major-General Barter reported up to HQ that the jagged tree-stumps of the woods would make it impossible for tanks to pass through. Barter was also less than impressed with the artillery plan for his part in the show. Because the British positions were so close to the wood, the artillery boys were instructed to leavethe German positions inside High Wood alone and target more distant positions instead.

Instead, he wanted to pull his men back a bit, to give the artillery space to smash ten-bells out of the woods. He would then send his tanks round the sides of High Wood to pinch the position while the infantry sneaked through the middle of the wood and over-run the beleaguered German defenders.

His ideas were rejected out of hand. The front line would stay where it was, the artillery would leave High Wood alone as planned, and he was to follow his orders regarding the tanks – they were to go through the wood.

The plan of attack had been meticulously worked out. The four tanks would set off early on pre-designated routes that had been timed for them to reach the German front line inside High Wood one minute before Zero. They were to create havoc and mayhem for three minutes and then move on to the Switch Line – reaching it at Zero plus 32 minutes or 6.52am.

But for the tank crews of 1916, trying to manoeuvre their behemoths quickly and correctly to their starting positions was a bit of a challenge. All four tanks lost their way, with at least one needing to call in at Battalion HQ to ask for directions. Consequently, they were very late, finally lumbering up to their starting positions at 6.20am – Zero hour. The should have been causing a nuisance in the German front line by that time, instead they were left behind as the first wave of infantry attempted to advance.

Without the tanks help and with no direct artillery support, the infantry were at the mercy of murderous German machine-gun and rifle fire as the tried to cross *No Man's Land* in front of High Wood. Wave after wave of attacks were thrown at the wood. Wave after wave of men were shot down.

By now, the four tanks had managed to get into High Wood, but they had all come to grief. One had ran into a rather stubborn tree stump and could venture on no further; another had broken the axle of its two-wheel steering 'tail' and became immobile; and another had veered so far off course it had ditched in a British front line trench on the south-eastern side of the the wood. Only one tank (Delilah) managed to get close to the German front line and was happily enfilading a support trench in the middle of the wood when it was hit by a shell and set on fire.

And so ended the tank's role at High Wood.

Further infantry attacks on the wood failed at the hands of merciless machine-gunners, until in the early afternoon the nod was given to the Trench Mortar battery of 140th Brigade to get busy. And busy they got, firing more than 750 rounds into the eastern part of High Wood in just fifteen minutes. Off the back of this bombardment, the remnants of two Civil Service Rifle companies re-attacked and soon afterwards Germans were moving *en masse* towards the British lines with their hands above their heads.

British bombing parties worked round the flanks and flushed out more prisoners. After more than two months of fighting, enemy resistance at High Wood was finally waning.

Attention now turned to the Starfish Line, some 700 yards beyond High Wood. Small pockets of men had managed to reach part of it while the Germans started to surrender, but there were insufficient in numbers to do anything other than survive and hold on.

At 3.30pm, orders were given for two fresh battalions – the 1st Surrey Rifles and the 24th Londons' – to get themselves ready for an attack on the Starfish Line. They moved up to their starting positions - the eastern side and north-western side of the wood respectively. Zero would be at 5.30pm

As they topped a crest in *No Man's Land* they came into full view of the enemy. Seconds later they were on the receiving end of a hurricane of artillery and machine-gun fire. Losses were catastrophic. Only 62 men from the Surrey Rifles got back unscathed from the 567 men who went into the attack. Yet, remarkably a small detachment managed to enter the Starfish Line and capture the strong hold.

The 24th Londons suffered similarly and were forced to dig in 200 yards from the enemy position. It was becoming a very costly day for the 47th London Division.

Ultimately, although High Wood and finally been captured, the 47th Division had failed in its objectives. The Division, exhausted and decimated, was relieved on 19th September. Divisional losses exceeded 4,500 officers and men. Rifleman Don Cree of 'C' Company, Post Office Rifles summed up the horror of High Wood perfectly:

> *We were a pitiful sight when we got back to safety and marshalled together. Our company was about two dozen strong, had no officers and only one sergeant.*
>
> *I will never forget High Wood[1].*

For his troubles, Major-General Barter was dismissed for a 'wanton waste of men' and sent back to Britain with his reputation in shreds.

67

---·---

BITE AND HOLD: THE BATTLE OF MORVAL

The evening of the 15th September saw Rawlinson very busy. He received battle reports from his ground commanders and, after coming to terms with the reality of the situation, penned and issued fresh new orders for the coming day.

He was demanding another full-scale attack to be launched immediately with the goal – yes, you guessed it – of enabling the cavalry to gallop through massive ruptures in the German line so they can put the kettle on for him in Bapaume by evensong.

His orders were ambitious, repetitive, and yet again unrealistic. The infantry divisions still in the line were simply in no fit state to carry out his wants. Instead of a decisive, thrusting attack, what followed were sporadic, small-scale token-gestures that were fully reminiscent of what followed the attack of 14th July. With the same results:

No territorial or strategic gains. Lots of dead and wounded.

Mercifully, the weather was now becoming decidedly autumnal, and even Rawlinson agreed nothing major could be launched any time soon. And anyway, Haig had bigger ideas.

Haig wanted Rawlinson's 4th Army, situated south of the Albert-Bapaume Road to work hand-in-hand with Gough's Reserve Army to the north of the road for a large co-ordinated attack from Thiepval in the north to Maurepas in the south. The French would

also be involved in the show which would have big prizes in its sights
– namely the village of Thiepval and the ridge it sat proudly upon in
the north and the original German third line (now the new front line)
from Martinpuich to Combles to the south of the Roman road.

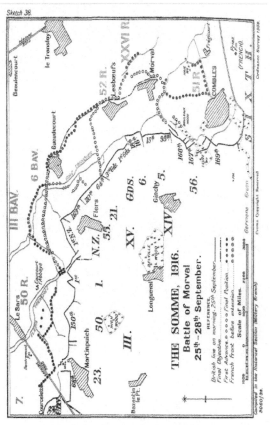

The Battle of Morval. September 1916

Weather problems and trying to co-ordinate the attack with the
French meant the offensive was delayed until 25th September. The
French insisted the attack took place during the afternoon, which

annoyed Gough, as he had planned to use tanks as part of his attack on Thiepval. Attacking in broad daylight would turn his tanks into sitting ducks for the enemy artillery, so he postponed his part of the attack until the following day so he can move his tanks up during the murky mists of the morning.

So much for a large co-ordinated attack on all fronts.

South of the Roman road, the plan was still to go ahead on the 25th. Rawlinson had ten infantry divisions at his disposal, and in a change to previous strategy, he concentrated them on capturing the German third line and the German third line only.

This was still going to be a significant ask for the men; the fortified villages of Morval, Gueudecourt and Lesboeufs were going to be tricky to nullify, plus there was still the small matter of the Quadrilateral strong point to contend with. There was scant mention of cavalry, with the advance limited to just 1,200 – 1,500 yards. This was going to be a classic 'Bite and Hold' advance of limited depth.

This small but meaningful change in approach meant that the supporting artillery could concentrate all its might on the actual infantry targets. It also meant that the infantry boys would not advance beyond the protective range of the big guns. These were two enormous advantages.

The artillery bombardment started on 24th September and over the following thirty-six hours, about 400,000 shells were thrown into 18,000 yards of enemy trench line. The enemy positions that were in the line of fire were much more rudimentary than their previous defensive positions had been, and because of the poor weather, there had been little opportunity to improve and reinforce them.

The shelling caused havoc. Also, the counter battery fire for this advance was one of the most effective of the Somme battles, knocking out 24 from 124 heavy batteries in the area.

After the big guns had done their worst, the plan was for the infantry to advance, hot on the coat-tails of a creeping barrage. The tanks were to follow behind to capture any enemy strong points that were still operating. This meant there was no need for those crazy tank lanes with no artillery support.

Zero was at 12.35pm. The main assault on the fortified villages of Morval and Lesboeufs would be taken on by men from the 5th, 6th and Guards Divisions. At the pointy end of the 5th Divisions advance on Morval were the 1st Battalion, Norfolk Regiment – they were led into battle by their Commanding Officer - Lieutenant Colonel P.V.P Stone – who treated the whole show like a glorified pheasant shoot. Regardless, backed up decent artillery coverage, his men took their first objective with relative ease:

> *Our artillery barrage was excellent and we advanced with it, practically in it, and got to the objective at the very second it lifted... The Germans had got out of their trenches and were largely in shell-holes, a few in front (who were killed as we went up), the majority were in rear of the trench. Germans were killed in the shelters and in the trench, and at first, some as they attempted to come forward from the shell-holes – the remainder surrendered (about 150).[1]*

To the immediate left of the Lieutenant Colonel and his merry band of Norfolks, the situation presented to the Guards Division at Lesboeufs was slightly different. Here, the artillery struggled to cut the copious amounts of enemy wire that hid in sunken roads and within crop filled fields, especially on the right side of the Guards attacking front. Guardsmen from 2nd Grenadier Guards were forced to risk everything by going out into *No Man's Land* under a hailstorm of machine-gun fire to cut it manually. The writeup in their war diary was slightly less positive towards the artillery boys...

> *... the co-operation of the Artillery was remarkable for its absence and a great deal of ammunition was use-lessly expended on ground where no Germans were, and places where Germans could be seen were left un-touched.*[2]

Harsh. But seeing as they lost scores of men, including all but one of their officers trying to cut through enemy wire, one can understand the sentiment.

Ironically, the battalion on the immediate left of the Grenadiers found their wire completely cut to pieces and had no problem making their advance. Overall, the Guards Division captured Lesboeufs and secured all their objectives on time – but their gains were expensive, with 1,900 casualties.

By late afternoon, the fortress villages of Morval and Lesboeufs had fallen. Gueudecourt was on the brink of capture (it would eventually fall the next day) and the important German transportation hub of Combles was isolated.

Not a bad day's work.

The bite and hold strategy of limited objectives over a narrow front, back up by copious amounts of artillery, had proved successful. This was very much an artillery and infantry show, with decent support from the RFC to help the artillery zone in on key targets. The tanks hardly made any real impact, and the cavalry never made it out of their stables.

In Somme terms, the advance of 25th September had been a re-sounding success. Now, it was time for Gough and his Reserve Army to replicate this achievement at Thiepval.

68

— · —

Back at Thiepval: 26th September

For the beleaguered German defenders of the shattered village of Thiepval, the writing had been on the wall for a while. The nearby villages of Ovillers, Pozieres, and Courcelette had all fallen since mid-July and the Allied war machine was relentlessly inching ever closer to this most coveted of villages.

On 23rd September, the British artillery guns (570 field guns and 270 howitzers spread across a 6,000 yard frontage) turned their full attention upon Thiepval for what was to be three days of uninterrupted shelling.

Yet the advance planned by Gough was fraught with danger. The ultimate objectives for the advance (Stuff and Regina Trenches) were on a reverse slope, out of sight of British observation, but before they got there, the attacking infantry would have to deal with no less than five formidable defences. In no particular order, these were Mouquet Farm – nothing more than a pile of brick dust, but home to three groups of underground cellars connected by a series of tunnels.

Thiepval village posed a similar puzzle, but on a slightly grander scale – British intelligence estimated there to be 144 underground cellars and dug outs deep beneath the rubble – any one of them capable of hiding an entire machine-gun team.

Then there were three redoubts – Zollern, Stuff, and the mighty Schwaben. They were some 1,000 yards distant from the British positions, which meant whoever was manning the strongpoint would get ample warning of any incoming attack. And these places were the kings of deep dugouts and long tunnels – even if they got smashed to bits above ground, an entire garrison could emerge at a moment's notice from underground.

For Gough and his men, this was one tricky assignment.

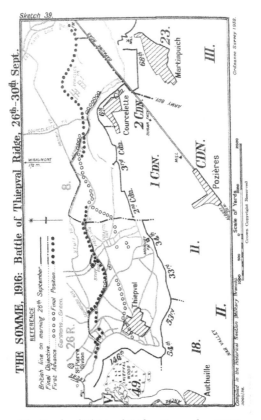

The Battle of Thiepval Ridge. September 1916

To cover the ground, Gough assembled four assault divisions. On the right of the attack would be the 1st and 2nd Canadian Divisions who would go after the Regina trench section. On their left would be 11th Division taking part in its first action since Sulva Bay back in 1915. They would tackle the tricky Mouquet Farm as well as Zollern and Stuff redoubts. The toughest gig was handed out to the 18th Division – they were tasked with silencing the Schwaben redoubt and taking the village of Thiepval – two positions that had taken a severe toll on many a British unit over the past few months.

On the extreme right of the attack, away from most of the strong German positions, the Canadians took their initial objectives with little ado, but they soon ran into significant resistance in the shape of enfilade fire from Mouquet Farm, Stuff and Zollern redoubts. Ultimately, Regina Trench stayed in German hands, despite repeated attempts to occupy it over several days.

To neutralise Mouquet Farm, a special bombing party from the 9th Lancashire Fusiliers was sent forward just before Zero to locate and block all the underground exits before the main attack went in. As they were going about their business, they were attacked by a machine-gun located in the rubble towards the north end of the farm and could not complete their tasks.

By late afternoon, several enemy machine-gun teams had turned Mouquet Farm into something of a fortress and were causing chaos among the many British units trying to capture the position. Two tanks were thrown into the mix, but they ditched before they could get to the farm. However, enterprising Tommies dismantled the machine guns from the tanks and used them as covering fire while bombing parties darted forward, throwing bombs down all known dugout entrances. By 5.30pm, the defending garrison finally gave up the fight and surrendered.

Meanwhile, more units from 11th Division were trying their hand at capturing Zollern and Stuff Redoubts. Zollern was around 750 yards from the British lines, but divisional intelligence was convinced the whole strongpoint had been obliterated by artillery. It did not take long for the infantry to figure out this was not the case. Enemy machine guns were alert and opened up a withering fire the moment they emerged from their trenches.

It was an impossible day for the would-be attackers. The battlefield in front of the redoubt became a dead zone – anything and anyone that moved was quickly hunted by machine-gun fire. By nightfall, just one officer and fifty-nine men had reached the southern perimeter of the redoubt, but they could do nothing but cling on to their position and hope to survive.

A fresh attack was prepared for the following day, but it was not needed. The Zollern was evacuated during the night.

500 yards beyond the Zollern position was Stuff Redoubt. It was still in German hands after the first day of fighting. Indeed, the closest British troops were those sixty men desperately hanging on to the edge of Zollern Redoubt. Once it was understood that Zollern was empty, it became the natural point from which to launch an attack on Stuff Redoubt. Such an attack was duly launched in the afternoon of the 27th, but despite bitter hand-to-hand fighting, Stuff Redoubt remained in German hands.

While this was all going on, men of the 18th Division were closing in on Thiepval itself. On the eastern top of the village, assaulting groups of men from the 10th Essex made decent progress. Following closely behind the creeping barrage, they found most defensive positions had been knocked out by the artillery. They could set about consolidating their positions quickly and had suffered negligible casualties.

The same could not be said for the other two attacking battalions - the 12th Middlesex and 11th Royal Fusiliers.

For these units, the attack got off to an ugly start. Progress was so slow the creeping barrage seemed to race off into the distance, leaving the men to clear numerous trenches, dug-outs, and tunnels without adequate artillery protection. The fighting quickly descended into violent hand-to-hand combat as the men inched their way to the centre of the village. As they approached the ruins of the Château, the men were hit by terrible machine-gun fire coming from the Château area itself. If it weren't for the timely appearance of a tank that dealt with the pesky machine gunner, the whole advance could have quite possibly dissolved there and then.

Despite having possession of the Château, progress was painfully slow and casualties mounted up quickly, courtesy of numerous snipers hiding out amongst the ruins. During this action, two members of the 12th Middlesex would win the Victoria Cross for their bravery in Thiepval – Private F.J. Edwards and Private R. Ryder, but their gallantry was not enough. By mid-afternoon, the advance had ground to a halt and the leading battalions were in real danger of being completely wiped out. They needed reinforcements, fast.

The reserve battalion had already been ordered forward by this time, but they had come under massive artillery bombardment as soon as they ventured out of their own positions. Only one company of men got into the village to help, but it was not enough to mount a fresh attack. The order instead was given to consolidate the captured ground in preparation to go again the next day. Thiepval simply had to be taken, otherwise it would be impossible to launch an attack on the Division's final objective – Schwaben Redoubt.

It turned out that the only group of men in position to finish the job at Thiepval were C Company, 7th Bedfordshire Regiment. So, they were ordered to capture the rest of the village. Led by 2nd Lieutenant Tom Adlam, the men from C Company lined up at 5.30am and charged across the open road, sweeping into the northern section of Thiepval despite heavy machine gun and rifle fire. Each shell hole, trench and building (or its remains) had to be taken individually with either bomb or bayonet. Hidden machine-gun nests were charged and overcame one by one.

Writing in the regimental war diary, Captain L.H. Keys describes the scene:

> *2nd Lt. Adlam... went across the open under extremely heavy rifle and machine-gun fire from shell hole to shell hole and organised an assaulting party... He collected a large quantity of German bombs and placing himself at the head of his party, commenced a whirlwind attack on the strong point. He personally out threw the enemy despite the fact they were using only egg bombs, and by the resolution and furiousness of his attack forced the enemy... (back). Realising this, 2nd Lt. Adlam... led a final attack on the strong point despite the fact that he had been wounded in the leg. This work was extremely successful and 40 dead Germans were carried into the trenches later on. This heavy loss being due to 2nd Lt Adlam's wonderful throwing.*[1]

And so, the rest of Thiepval finally fell and 2nd Lieutenant Adlam was awarded the Victoria Cross.

The path was now open for another go at the mighty Schwaben Redoubt. This was a formidable defensive unit that sat on top of miles of underground tunnels and scores of deep dugouts large enough to house hospital facilities and a telephone exchange.

In the end, it took eight different battalions from the 18th Division nine days at a cost of 2,000 men to grab a foothold of the position, and even then, the Germans still held onto the north-western corner.

After the fighting on Thiepval Ridge had died down, the results were a decidedly mixed bag. Territorially, the British had snatched just over five square miles of tortured ground from the Germans, including the important village of Thiepval. However, Regina Trench and portions of Stuff and Schwaben Redoubts were still held by the enemy. And at what cost? Around 12,500 British and Canadian men were listed as killed, missing or wounded. German casualty numbers are not known, but best guesses suggest similar numbers.

Back at British HQ, Haig was delighted with progress. The fighting between 15th and 30th September had captured as much ground as all the attacks from 1st July to 14th September combined. With all the advances, the German first, second and third lines of trenches had already been captured, and he was seeing his new wonder weapon – the Tank - finally start to make a real difference on the battlefield.

He was so excited he started working on his 'Grand Design' for October which would see the Fourth and Reserve Army link arms and attack as one towards Bapaume and beyond, before finally advancing on Cambrai, some twenty-four miles away from their current positions.

What could possibly go wrong?

69

2ND LIEUTENANT THOMAS EDWIN ADLAM VC

T om Edwin Adlam was born in Waterloo Gardens, Milford, Salisbury, on 21st October 1893, the son of John and Evangeline Adlam. Following his education at Bishop Wordsworth's School, Salisbury, he trained to be a teacher at Winchester Training College from 1912 to 1914, before becoming a teacher at Brook Street Council School in Basingstoke. While attending college, Adlam joined the 4th Hampshire Territorial Force and when war broke out enlisted with 2/4th Hampshire Regiment.

The 2/4th Hampshire's served in India during the initial stages of war, setting sail from Southampton on 13th December 1914 and It is likely that Adlam served a short while in India, working his way up to Sergeant, before returning to Britain later in 1915.

On 16th November 1915 he was Commissioned as a Second Lieutenant into the Bedfordshire Regiment, originally being posted with the 9th (Reserve) Battalion before ultimately being posted to the 7th Battalion where he was soon trained up as a Bombing Officer as he had the unusual talent of being able to throw Mills bombs a significant distance with both arms, which he put down to years spent playing cricket.

Adlam joined the 7th Battalion in the field on 18th July 1916 as part of a large draft of reinforcements after the regiment had suffered badly during the early fighting on the Somme.

They had been one of the few units to actually capture enemy positions (including the heavily fortified Pommiers Redoubt) on the first day of the battle and had also been thrown into the crucible at Trônes Wood — with predictable consequences. He was posted to 'C' Company and, other than two weeks in August, spent in the front lines opposite Lille, spent the next couple of months in reserve positions. Here the battalion initially rested after their ordeal on the Somme, then started training for their future role at Thiepval in September.

His mother died while he was in France that summer, but as the burial and service would have been finished by the time he returned to England, he remained with his platoon. This innocuous decision would ensure he was with the battalion while they stormed Thiepval and the Schwaben Redoubt, the action where he would win the Victoria Cross.

Thiepval stood on a prominent ridge that dominated the surrounding countryside. The fortified village itself sat in the middle and on either shoulder of the ridge, and the defenders had built redoubts to repel any attempts to overrun the position.

These redoubts were complex tangles of barbed wire, trenches, reinforced machine-gun posts and dugouts in which the defenders could shelter from shelling. Two big attempts had already been made to storm the ridge, but only succeeded in nearly wiping out both assaulting divisions.

The 26th September would see a third attempt at taking Thiepval, and the 7th Bedfords would be held back in reserve in case needed. After initial success, the attack broke down and the call did indeed go out to the Bedfordshire men to prepare to assault the northern part of the village. In the early hours of 27th 2nd Lt. Adlam and his 'C'

Company swept into the village but quickly ran into a wall of enemy snipers and machine gunners that had to be taken care of individually. At about 7am, the right platoon of 'C' Company was pinned down by enemy fire coming from multiple defensive positions – it was a critical moment. If 'C' Company failed, the whole attack was in jeopardy.

The company went to ground and Adlam sought the Company O.C. in another shell hole, nicknamed *Father*, to debate what the best course of action was. Adlam decided to have a go at getting into the German trenches, to which *Father* solemnly shook his hand before departing, expecting to not see him again.

But Adlam had other ideas and led his platoon into the enemy trench, charging and bombing individual defensive posts, including a well-defended machine-gun position.

> *We were in this narrow bit of trench and by this time we had no bombs. There were bags of German bombs like a condensed milk tin on a stick. On them there was written '5 secs'. You had to unscrew the bottom, and a little toggle ran out. You pulled that and you threw it. I'd noticed that the Germans were throwing them at us, seen them coming over, wobbling about as they did, pitching a bit short of me, luckily. I could count up to nearly three before the 'Bang!' came. So, I experimented on one. I pulled the string and took a chance, counted 'One, two, three...' My servant beside me was looking over the top of the trench and he said, 'Bloody good shot, Sir, hit him in the chest, hit the bugger!' The Germans found their own grenades coming back at them, I think it rather put the wind up them. There were bags of them in the trench. With my few men behind me, I got them to pick up all the bombs.*

*I dumped all my equipment except my prismatic com-
pass, I thought, 'I bought that myself and I don't want to
lose it!' I kept that over my shoulder. The men brought
these armfuls of bombs along. I just went gaily along,
throwing bombs. I counted every time I threw, 'one, two,
three...' and the bomb went – it was most effective. Then
we got close to where the machine gun was, and it was
zipping about. We daren't look up above. I got a whole
lot of bombs ready, and I started throwing them as fast
as I could. My servant, who was popping up every now
and again, said, 'They're going, Sir! They're going!' I
yelled, 'Run in, chaps, come on!' We just charged up
the trench like a load of mad things, luckily they were
running, we never caught them, but we drove them out.[1]*

Adlam and his merry bunch of men carried on deep inside German
territory and cleared out another machine-gun post that was stopping
the platoon on the right from joining in the fight. With this nuisance
out of the way, more men could get across and help mop up, taking
hundreds of prisoners in the process.

By now, Adlam's CO had also managed to get across and saw a
couple of trenches leading up towards the Schwaben Redoubt. He
arranged for a small group of men to investigate and set up an advance
post, but as they set off on their task, they immediately took casualties.
Cue Lieutenant Adlam. Again.

*I said 'Oh, damn it! Let me go, I can do it, I've done the
rest of it, I can do this bit! So I went on. I bombed up the
trench, put some men to look after that, bombed along
this one there, it wasn't much of a trench at all, nearly
all blown to pieces, that was an easy job. Then I got to*

> *the other corner, bombed them out of there, bombed back*
> *down the way. We took more prisoners down there in*
> *dugouts. So we had our two advanced posts out towards*
> *the enemy.*[2]

During all this excitement, Adlam received a leg wound, but seems to have hardly noticed it. Without Adlam's leadership and courage, it is unlikely the starting positions for the important attack on the Schwaben Redoubt would have been established. For this, and for his handy work with the bomb, he would be put forward for the Victoria Cross. the Citation for which appeared in the Supplement to The London Gazette of 24th November 1916. (25th November 1916)

> *For most conspicuous bravery during operations. A por-*
> *tion of a village which had defied capture on the previ-*
> *ous day had to be captured at all costs to permit subse-*
> *quent operations to develop. This minor operation came*
> *under very heavy machine gun and rifle fire. Second*
> *Lieutenant Adlam, realising that time was all impor-*
> *tant, rushed from shell hole to shell hole under heavy fire*
> *collecting men for a sudden rush, and for this purpose*
> *also collected many enemy grenades. At this stage he*
> *was wounded in the leg, but nevertheless he was able to*
> *out-throw the enemy and then seizing his opportunity,*
> *and in spite of his wound, he led a rush, captured the*
> *position and killed the occupants. Throughout the day,*
> *he continued to lead his men in bombing attacks. On the*
> *following day, he again displayed courage of the highest*
> *order, and though again wounded and unable to throw*
> *bombs, he continued to lead his men. His magnificent*

example and valour, coupled with the skilful handling
of the situation, produced far-reaching results.

But that was not the end of it. The next day he was back in the thick of the action again, this time in a direct assault against the Schwaben Redoubt. Once again, Adlam resorted to bombing his way out of trouble, until, when within touching distance of the Redoubt he took a decent whack on his throwing arm, but this didn't deter him, he simply threw the bombs with his other arm and continued to lead his men deeper into German territory.

When the CO arrived in Adlam's section, he insisted Tom retired because of his wounds. He did so, escorting a dozen POW's to the rear as he retired. After all the effort and sacrifice, they had secured a toehold in the Schwaben redoubt, but it would be October before the position would be fully captured.

Lieutenant Adlam was in Colchester recovering from his wounds when news of his VC reached him. No one had mentioned him even being proposed for a medal, but he returned to the Orderly Room one night to find himself swamped with telegrams. Calling home to ask what everyone was congratulating him for and why newspaper people wanted to get his photograph, his father was the one to give him the news!

Adlam travelled to Buckingham Palace on 2nd December 1916 to receive his Victoria Cross from the King. Two weeks later, he received a gold watch by the Mayor of Salisbury.

Adlam was not deemed fit enough to return to the trenches and instead became an instructor at No.2 Officer Cadet Battalion, Cambridge and by the end of the war he had reached the rank of Captain. He joined the Army Educational Corps in December 1920 before moving back to Hampshire a few years later to resume his teaching career.

On 24th August, 1939, Adlam was recalled to service as a Staff Captain with the Movement Control Section of the Royal Engineers at Avonmouth Docks, Somerset before being appointed Deputy Assistant Quartermaster General at Glasgow – a position held until August 1943. He was then promoted to temporary Lieutenant Colonel and Commandant at Dover, where he was involved in the organisation of Operation Overlord.

Tom continued his love of cricket well into his retirement, being the wicket keeper for his local team until he was 71! He attended every VC/GC reunion and ceremony between 1920 and 1974 and in 1933 led the Remembrance parade past the Cenotaph with fellow VC and 7th Bedfordshire comrade, Christopher Cox VC.

Tom Adlam died on the 28th May 1975, during a family holiday on Hayling Island, Hampshire. He was 81 years old and is buried in St Matthew's Churchyard, Blackmoor, Hampshire.

70

HAIG'S GRAND DESIGN

S purred on by the successes during the second half of September, Haig immediately got to work on his 'Grand Design'.

On 29th September, Haig visited Rawlinson to explain his ideas. This would be a three-army affair. Rawlinson would attack the Transloy Line before turning north-east to Beaumetz (some eight miles from the recently captured village of Flers) and then swing east to encircle Cambrai – twenty-four miles distant.

To put that into perspective, Haig was asking Rawlinson to advance in one month six times the distance achieved in the previous three.

Gough and his Reserve Army were to capture Achiet-le-Grand before advancing towards Cambrai on Rawlinson's left shoulder – again another advance of twenty-four miles. General Allenby and his Third Army would be the northern point of the attack – he would attack south of Arras, capture the high ground around Beaurains-Monchy, cut off the enemy from the north and push them up against the Canal du Nord with nowhere to go. Allenby would 'only' need to cover twenty miles but would need to move his entire artillery machine quickly to the Canal du Nord to effectively plug any gaps and trap the enemy as desired.

With these three sweeping moves, Haig would achieve in October what had proved an impossible task in July. And then some.

It was a bold idea. Some might have called it extravagant. Others might have called it ludicrous. But Haig was convinced that he was on the brink of a Napoleonic-style pivotal victory that could decide the outcome of the entire war. And such decisive moves could only be achieved after an infantry-led break through was exploited by rampant cavalry.

However, despite the Chief's free-flowing optimism regarding a decisive breakthrough, there were one or two (or three) tiny challenges to Haig's Grand Design that threatened to bring it all crashing down before it even got going...

First, there was the weather. The back-end of September had been glorious on the Somme, with only a couple of days of rain. However, October often saw prolonged heavy rain, which would quickly turn the battlefield into a sea of deep, sticky mud, which made moving artillery into position quite impossible and made life simply miserable for the ordinary man in the trenches.

Second, the positions the British found themselves in at the end of September were very favourable from a strategic point of view. Apart from a few isolated positions, such as the Schwaben Redoubt and Regina Trench, the British occupied the high ground, overlooking their enemy. Any advance would see the men move down the reverse slope and into the next valley – restoring the advantage of observation to the Germans and, if / when the rains came, it would mean forcing the attacking infantry through some pretty mucky conditions at the bottom of the valley where all the rainwater would collect. Not ideal.

Finally, there were the Germans themselves. Yes, the original three lines of defensive positions were now in British hands, but they had already got busy building a fourth line through Le Transloy opposite Fourth Army and aerial reconnaissance was showing construction of a fifth line just in front of Bapaume and a sixth line a few miles beyond. Now, none of these positions were as strongly fortified as the original defensive lines, but they were still going to need taking care of.

Any kind of attack towards Bapaume would be fraught with danger, especially with the large distances involved.

In the end, not one section of Haig's Grand Design was successfully implemented. What took place, however, were several badly thought out isolated and costly attacks that didn't really move the needle strategically at all.

Sound familiar?

71

— . —

MUDDY ATTRITION: LE TRANSLOY & REGINA TRENCH

Haig was eager to keep up the momentum of September and urged his commanders to take the necessary steps to capture close-by enemy positions as quickly as possible. For Gough and his Reserve army, that meant Regina Trench – a formidable position which had resisted two separate Canadian attacks in September, but as it overlooked the Ancre valley, it needed to be captured if there were any hope of any grand advance.

On 1st October, the 2nd Canadian Division tried to make it third time lucky, but they were hit by artillery and machine-gun fire the minute they stepped into *No Man's Land*. Those men that survived long enough to make progress towards the enemy lines then found themselves held up by uncut wire. Only a handful of men got themselves into the German front line, but they were soon bombed back out of it.

Later that evening, it started to rain and did so for the next four days, making further attacks impossible.

While Gough's Reserve Army struggled in front of Regina Trench, Rawlinson had his eye on the Transloy Ridges. Even though it was officially only a pre-cursor to Haig's *Grand Design*, this was a big enough gig in its own right with seven infantry divisions taking part – six British and one French.

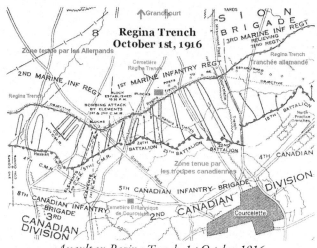

Assault on Regina Trench. 1st October 1916

This Anglo-French affair was originally pencilled in for 5th October, with the objective of capturing a number of disconnected enemy trenches and establishing a line on the forward slope of the ridge, from which the Transloy Line could be observed. But owing to the poor weather, the attack was postponed for forty-eight hours. At 3.15pm on 6th October, the preliminary artillery show finally fired up with the infantry assault kicking off at 1.45pm the following day.

The attack was a failure. The weather had not allowed sufficient aerial spotting to help the artillery boys zero in on their targets, and they had failed to spot German trenches that were completely unknown to the infantry – who subsequently got the shock of their life when they ran into them.

In other parts of the attack, the enemy cleverly placed defensive machine-gun positions in shell holes wide on the flanks of the attacks, out of the way of the main barrage.

The only registered success was the capturing of the village of Le Sars – here the men of the 23rd Division attacked with speed right behind a creeping barrage that gave the defenders no time to get organised. They were over-run before they could say *Bratwurst*.

After the day was done, the order immediately went out for a renewed assault on 8th October, but even Rawlinson had to concede to yet more rain, and he begrudgingly settled on 12th October for Zero part *deux*.

The weather didn't stop Gough sending in yet more Canadians to finally capture Regina Trench. But, in a distinct case of *Deja-vu*, the bombardment again failed to cut the enemy wire (in some places German defenders even pushed fresh rolls of wire out into *No Man's Land* as the first waves of Canadians began their advance). The Canadians struggled to make progress and were simply picked off by German machine-gun and small arms fire.

Gough was not impressed. Haig travelled to Reserve Army HQ after the attack and noted Gough's grumpiness in his diary:

> *Gough... was of the opinion that the Canadians (3rd Division) had not done well. In some parts they had not left their trenches for the attack yesterday. The Canadian 1st Division, which had attacked northwest of Le Sars and gained some ground, had been driven out again.*[1]

Meanwhile, the multi divisions of the Fourth Army were preparing themselves for another shot at the outer defensives of the Transloy Line – earmarked for 12th October. The days in the run up to the attack were full of low cloud which once again made aerial observation difficult, if not impossible. But it wasn't raining, and on that principle alone, the attack went ahead as planned. The results were predictable. Yet again, German machine-gunners reigned supreme - not one attacking division captured their first objective. A review of the battle written for the war diary of 30th Division summed up the situation nicely:

> The principal cause of failure appears to me to have been due to a well organised enemy employment of machine-gun fire. It remains to be discovered how we can deal with enemy machine-guns, scattered all over evenly but not placed in trenches, which by indirect or long range fire can erect a 'barrage' on No Man's Land.[2]

These failures put a severe dent in Haig's *Grand Design*. But was he deterred? Not a chance. Another attack on the Transloy Ridge was ordered for 18th October. The continuing bad weather made any kind of artillery support difficult. For the men on the ground trying to force the German's hand, conditions were awful, as described in this account taken from the 1st Battalion, East Lancashire Regiment's diary:

> At Zero hour 3.40am the weather conditions were appalling, pitch black, extremely cold, and pouring with rain. The waves advanced... No organised line held by the enemy was met, but heavy machine gun and rifle fire was directed on to our waves from front and flanks...
>
> The ground was terribly torn up by shell fire, and as

*slippery as ice. The men kept on slipping and falling into
the holes in the dark. The few who returned were a mass
of mud from head to foot, and completely exhausted.*[3]

Back at HQ, Haig was more upbeat. Later that day, he wrote a letter
to King George V summarising the day's work.

*The Fourth Army attacked in places this morning at
3.45am to straighten up their line with a view to getting into a more suitable position for a more serious
effort later on... the ground was very slippery and unfavourable for the advance of the infantry. However, the
majority of the objectives for this morning's attack were
no great distance, and about 60 per cent of them were
taken. In many places the enemy is reported as running
away as soon as our infantry were seen advancing!*[4]

Despite Haig's spin to the King, the grim fact was that the attack
was never going to succeed in those conditions. By now the conversation between Haig, Gough and Rawlinson should have been about
calling it a day on the Somme for the winter. But, although Haig did
concede that his *Grand Design* of motoring into Cambrai in October
was now out of the question, – and he did tell the Third Army to the
north to stand down – he still wanted the Reserve and Fourth Armies
to keep going at the objectives that were facing them in the Somme
sector. Namely the Miraumont Spur and the Transloy Line.

Unfortunately, even these much smaller objectives were now just
as unrealistic as Bapaume, Cambrai, and the Canal du Nord. But
such minor details were not going to stop the British *grande fromages*
planning another massive attack on Regina Trench. And on 21st October thousands of men huddled together in what used to be assembly

trenches waiting for the whistles to blow. It was the coldest day of the Somme campaign so far with the temperature dropping below zero degrees Celsius. Even the Somme mud had frozen over.

Supported by the field artillery of seven divisions, the attack began with the 4th Canadian Division on the right and the 18th, 25th and 39th divisions in line to the left, across a 5,000 yard front. This time, the artillery managed to do significant damage to Regina Trench and even cut the wire in many places. Consequently, several parts of Regina Trench were captured and consolidated, some brave souls even pushed on some 500 yards in front, and over one thousand German prisoners were captured in the process.

Two days later, Rawlinson launched his fourth attempt to capture the Transloy Ridge. The results were sadly similar to the previous three. A few isolated gains here and there, but nothing of strategic value – and another couple of thousand names added to the casualty list.

By now, the men on the ground (and those supervising them) had had enough. When orders came down the line to prepare for yet another go at the Transloy Line, the reaction was one of pure anger. Lord Cavan, whose XIV Corps were right in the thick of it, wrote to Rawlinson and told him what he thought of his new orders:

> *With a full and complete sense of my responsibility I feel it my bounden duty to put in writing my considered opinion as to the attack ordered to take place on Nov 5th...*

> *An advance (on Le Transloy) from my present position with the troops at my disposal has practically no chance of success on account of the heavy enfilade fire of machine guns and artillery from the north, and the enormous distance we have to advance against a strongly*

*prepared position, owing to the failure to advance our
line in the recent operations...*

*No one who has not visited the front trenches can really
know the state of exhaustion to which the men are reduced.*[5]

In 1916, writing such words to a superior officer was really not the
done thing. This kind of riposte took guts and conviction to write and
deliver as it could have been extremely career limiting.

Rawlinson chose to ignore Cavan's points. Instead, he urged him to
use the minor attack planned for that day (3rd November) as a cheeky
little test-run for the main event on the 5th. So, the attack went ahead
and did indeed prove to be a useful test. It achieved nothing but more
casualties. Predictably, Rawlinson and Haig chose to ignore the results
of this useful test – the main attack would go ahead as planned on 5th
November.

Cavan could have easily yielded. Indeed, it would have been what
his superiors would have expected him to do. But he didn't. He replied
to his boss, telling him he refuses to attack until he (Rawlinson) tore
himself away from his comfortable Château and visited the front line
for himself. To his credit, Rawlinson visited Cavan and agreed with
him that conditions were completely unsuitable for any further advances. He even convinced Haig that they should limit activities in the
region to trench raids and artillery shelling only.

Remarkably, Cavan won the argument. At least for a couple of
hours. That same day, Haig met with Foch and changed his mind. The
attack would go ahead on 5th November, after all.

Unsurprisingly, the attack failed. The only thing the British Army
gained were another 2,000 casualties.

72

THAT MINIATURE GIBRALTAR: THE BUTTE DE WARLENCOURT

T he Butte de Warlencourt is an ancient burial mound situated about half-a-mile north of the village of Le Sars, and about four miles south of Bapaume. Up close it doesn't look much - a British Army Intelligence report of 20th July 1916 dismissed the strategic importance of the position, describing it as nothing more than a *Roman tumulus at most fifty yards in diameter by twenty yards high. It commands nothing, being at the bottom of a hollow and cannot be seen from Le Sars owing to a row of trees along the road leading from the main road to Eaucourt l'Abbeye.*[1]

The Germans, in possession of the position, begged to differ:

> *The commanding ridge of the Butte afforded us unobstructed views as far as the Windmill Hill at Pozières, the hotly contested Hill 154, and the short stumps that were all that left of High Wood and Delville Wood. From the Butte we could see into the intervening No Man's Land, and our artillery was able to take in enfilade the deep hollow of Martinpuich which constituted the best approach for enemy forces to the battlefront. The distance to the elevations which formed the horizon was*

*5 or 6 kilometres, which meant the British had to bring
all but the longest ranged of their offensive batteries
forward into this ground.[2]*

The first attempt to kick the Germans off the Butte took place in
early October. Three Battalions of the 47th (London) Division tried
earnestly, but the attack was an utter disaster. The attacking troops
were subjected to horrendous crossfire directed upon the slopes leading up to the Butte. The Germans, as you would expect, were making
full use of their elevated positions.

*The Butte de Warlincourt
and Surrounding Area*

The 47th Division was replaced in the line by the 9th (Scottish)
Division and a renewed attack on the Butte was pencilled in for 12th

October. Led by the 2nd and 4th Regiments of the South African Brigade, this attack would have two principal objectives - the two trenches leading up to the Butte called Snag Trench and The Tail respectively, before moving through to the German defensive system behind, including the Butte.

The South Africans climbed over the parapet at 2.05pm during a heavy mist that should have offered them a small piece of protection. Alas, the second they appeared in *No Man's Land*, they immediately came under a furious fire from long-range enemy machine-guns. As a result, the attack failed before it really got started.

Ignoring the rain, the conditions, the mounting number of casualties and almost all sense of normal reasoning, the orders went out to plan for an immediate replay. So, six days later, South African whistles blew again to signal the start of another attempt to boot the Germans off the Butte. Zero was 3.40am on 18th October – would this be a case of third time lucky for Gough?

In short, no.

Three companies of the South Africans advanced, immediately disappearing into the rain, and for hours there was no news whatsoever of progress. When, finally, updates did start to trickle back to HQ, the reports were of failure and of high casualty rates.

In the ten days of fighting from 9th to 19th October, the South African casualties amounted to a staggering 1,150 men.

During the night of the 19th, fellow units of the 9th Division struggled to get into position and relieve the beleaguered South Africans. After an exhausting struggle to get to the front line, passing through log-jammed communication trenches waist deep in mud, the 6th Battalion King's Own Scottish Borderers were deemed fit enough to go *Over the Top* the very next day at 4pm. Bitter fighting ensued, and confusion reigned.

Positions in front of the Butte were won, lost, and won again. By night fall Snag Trench was Scottish, but in reality, the British were no closer to gaining control of the Butte. Strewn across the open ground in front of Snag Trench were a long line of dead Londoners serving as grim evidence as to the dominance of the German machine gun on this piece of the Somme battlefield.

Meanwhile, back at GHQ, far away from the mud and blood, Haig, Rawlinson and Gough were discussing the future direction of the Somme campaign. It was decided that the Fourth Army would attack the Butte again on 25th October, weather permitting. Unsurprisingly, the weather gods were not playing ball with the British top brass.

The ground was so deep with mud that to move an 18-pound field gun required ten or twelve horses. In the forward trenches, mud was three feet deep in many places and they offered absolutely zero cover from the elements. The men were freezing, sodden, and hungry, with very little food getting through. Stretcher bearers often needed a crew of eight to carry one man on one stretcher, and runners were taking up to six hours to cover 1,000 yards.

Recognising that asking the Borderers to launch another charge at the Butte would be beyond their current capacity, they were relieved by the 50th Division on 24th October in preparation for attempt number five. The attack was moved from the 25th to the 26th October, but the conditions were so bad the generals finally agreed on the 5th November with objectives also including Gird Trench - running behind the Butte - and the Gird Support Line beyond. The battalions being asked to perform what many before them had been unable to do were the 6th, 8th, and 9th Durham Light Infantry. The 6th and 8th were to capture Gird Trench and Gird Support, with the 9th Battalion on the left being given the orders to capture the Butte and a nearby Quarry.

The night before the attack saw horrendous rain and howling wind and in parts of the line, the Somme mud was waist high.

At Zero Hour, the mud was so bad the assaulting troops had no choice but to crawl out of their jumping-off positions in what was left of Snag Trench, Tail Trench and Maxwell Trench, and stumble into *No Man's Land*. Progress for the men was painfully slow. Deadly slow. It was impossible to advance with any kind of haste and as a result, they were sitting ducks for the enemy machine gunners.

On the right-hand side of the attack, the 8th DLI gallantly ploughed on through the mud, hopelessly disconnected from their protective creeping barrage. Some brave souls got tantalisingly close to the German front line before being cut down by machine-gun fire from both flanks. Finding further advance impossible, they were ordered to retreat to Snag Trench. Their fight was over. It was a similar story with the 6th Battalion; however, they did manage to breach Gird Trench in a couple of places, but couldn't hang on.

On the left of the attack, the 9th DLI had the toughest gig on paper, yet they carried all of their objectives and broke through two lines of German defences. Forward observers reported seeing men of the 9th DLI on top of the Butte and advancing on towards the Gird Lines.

Was this it? Was the Butte finally conquered? Had the men from the Durham Light Infantry achieved what many thought was impossible given the catastrophic battle conditions?

Writing in the Regimental War Diary, Commander of the 9th, Lt Colonel Roland Bradford, describes the attack very eloquently for us.

> *9.10am – A, B and C Companies crept forward under the artillery barrage and assaulted the enemy's trenches. The assault was entirely successful. By 10.30am we had taken the quarry and had penetrated the Gird Line, our objective. A post was established on the Bapaume Road, i.e north west of the Quarry. A machine-gun in a dug-out on the north-eastern side of the Butte held up our advance somewhat, and we attempted many times to bomb this dug-out...*

By noon... the enemy still had a post on the north side of the Butte. We held Butte Alley and the Quarry strongly, telephonic communication with the Quarry still holding. On our right, the 6th Durham Light Infantry had been held up by machine-gun fire and could not advance much beyond Maxwell Trench.

Independent witnesses stated that our advance was very finely carried out and that our men could be seen advancing very steadily. They passed right over the Butte and straight on to the Gird Line...

From noon up to 3pm, the position remained unchanged; the enemy delivered several determined assaults on the Grid Line, but these were all repulsed. Fighting still continued on the Butte, where we tried to capture the fortified dug-out on the north side.

At about 3pm, the enemy, strongly reinforced, again counter-attacked and at 3.30pm we reported as follows: ' We have been driven out of the Gird front line and I believe my posts there were captured and have tried to get back but the enemy is in considerable force and is still counter-attacking. It is taking all my time to hold Butte Alley. Please ask artillery to shell area north of Bapaume Road in M. 10d and M. 11C as Germans are in considerable force there. Enemy is holding Gird front line strongly on my right, and in my opinion a strong advance to the right of the Butte would meet with success. I have a small post in a shell hole at the north-western corner of the Butte, but the enemy still has

> *a post on the Butte on the north side. I am just going to*
> *make another effort to capture this post.*[3]

That afternoon and evening, the battle menu being served up on the Butte comprised copious amounts of nasty hand to hand fighting. Yet, the Germans stubbornly clung on to their fortified position on the north side despite Bradford's best efforts.

Late into the night, the Germans launched yet another fanatical counter-attack. This time it worked and by 12.20am on 6th November Lt Colonel Bradford and his men were being driven back to their own lines. By 1pm that afternoon, all three battalions from Durham were back in the same forward trenches they had been in twenty-four hours earlier. The only difference was there were 967 fewer people to take the roll call.

That wasn't quite the end of the action here, though. Before being moved into reserve, the 50th Division had time to sneak in one last show on the Somme. It would be another go at Gird Trench, along with a few cheeky new positions the Germans were busy building. The attack went in on 14th November – it was a disaster. Thirty-seven officers and 852 other ranks were killed, missing, or wounded.

In a retrospective report, Colonel Bradford bemoaned what he saw as an unhealthy fixation with capturing the Butte...

> *Looking back at the attack on the 5th November, it seems*
> *that the results which would have been gained in the*
> *event of success were of doubtful value and would have*
> *hardly have been worth the loss which we would suffer.*
> *It would have been awkward for us to hold the objectives*
> *which would have been badly sited for our defences.*
>
> *But the Butte de Warlincourt had become an obsession.*

Everyone wanted it. It loomed large in the minds of the soldiers in the forward area, and they attributed many of their misfortunes to it. The newspaper correspondents talked about 'that miniature Gibraltar'. So it had to be taken.

It seems that the attack was one of those tempting, local operations which are so costly and which are rarely worthwhile. But perhaps that is only the narrow view of the Regimental Officer.[4]

73

BRIGADIER-GENERAL ROLAND BRADFORD VC MC

H e didn't yet know it, but while Lt Colonel Bradford was struggling to secure the Butte de Warlencourt, he was being put forward for the Victoria Cross for his actions a few weeks earlier at Eaucourt-L'Abbaye.

Born on 23rd February 1892 in County Durham, Roland was the youngest son of a mining engineer. He was educated at Queen Elizabeth Grammar School, Darlington and Epsom College, where he captained his house rugby XV and was part of the college's first XV in his final year. He was also in the Epsom Cadet Corps, rising to Lance Corporal and Section Leader.

On 15th April 1910, he was commissioned into 5th Durham Light Infantry (Territorial Force). He loved the territorials so much he gave up on his original idea of studying for a medical degree and joined the army instead. He was commissioned into 2nd Durham Light Infantry on 22nd May 1912.

After the outbreak of war, he soon sailed from Southampton with his battalion, landing at St Nazire on 10th September 1914 where they were quickly in the thick of the action on the Aisne front. He served as a Platoon Commander during the winter fighting around

Armentieres and quickly showcased his outstanding military ability and tactical awareness as a leader.

He was Mentioned in Sir John French's Dispatch dated 14th January 1915 and awarded the Military Cross in February 1915 – possibly for fighting in October where his Battalion advanced near Bieux Berquin. On the third night of continuous fighting, Bradford's platoon was practically surrounded in the Bois Grenier area until he skilfully extracted them from a most deadly situation. With his award came a promotion to Captain.

During the rest of 1915 and the first half of 1916, the Battalion was not engaged in any major operation. Before the Battle of the Somme began, he was transferred as Second-in-Command to another battalion in the same division - the 1st/9th Durham Light Infantry. He was Mentioned in Sir Douglas Haig's Dispatch of 30th April 1916 by which time he had been made Temporary Major.

On 4th August 1916, he was given full command of the battalion. Three years of war had seen Roland, at the age of just 24, promoted to the rank of Lieutenant-Colonel. He forged close links with his battalion – he went out of his way to spend time with his men and led them in combat from the front. He was wounded by a shell splinter on 15th September 1916 at Mametz Wood, but continued forward with the attack and carried a wounded man back under heavy fire to the assembly trench. Bradford's wound still required regular treatment two months later.

On 1st October 1916, the 1/9th Durham Light Infantry was ordered into action at Eaucourt l'Abbaye. Bradford's men went into action at 3.15pm and it was for his actions during this battle that he would be awarded the Victoria Cross. The London Gazette recorded the following:

> *For most conspicuous bravery and good leadership in*
> *attack, whereby he saved the situation on the right flank*

of his Brigade and of the Division. Lieutenant-Colonel Bradford's Battalion was in support. A leading Battalion having suffered very severe casualties, and the Commander wounded, its flank became dangerously exposed at close quarters to the enemy. Raked by machine-gun fire, the situation of the Battalion was critical. At the request of the wounded Commander, Lieutenant-Colonel Bradford asked permission to command the exposed Battalion in addition to his own. Permission granted, he at once proceeded to the foremost lines. By his fearless energy under fire of all description, and his skillful leadership of the two Battalions, regardless of all danger, he succeeded in rallying the attack, captured and defended the objective, and so secured the flank.

It was just a matter of weeks before Bradford and his boys were back in the firing line on the Somme, this time in early November at the Butte de Warlencourt. He was again Mentioned in Field Marshall Sir Douglas Haig's Dispatches on 13th November 1916.

Having witnessed first-hand the terrible conditions on the Somme, Bradford wrote to Lord Northbourne, the honorary Colonel of his Battalion, requesting warm weather clothing and food parcels. Lord Northbourne duly obliged, sending food and clothing parcels to the men. As Christmas 1916 approached, Bradford organised a football tournament for his men with Lord Northbourne providing medals for the winners and runners up. Those medals arrived in February 1917 and were duly presented to the men – much to their delight.

Roland was presented with his Victoria Cross by King George V during an open-air ceremony in Hyde Park on 2nd June 1917. On his return to the front, he ordered that the hymn 'Abide with Me' be sung every night by his men. The tradition grew and was taken up by the entire Durham Light Infantry (DLI), and it remains the hymn of the regiment to this day.

On 10th November 1917, Roland was given command of the 186 Brigade of the 62nd (2nd West Riding) Division. At 25-years-old, he was the youngest Brigadier General in the modern history of the British Army to lead a combat formation. Just twenty days later, on 30th November 1917, during the Battle of Cambrai, he was killed by a shell fragment. On hearing the news, the 1st/9th DLI sang 'Abide With Me' in remembrance and respect for their former commander. Roland is buried in Hermies British Cemetery.

His other brothers had equally impressive military careers, making the Bradford family one of the most highly decorated families in British military history. Sadly, out of the four Bradford brothers, only one survived the war.

One brother, Captain Thomas Andrews Bradford, of the 8th Durham Light Infantry (and later of the York and Lancaster Regiment), won the Distinguished Service Order at the First Battle of Ypres. Another brother, Lieutenant. James Barker Bradford, of the 18th Durham Light Infantry, won the Military Cross, but fell in the Arras fighting of May 1917.

A third brother, Lieutenant-Commander George Nicholson Bradford (Royal Navy) was awarded a posthumous Victoria Cross for his work during the great raid at Zeebrugge on St George's Day, 1918.

They were the only brothers to both be awarded the Victoria Cross during the war.

74

_—•—_

CHANTILLY RACE

During early November, Haig began to prepare for a large conference of all Allied Commanders, to be held at Chantilly – French Army HQ – on 15th November. Haig planned to present to his French, Italian, Russian and Serbian colleagues the story of a successful British undertaking on the Somme and the icing on his cake would be one last success he could point to and smile.

With this in mind, he sent his Chief of Staff, General Kiggell, to see Gough at Reserve Army HQ on 8th November to fill him in on the situation. Gough was so taken aback by the request from the Chief that he brought in his senior Staff Officer, Lieutenant Colonel Malcolm, to transcribe the conversation. The bottom line was that regarding the Chantilly Conference of 15th November, Haig's (and therefore Britain's) standing would be significantly strengthened if Gough could sneak in a decent win beforehand – i.e. within the next week.

To say this was putting Gough in an uncomfortable position is a big understatement. He immediately called together his three Corps Commanders to deliberate over the options. With conditions of men and ground distinctly unfavourable, it was quickly agreed that any attack should carry only limited objectives of no more than 1,000 yards.

The men revisited orders received at the end of September for a renewed attack against Beaumont Hamel from their current positions at Thiepval. If (and it was a big if at that point) Beaumont Hamel could be taken, there was a good chance the next set of objectives – Serre and Beaucourt – could also be taken. The main deciding factor for all of this would be the weather.

The next couple of days were overcast and misty, but dry in the main and the ground was firming up quickly. Gough gave the attack the green light for 13th November – just in time for Haig's Chantilly presentation.

Haig was delighted. Although Beaumont Hamel should have been captured way back on the 1st July, a successful attack in November would, in his mind, energise the Romanians, prove to the Russians that he knew what he was doing and improve the general perception of Britain amongst the Allies. But more than that, with winter fast approaching, Haig himself was desperate for his *Big Push* on the Somme to have some kind of triumphant conclusion.

75

THE FINAL FIGHT: ASTRIDE THE ANCRE

T he Ancre River practically dissects Thiepval to the south and Beaumont Hamel to the north, before it turns south towards Albert, and it would be astride this river that Gough and his Fifth Army (previously the Reserve Army) would play out the final acts of the Somme battle of 1916.

The main objective of this final fling was Beaumont Hamel, a target of the first day of battle with such a formidable reputation that, even four months on, the mere mention of its name struck fear into the hearts of the men. Men such as Ordinary Seaman Joe Murray of the Hood Battalion, Royal Naval Division, who had just heard the delightful news that he was going to be part of the new attempt to take the village:

> *We've got in mind what we go to do. We know we're for the slaughterhouse. We know that the 29th Division, the Newfoundlanders, the Essex and everybody else got slaughtered. We know that! We knew that since then there'd been five attempts all beaten back. Five!*[1]

The puzzle that was Beaumont Hamel was a fearsome one. *No Man's Land* tapered from south to north from 500 to 200 yd and was devoid of cover, except for the infamous sunken lane of Lancashire Fusiliers' fame. The village itself had been fortified to within an inch of its life and from it, German machine-gunners commanded the approaches in front. Artillery observers on nearby Beaucourt Ridge had a magnificent view over the British lines, including being able to see field gun positions. Conversely, from the British front line, only the German front and support trenches were visible down the slope.

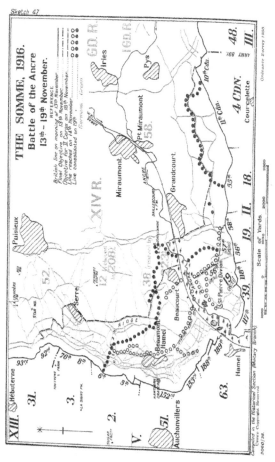

The Battle of the Ancre. November 1916

Every aspect of the terrain was in the defender's favour, but Haig was desperate. Gough was compliant. The weather was abysmal, but the final question of 1916 was about to be answered: Could Serre and Beaumont Hamel be captured in such unfavourable conditions?

The bombardment kicked off during the early morning of 6th November. Zero hour was set for 5.45am on 13th November.

Gough arranged his Fifth Army on either side of the Ancre river for the attack. On the right flank of the attack, south of the Ancre, the II Corps were to line up with the 19th and 39th Divisions. North of the river was the 63rd (Royal Naval) Division, 51st, 2nd, and 3rd Divisions of V Corps. On the extreme left of the attack was the 31st Division from XIII Corps.

In the final hours before the attack, the men tried to get a bit of sleep. But because of the cold and the thoughts of what the next day might hold, sleep was difficult to come by for many, including our friend Joe Murray of the Royal Naval Division who only snatched a couple of hours of rest using a bag of bombs as a pillow:

> *In the early hours of the morning, round about five o'clock, we were all woken, perishing cold... The official record says that someone brought round some tea at five o'clock, quarter past five. I never saw any tea. I'm not saying they didn't have it, but I didn't have any! About 5.30 most of us started getting warmed up a bit, dancing about, quietly! Then we had to fix bayonets, a clink, a metallic noise, so you put your tunic around it to deaden it...*[2]

The first waves of men began their advance as planned at 5.45am. It was dark and there was a heavy mist laying across big chunks of the battlefield, both of which added extra layers of complication to the already tedious battle conditions. Results were decidedly mixed.

On the very left (north) of the attack, in a distinct and deadly case of *Deja-Vu* the same division (31st) – although definitely not the same men - were crossing the same piece of *No Man's Land* in an advance against the same objective (Serre) as they did on 1st July. The results were also sadly similar. The mud was so bad it was almost impossible for the men to follow the creeping barrage.

Without its protection, and unable to move quickly across *No Man's Land*, many men were shot in front of the German lines before they could move away. That being said, small detachments of men did manage to wriggle their way into Serre, but they were quickly driven out.

The divisions next to the 31st also had a rough time of it – in essence, uncut wire, unpassable ground, and the loss of artillery protection meant that the northern portion of Goughs attack literally died in the mud.

Fortunately, the southern two-thirds of the attack fared a bit better. Firmer ground and improved visibility meant more of the wire was cut and it was easier for the infantry to follow closely behind the creeping barrage. In places, the assaulting groups penetrated towards the German third line. Then there were the pivotal attacks on Beaumont-Hamel and Serre – these were going to be the key to the success or failure of the entire show.

It was the job of 51st Division to take control of Beaumont Hamel and the strong defensive positions beyond. As was done on 1st July, a large mine was exploded near the old Hawthorn Redoubt to curtail enfilade machine-gun fire from that position. Unlike the attempt on the first day, this time the British occupied the mine crater before the Germans could get their hands on it and successfully nullified the machine-gun risk from that direction.

Saying that, the village itself was still a nightmare for the attacking infantry. Even though the village had been practically razed to the ground, the myriad of underground dugouts and tunnels had remained intact and up popped copious numbers of armed defenders, stopping the attack in the west portion of the village. However, thanks to the success of the mine, attacking reinforcements could be brought up safely and by 10.45am the daunting position of Beaumont Hamel was in British hands.

While the 51st Division were wrapping things up in Beaumont Hamel, the 63rd (Royal Naval) Division was also making decent progress in what was its first fight in anger on the Western Front.

> *It was very dark and misty, and several times got hung up in the Huns' barbed wire. I eventually lost touch with our battalion and arrived in the Huns' first line trench by myself and found a chap belonging to the RND there. We at once started bombing and throwing smoke bombs down into the dugouts and it was some time before we got them out. The first one to come out went down on his knees and cried for mercy. I did not have the heart to stick him although I would have liked to. Between us two we took forty or more prisoners.[3]*

The Royal Naval Division captured the German front-line positions in relative sort order, but the Germans were putting up a hell of a fight in some parts of the line, which caused the momentum of the initial push to be lost. While the battle raged either side of him, Lt Colonel Bernard Freyberg pondered how to move towards their objective – what was left of Beaucourt railway station. Once again, Joe Murray was right in the thick of it.

I forget how long we had to wait, but the time was getting on. Freyberg decided the Drakes can't go by themselves so we'll have to go... The barrage lifted and off we go again. There was firing going on all over the place: our own shells falling short, Jerries firing from left and right, our left flank was vacant. They say run but you stumble, there's shell holes - you can't go direct, you go this way and that way, picking your way round the shell holes. Sometimes there are two or three of you together, sometimes there was nobody. They'd got behind or blown up, you don't know. All the time there was these fumes and the shelling going on. We get to this point on the other side of the sunken road, and we capture it. I was almost near the station. We had to go down this road and up the side. There was a lot of dugouts there, well we got our 'P' bombs out and chucked them down there...[4]

In the end, the Royal Naval Division made the largest territorial gains of the day, but eventually German resistance stiffened, and the assault was forced to a standstill.

South of the Ancre, the 39th Division captured the fortified village of St-Pierre Divion, aided greatly by some clever deployment of howitzers. All in all, there was enough positive news for Haig to take to Chantilly, but not content with these gains, as Haig made his way to the conference on the 14th, the orders were flowing on both sides of the Ancre to continue the push in all areas towards the original objectives.

All attacks failed. The artillery had lost touch with the forward units and could not safely fire into the German positions. Men were dispersed all over the place and co-ordination of any meaningful advance was impossible. Undeterred, Gough issued repeat orders for the 15th – the fight must continue.

Meanwhile, Haig enjoyed a very splendid dinner with the Prime Minister at Chantilly, who seemed pleased with progress. Haig was happy. In his mind, the push astride the Ancre had done its job. He arranged a message to be sent to Gough that night, stating that no further attacks on the Somme should begin until he returned to the battlefield.

That, then, should have been it. The end of the fighting on the Somme in 1916. But it wasn't. Gough was convinced that, as the weather had improved (i.e it had not been chucking it down with rain all day every day) he could still push on and achieve great things, and sent a message back to Haig telling him such.

Haig conceded and operations resumed on the 18th. Some ground was captured around Serre, and Lt Colonel Freyberg's Royal Naval Division completed the occupation of Beaucourt. But elsewhere, the fresh attacks were met with fierce resistance and failed. Expensively. Gough's 5th Army took on another 10,000 casualties in one day for no apparent strategic reason.

By now, the morale of the men was at rock bottom. They had had enough of the weather; they had had enough of the conditions; they had had enough of the death. The battle was threatening to take the very soul of the British Army.

> *The suffering is terrible and some of the men are about mad with the cold and exposure. Snow in the morning followed by rain all day has made things pitiable. What I am seriously thinking now is that those boys lying stiff and cold all around Beaumont Hamel, insensible to it all, are perhaps lucky, and better off now than we are.*[5]

Everyone realised – even Haig and Gough - that the weather could not be beaten. It was simply impossible to move men and machines forward in such terrible conditions.

Apart from a few isolated skirmishes and the day-to-day attrition that was trench warfare, the British-led offensive on the Somme battlefield, at least the 1916 version, was over.

76

THE GREATEST BATTLE OF ALL WARS

If we take the 18th November as the end date of the battle, the whole Somme saga of 1916 lasted 141 days. With over a million casualties during this time, this equates to over 7,000 names added to the casualty list each and every day. That's almost 300 men an hour. Every hour. For four and a half months straight.

But could either side claim victory on the Somme in 1916? And did any of this death and destruction move anyone any closer to the ultimate finishing line and overall triumph?

On paper, you would have to say the Germans edged it. Over those 141 days, the deepest Anglo-French breach of German lines ran just shy of six miles. By mid-November, the British line was still three miles short of Bapaume, which Haig had wanted to call his own within days of the first attack.

Sadly, for Haig there was to be no thrusting cavalry charge. Not one major French town had been liberated. No disruption of German supply chains and communication links had taken place and the enemy line was still very much intact. German defenders were still fighting hard – despite Haig repeatedly convinced that just 'one more push' would shove the beleaguered German defenders over the edge and have them running back to Berlin with their tails between their legs.

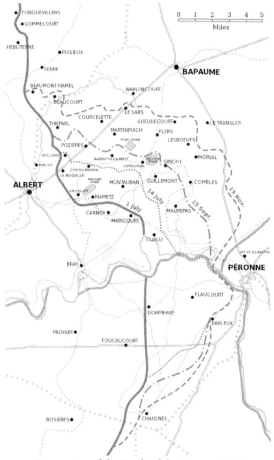

Progression of the Battle of the Somme 1916.

Haig and his leadership team have come in for an awful lot of criticism over the years from historians and the media for their handling of the Somme battle. The concept that the British Army were 'Lions led by donkeys' has been well perpetuated over the years. Haig himself was given the moniker of 'The Butcher of the Somme'. But are these tags justified?

Hindsight is always 20/20 and there are dozens of opportunities for historians and commentators to pick holes in the decision making. Even within this book, my frustration with some of the senior decision makers is evident. Yet, it is practically impossible for us to appreciate just how tough a job they had.

Haig didn't want to have the fight on the Somme in the first place, and he had never planned a battle on such a large scale before. In fact, no one in the British Army had – including the artillery boys, who were to be put under a strain and spotlight like never before. Then add in the reduction in French help due to Verdun and what we have is an under resourced attack in a less-than-ideal position.

One of the biggest criticisms has been the fact that senior British generals spent too much time far away from the action, shacked up in peaceful stately homes, miles behind the action. For the men in the trenches it is easy to see what this would be frustrating. Receiving orders from invisible officers who had no clue what conditions were like on the ground. But with the length of the attacking front, the senior generals had to hang back so they could see the complete picture. They couldn't afford to get caught up in details.

It didn't help that battlefield communications in 1916 were incredibly primitive, and decisions were being made based on incomplete information that often didn't reach HQ for hours after the event. It must have been a very frustrating time for those men burdened with making the strategy calls.

Were Haig, Rawlinson, Gough and Co. too optimistic in how they expected the battle to pan out? Yes.

Could they have reigned in their objectives? Most definitely.

Should they have stopped the battle in October rather than let it continue? Absolutely – those final weeks of the battle were hell for the men on both sides of the wire and prolonging the battle gained very little of strategic importance.

But was Haig a butcher? No. Not for me.

Back in Germany, the battle was spun as a victory for the tenacity and strategic ability of the German defensive machine. Fritz von Lossberg, Chief of Staff Second Army declared afterwards that:

> *The Allied plans foundered in the face of sacrificial, in-*
> *destructible courage and faithfulness of our army. Each*
> *Sommekämpfer can take pride in having contributed*
> *to the fact that the greatest battle of all wars ended with*
> *enemy failure and German victory.*[1]

However, in the corridor of powers in Berlin, there was a quiet, unspoken realisation that, like a heavyweight boxer who had just taken part in a bruising twelve round smash-up, the German Army had left a big chunk of themselves out on the Somme battlefield in 1916. British pressure in the high summer of 1916 had led to so many German losses that they were forced to change their defensive tactics. They started to fight in zones, which allowed the British to gain territory that would previously would have been hotly contested in endless counter-attacks. By doing this, they gave up ground but saved lives.

One of the first things Hindenburg & Ludendorff signed off on when they re-took their places at the German top table was the construction of the *Siegfried Stellung* (known to the British as the Hindenburg Line). Construction started on 23rd September, after the battle of Flers-Courcelette. Some 90 miles long and several miles deep, it may look like the action of a defeated army, but it was a extraordinary feat of military engineering that cleverly shortened the German defensive line, freed up large amounts of manpower, supplies and resources, and allowed the Germans to further improve and enhance defence-in-depth on tactically favourable ground of their own choosing.

The retirement back to the Hindenburg Line began in February, 1917.

Despite a massive recruitment drive during the winter of 1916, along with some significant industrial mobilisation to increase production of guns and ammunition, the German army would never really be the same outfit again - they would never have the same quality of men or materials they had that summer. And with America slowly coming to the aid of the Allies, the resources gap between the two sides would only grow wider.

No one knew it at the time, but the Battle of the Somme could well be seen as the beginning of the end for the German Army in the First World War.

THE FINAL WORD: DEATH IS A DREADFUL THING.

Death is a very dreadful thing to those who are not flung into slaughter. It will take months for me to gain a truer perspective. When the dead lie all around you, and the man next to you, or oneself, may puff out, death becomes a very unimportant incident. It is not callousness, but just too much knowledge. Like other things, man has ignored death and treated it as something to talk of with pale cheek and bated breath. When one gets death on every side, the reaction is sudden.

Two chaps go out for water, and one returns. Says a pal to him, 'Well, where's Bill?' 'A bloody "whizz-bang" took his bloody head off' my not appear sympathetic, but it is the only way of looking at the thing and remaining sane. You may be certain however, that the same man would carry Bill ten miles if there was any chance of fixing his head on again.

Captain Charles McKerrow, 10th Northumberland Fusiliers, 68th Brigade, 23rd Division

REFERENCES, SOURCES AND FURTHER READING

B elow is a list of sources I have used when I have quoted directly from their works.

Niederwerfungstrategies and *Schwerpunkts:* Imperial German Strategy

1. Clausewitz; *On War Book III* Chapter 11

2. Gehre; *Die Deutsche Kräfteverteilung* pp. 15-16

Big Guns. Artillery

1. Macdonald; *Somme* p. 44

Just Let Them Come! The German front line – June 1916

1. Gilbert; *Somme. The Heroism and Horror of War* pp. 42

Reconnaissance and Dominance: The Role of the Royal Flying Corps

1. IWM's sound archive: Archibald William Henry James. Catalogue number 4.

Red Tabs and Long Days: The view from HQ

1. Douglas Haig; *War Diaries and Letters (1914-1918)* pp195

Countdown to Zero
1. Living; *Attack on the Somme* pp26-28

Over the Top
1. Levine; *Forgotten Voices of the Somme* pp. 113

The British Burden of Battle
1. Levine; *Forgotten Voices of the Somme* pp 110-111

The Film Men. Documenting the Battle
1. Mallins; *How I Filmed the War* pp. 157

2. Mallins; *How I Filmed the War* pp. 162

Lt Downman's Damning Decree on the Disaster of Gommecourt
1. War diary of 1/5 Battalion Sherwood Foresters (Nottinghamshire and Derbyshire Regiment); The National Archives WO 95/2695/1

1st July. Premature Detonation at Serre and Beaumont Hamel
1. Sheen; Durham Pals: 18th, 19th, & 22nd (Service) Battalions of the Durham Light Infantry pp.99

2. Middlebrook; *The First Day on the Somme* pp157

3. Sparling; *History of the12th (Service) Battalion York and Lancaster Regiment* pp.63

1st July. 'For Goodness Sake, Send Reinforcements!' Attacking the Quadrilateral.
1. War diary of 1st Battalion, The Rifle Brigade; The National Archives WO95/1496

1st July: Beaumont Hamel

    1. Regimental History of Infanterie-Regiment No.119 (pub 1920)

1st July. 'To you has been set the most difficult task.' The Sunken Lane

    1. The National Archives, CAB 45/191 Capt E.W. Sheppard

    2. IWM Sound Archive AC9875 – Reel 15: Corporal George Ashurst

    3. War diary of 1st Battalion Lancashire Fusiliers; The National Archives WO95/2300

    4. IWM Sound Archive AC9875 – Reel 15 & 16: Corporal George Ashurst

1st July. Dead Men Can Advance No Further. Y-Ravine

    1. War diary of 1st Battalion Newfoundland Regiment; www.therooms.ca (virtual exhibit)

    2. Kershaw; *24Hrs at The Somme 1 July 1916* pp 189

Feste Schwaben: The Schwerpunkt of Schwerpunkts

    1. Sheldon; *Fighting the Somme* pp.45

    2. Gerster; *Die Schwaben und der Ancre* pp.117

    3. Sheldon; *Fighting the Somme* pp.130

1st July. Bulletproof Soldiers. The 32nd Division at Thiepval

    1. Edmonds, Sir James; *Military Operations France and Belgium, 1916 (Vol 1)* pp.398

    2. Hart; *The Somme*, pp.152

3. Brown; *The Imperial War Museum Book of The Somme* p p.66-7

4. IWM Docs. J.L.Jack type written memoir, pgs 5-6

5. Yatman; *Letter written 23rd May 1930,* The National Archives CAB/45/132

1st July. Morituri te Salutant. The Ulsters Attack
1. Blacker; *Letter written 20th March 1930,* The National Archives CAB/45/132

2. Gardiner, *Three Cheers for the Derrys!* pp.116

1st July. So Ends the Golden Age. Ovillers
1. Macdonald; *First Day of the Somme* pp.202

2. War diary of 11th (Service) Battalion, Sherwood Foresters; The National Archives WO95/2187

3. Gilbert; *Somme: The Heroism and Horror of War* pp.72

4. War diary of 2nd Battalion, Lincolnshire Regiment; The National Archives WO95/1730

5. War diary of 2nd Battalion, Devonshire Regiment; The National Archives WO95/1712

6. Macdonald; *First Day of the Somme* pp.223

Lieutenant-Colonel E T F Sandys, DSO
1. Middlebrook; *The First Day on the Somme* pp 98

2. The Times; Friday, September 15, 1916 pp. 3

1st July. The Glory Hole. Ovillers La Boisselle

1. Papers of Major W.A. Vignoles DSO & Bar; IWM Documents, Ref 6968

2. War diary of 11th Battalion, Suffolk Regiment; The National Archives WO95/2458

3. War Diary of 34th Division; The National Archives WO95/2457

4. Macdonald; *First Day of the Somme* pp.197

1st July. XV Corps at Fricourt

1. Middlebrook; *The First Day on the Somme* pp 156

2. Gee; *In case I cannot write again – The New Chequers No.2* pp. 20-21

1st July. Mostly Successful at Mametz

1. Aggett; *The Bloody Eleventh, The Devonshire and Dorset Regiment Vol III* pp. 44

1st July. Kicking Off at Montauban

1. Reymann; *Das 3. Oberschlesische Infanterie-Regiment Nr.62 im Kriege 1914-1918* pp. 90

2. Barton; *The Somme, A New Panoramic Perspective* pp.169

3. IWM Docs. C.W. Alcock manuscript letter, 15/7/1916

4. Andrews; *Orders are Orders* pp.49

1st July. South of the Somme. French Success

1. Sumner; *The French Army on the Somme 1916,* pp. 39

'Hold our current positions without fail.' German reaction to the 'Big Push'

1. Middlebrook; *The First Day on the Somme* pp.162

2. Kershaw; 24hrs at The Somme pp.180

3. Falkenhayn; *General Headquarters 1914-1916 and its Critical Decisions* pp. 264-5

4. Sheldon; *The German Army on the Somme 1914-1916* pp. 179

Medic! Coping with the Wounded

1. IWM Docs: F.H. Drinkwater, Typescript diary, 2/7/1916

2. Mayhew; *Wounded: From Battlefield to Blighty 1914-1918*, pp. 66-67

The Morning after the Day Before

1. Rawlinson Diary, 1/7/1916, Churchill College, Cambridge

2. Haig; *War Diaries and Letters 1914-1918* pp.197

The Unkillable Soldier. Lieutenant-Colonel Adrian Paul Ghislain Carton de Wiart

1. BBC news; *Adrian Carton de Wiart: The unkillable soldier* published 6/1/2015

2. BBC news; *Adrian Carton de Wiart: The unkillable soldier* published 6/1/2015

Private Thomas George Turrall VC, Worcestershire Regiment

1. The Birmingham VCs - http://www.birminghamvc.co.uk/the-vc-holders/thomas-george-turrall/

2. The Birmingham VCs - http://www.birminghamvc.co.uk/the-vc-holders/thomas-george-turrall/

Another Expensive Diversion. Thiepval and Ovillers

    1. IWM Docs: S.T. Kemp, Tyoescript account, pp 48-49

    2. IWM Docs: W.A. Gates Collection, S. Steveson-Jones, Edited from typescript letter, 13/7/1968 & Thiepval article

    3. IWM Docs: W.A. Gates Collection, S. Steveson-Jones, Edited from typescript letter, 13/7/1968 & Thiepval article

Random Acts of Warfare (Part 1). Contalmaison

    1. IWM Docs: R. D. Mountfield, Manuscript letter, 23/7/1916

Random Acts of Warfare (Part 2). Mametz Wood

    1. https://www.inthefootsteps.com/blog/histiry/38th-welsh-division-at-mametz-wood/

    2. Dudley Ward; *Regimental Records of the Royal Welch Fusiliers*, pp.210

Random Acts of Warfare (Part 3). Trones Wood

    1. IWM Docs: W.H.Bloor, Typescript diary, 11/7/1916

The Horror of High Wood

    1. Norman; *The Hell They Called High Wood* pp.120

'At All Costs.' Delville Wood

    1. Mallett; quoted in Uys; "The South Africans at Delville Wood" *South African Military History Journal,* Vol VII, No.2

    2. De Burgh Thomas; quoted in Uys; "The South Africans at Delville Wood" *South African Military History Journal,* Vol VII, No.2

Fromelles. The worst 24hrs in Australia's entire history

    1. Gilbert; *Somme: The Heroism and Tragedy of War*, pp. 121

23rd July. An organised attack on a broad front. Or not.

    1. Fourth Army Papers. V2. IWM

    2. Andrews; *Orders Are Orders* pp. 58-59

Pozières. ANZAC attack

    1. Bean; *The Australian Imperial Force in France: 1916. Official History of Australia in the War of 1914–1918. Vol. III* pp.599

    2. Haig; *War Diaries and Letters 1914-1918* pp.210

OHL. Trouble at the Top

    1. Lossberg; *Meine Tätigkeit* pp.234-235

    2. Rupprecht Kronprinz; *op.cit.* Bd 2 pp. 1

Tension at Home. A Blighty Back and Forth

    1. Churchill; Memorandum 1/8/1916. Taken from Hart; *Somme* pp. 325

Grinding it Out at Guillemont

    1. Rawlinson Diary, 8/8/1916, Churchill College, Cambridge

    2. IWM Docs: A. Russell, Typed manuscript, pp.60-61

    3. IWM Docs; Fourth Army Papers, OAD 91, p1

Sit Rep Germany. Lurching from one crisis to another

    1. Hindenburg; *Aus meinen Leben* pp.124

Metal Monsters. Tanks

    1. Pidgeon; *Flers and Guedecourt* pp.74

'As Strong and as Violent as Possible.' The Battle of Flers-Courcelette

1. Haig; War Diaries and Letters 1914-1918 pp.225

2. Fletcher; *Tanks and Trenches: First Hand Accounts of Tank Warfare in the First World War,* pp. 12-13

A Wanton Waste of Men. 47th Division at High Wood

1. Norman; *The Hell They Call High Wood* pp.233

Bite and Hold: The Battle of Morval

1. War Diary of 1st Battalion, Norfolk Regiment 25/9/1916. The National Archives WO95/1573

2. 2nd Grenadier Guards; *Narrative of events for 24th-25th Sept 1916.* The National Archives WO95/1215

Back at Thiepval. 26th September

1. War Diary of 7th Bedfordshire Regiment 27/9/16; The National Archives WO95/2043

2nd Lieutenant Thomas Edwin Adlam VC

1. IWM Sound Archive; T.E. Adlam, AC34, Reels 3 & 4

2. IWM Sound Archive; T.E. Adlam, AC34, Reels 3 & 4

Muddy Attrition. Le Transloy & Regina Trench

1. Haig; *War Diaries and Letters 1914-1918* pp.239

2. 30 Division War Diary, October 1916. WO95/2311

3. 1st East Lancashire War Diary, 18/10/1916. WO95/1498

4. Haig; *War Diaries and Letters 1914-1918* pp.243

5. Letter from Cavan to Rawlinson, 3/11/1916. AWM 45,

Bundle 31

That Miniature Gibraltar. The Butte de Warlincourt

1. Intelligence, III Corps; *Report on country between Bazentin and Bapaume. 20th July, 1916.* National Archives WO157/318

2. Maude; The 47th (London) Division, 1914-1919

3. War Diary of 9th Battalion, Durham Light Infantry, November 1916. The National Archives WO95/2840/4

4. War Diary of 9th Battalion, Durham Light Infantry, November 1916. The National Archives WO95/2840/4

The Final Fight. Astride the Ancre

1. Imperial War Museum sound archive. J. Murray. A.C. 8201, Reel 35

2. Imperial War Museum sound archive. J. Murray. A.C. 8201, Reel 36

3. Imperial War Museum Docs. S. C. Hawkins, Manuscript diary, 13/11/1916

4. Imperial War Museum sound archive. J. Murray. A.C. 8201, Reel 36 &37

5. Imperial War Museum Docs. A. E. Wrench, Typescript diary, 18/11/1916

GRAB A FREE WW1 FACTBOOK!

Get your hands on this exclusive ebook packed with 500 WW1 facts not found in any of my other books!

Visit www.wordsofwarfare.com to claim your free book now!

By the same author:

WW1: A Layman's Guide

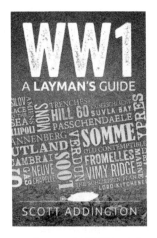

"First time I have understood WW1 without having to read War and Peace. Now onto the next book from this author, WW2."

By the same author:

WW2: A Layman's Guide

"This is indeed an excellent read. It lays out the events of World War Two in a way that the ordinary reader could understand. The book is written using plain but effective language. A true Layman's guide.."

By the same author:

THE THIRD REICH: A LAYMAN'S GUIDE

"The Third Reich is one of my favourite subjects and I have read and researched extensively. Many of my friends who want to read about the topic do not have the patience to read such long books. Scott Addington has reached out to these people and helped them understand the subject in a bite size format. I now pass on my copy to my friends so they have a basic understanding of the subject. A worth while book to read!!"

Printed in Great Britain
by Amazon